ENGLISH
Essentials

What you need to know about grammar, punctuation, and usage

Canadian Edition

John Langan
ATLANTIC CAPE COMMUNITY COLLEGE

Beth Johnson

Lisa Salem-Wiseman
HUMBER INSTITUTE OF TECHNOLOGY AND
ADVANCED LEARNING

**McGraw-Hill
Ryerson**

Toronto   Montréal   Boston   Burr Ridge, IL   Dubuque, IA   Madison, WI   New York   San
Francisco   St. Louis   Bangkok   Bogotá   Caracas   Kuala Lumpur   Lisbon   London   Madrid
Mexico City   Milan   New Delhi   Santiago   Seoul   Singapore   Sydney   Taipei

English Essentials
Canadian Edition

ISBN-13: 978-0-07-098040-2
ISBN-10: 0-07-098040-3

1 2 3 4 5 6 7 8 9 10 TCP 0 9 8

Printed and bound in Canada

Care has been taken to trace ownership of copyright material contained in this text; however, the publisher will welcome any information that enables them to rectify any reference or credit for subsequent editions.

Editorial Director: *Joanna Cotton*
Sponsoring Editor: *Lisa Rahn*
Marketing Manager: *Michele Peach*
Senior Developmental Editor: *Suzanne Simpson Millar*
Editorial Associate: *Marina Seguin*
Supervising Editor: *Graeme Powell*
Copy Editor: *Evan Turner*
Senior Production Coordinator: *Jennifer Hall*
Cover Design: *Sarah Orr*
Cover Image: *© Stockbyte; Brian Wilson Photography Inc.; Ashley Watson Images; BananaStock/Punch Stock; Courtesy of Rosarina Saw; Ashley Watson Images; CP Photo/Peterborough Examiner-Clifford Skarstedt; Brent Richter*
Interior Design: *Sarah Orr*
Page Layout: *Aptara Inc.*
Printer: *Transcontinental Gagne*

Library and Archives Canada Cataloguing in Publication

Langan, John, 1942-
 English essentials / John Langan, Beth Johnson, Lisa Salem-Wiseman.
 Includes index.
 ISBN 978-0-07-098040-2

 1. English language–Grammar–Problems, exercises, etc. 2. English language–Punctuation–Problems, exercises, etc.
 3. English language–Usage–Problems, exercises, etc.   I. Johnson, Beth   II. Salem-Wiseman, Lisa   III. Title.

PE1112.L26 2008   428.2   C2008-902302-1

CONTENTS

ABOUT THE TEXT

When you first looked at this textbook, did you notice the photographs on the cover? As you flip through the text, you'll spot these photos inside, accompanied by stories. What do these photographs and stories have to do with learning grammar?

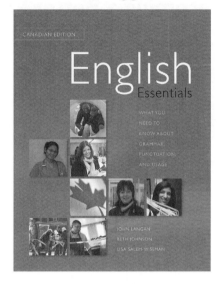

While you work on mastering practical English skills that you will use every day, you will share in the real lives of interesting people – people like you or your classmates – whose lives have been enriched through reading, writing, and learning. The photographs and the stories feature Canadians who are pursuing their personal, academic, and career goals through the acquisition and improvement of English writing skills.

Student photographers took the photos. The photo shoots were a great way for students in different programs to meet and work together on something that will be useful to you and your peers at colleges and universities across Canada. The pictures and stories add a human dimension to the subject of grammar, making it interesting…and fun!

This text provides a full treatment of the essential English skills that you need to know in an accessible way. Parts Two through Six begin with a list of objectives that will assist you in identifying the skills that you can expect to have acquired by the end of the unit. A diagnostic pre-test will identify the skills with which you may be familiar and those skills that require more attention. Every chapter presents the need-to-know information on the first page followed by activities that reinforce what you learn. Each chapter concludes with a series of tests to help you track your progress. You will be learning through doing – the most effective way to learn.

English Essentials includes the following icons, making the book easy-to-navigate:

 Specifies those skills that are useful for those whose first language is not English, but also for native English speakers.

 Indicates that, after reading about a skill, you can practise it with a "Do It Yourself" exercise.

 Identifies a helpful tip to improve your writing.

TEXT WALKTHROUGH

Here is an overview of what you will find on the following pages:

PART ONE: Becoming a Better Writer

The first part of this text presents the writing process in a brief, clear, and easy-to-understand manner. The information covered in this section includes:

- The basic goals of writing
- Paragraph and essay structure
- The importance of supporting your points
- Different patterns of organizing your support
- The writing process, from prewriting to formatting and proofreading
- Topics for writing paragraphs and/or essays

PART TWO: The Basics

This section introduces you to some basic grammar skills, including:

- Recognizing the various parts of speech and types of sentences
- Working with subjects and verbs
- Using the correct pronoun form, article, and modifier (adjective or adverb)

PART THREE: Beyond the Basics

Once you have mastered some of the basics, it's time to move on to the next level of essential skills. These include:

- Making verbs agree with their subjects
- Avoiding common sentence errors such as fragments, run-ons, comma splices, misplaced and dangling modifiers, and faulty parallelism

PART FOUR: Punctuation

Now it's time to introduce some rules for using punctuation marks such as:

- Apostrophes
- Quotation marks
- Commas
- Colons and semicolons

PART FIVE: Mechanics and Spelling

This final section covers some important but often-overlooked skills, such as:

- Improving spelling
- Correctly using frequently misused words
- Learning when to capitalize words
- Correctly using numbers and abbreviations

PART SIX: Proofreading

An important part of becoming a good writer is learning to proofread—to check the next-to-final draft of a paper for grammar, punctuation, and other mistakes carefully. This chapter provides you with some hints for improving your proofreading skills, as well as ten proofreading tests with which to practise those skills.

FOR THE INSTRUCTOR

"What's the catch?" you might be asking. "What are people's photographs doing in this textbook? And just how will they help me teach *English Essentials: What You Need to Know about Grammar, Punctuation, and Usage?*"

The student photographs are just one of the number of features that distinguish this book from other grammar texts on the market:

1. Personal photos and stories. All too often, grammar texts are dry, dull affairs, about as interesting as a study of rock dust on the planet Mars. As educators, we sometimes felt we were leading our students on a death march when we moved them through a traditional grammar text. So we have added a strong human dimension to this text by illustrating the grammar skills with photos and stories of interesting people from all walks of life. The stories describe not only their personal lives but also their involvement with reading and writing. Some of these people are pictured on the cover of the text.

2. Ease of use. All of the following make the textbook easy for students to understand and use:

- The essentials are presented in a highly accessible way. Look at any of the one-page reviews that open each of the skill chapters in Part Two. Only the basics of each skill are presented on this page, which students can read and understand quickly. Once they grasp this basic material, they go on to learn more and then practise applying the skill. It is better to learn a step at a time than to risk confusion by trying to learn everything at once.

- The chapters are self-contained, so that students focus on a particular skill set.

- Explanations are written in simple, clear language, with a minimum of grammatical terminology.

- An inviting two-colour design with headings and other graphic elements make the content accessible.

- Finally, the book is written in a friendly and helpful tone – a voice that never condescends to students, but treats them as adults.

3. Abundant practice. Students learn best when clear explanations are followed by multiple opportunities to practise which this text includes.

4. Engaging materials. In addition to the photos and true stories, lively and engaging examples and practice exercises will maintain student interest throughout the book.

5. **Inclusiveness.** A combined forty years of teaching experience taught that applying the skills in actual writing situations helps students master them. Part One focuses on how to become a better writer and the writing process. Part Two presents basic information about grammar and also covers topics not addressed in Part One. Parts Three, Four and Five go beyond the basics and deal with areas that some other grammar texts neglect: spelling improvements, parts of speech, and subject-verb agreement. Part Six offers guidance and practice in the crucial skill of proofreading. Within the covers of *English Essentials* are all the basic writing materials that instructors and students need.

6. **Superior supplements.** The following supplements are available:

   - For instructors:

       - An Instructor's Edition, which is identical to the student text and includes answers to all the practices and tests, is available online to instructors at www.mcgrawhill.ca/olc/langan.

       - An Instructor's Manual and Test bank, password-protected and available online at www.mcgrawhill.ca/olc/langan, includes teaching hints, diagnostic and achievement tests, a full answer key, and additional tests.

       - PowerPoint® Slides provide lecture presentation visuals that may be tailored to your work. Also available at www.mcgrawhill.ca/olc/langan.

       - A Student Answer-Key, also available online to instructors, consisting of the answers for all activities and to the practises and tests in the rest of the book.

   - For students: Online exercises and additional resources are available at www.mcgrawhill.ca/olc/langan.

In short, *English Essentials,* Canadian edition, is designed as a core textbook that will both engage the interest of today's students and help them truly master the skills they need to write well.

John Langan   **Beth Johnson**   **Lisa Salem-Wiseman**

Acknowledgments and Reviewer Names

First, this text would not exist without the contributions of the following people: Jo Altilia and Literature for Life, Sandeep Chahal, Samantha Conte, Ronda Franco and her students, Farzana Jamal, Jessica Lambert, Bryan Nedham, Laura Pettersen, Kinda Rodrigues, Kin Sambath, and Rosarina Saw. Hearing about their remarkable experiences was the best part of writing this book, and I thank them for their willingness to share, their honesty, and their humour. I am also grateful to my friends, colleagues, and students at Humber College, who were always generous with ideas, support, and encouragement.

I also thank my editors at McGraw-Hill Ryerson—Lisa Rahn and Suzanne Simpson Millar—for their unflagging enthusiasm for this project, and for patiently holding my hand throughout what was, for me, a new and somewhat overwhelming process.

In addition, I would also like to thank the following reviewers who provided valuable and insightful comments about the manuscript:

Barbara Danbrook, *Humber College*
Tony Gremaud, *Fanshawe College*
Donald E. Holmes, *Humber College*
Peter C. Miller, *Seneca College*
Shelly Lyck, *Loyalist College*
Colleen Mahy, *George Brown College*
Kathleen Moran, *Conestoga College*
Nina L. Padden, *Concordia University*
E. Alex Pierce, *Cape Breton University*
Mary Ann Pruyser, *North Island College*
Bruce Raskob, *Kwantlen University College*
Diane Ridout, *Kwantlen University College*
Melanie A. Rubens, *Seneca College*
Mike Tiittanen, *Seneca College*
Marju Toomsalu, *Ryerson University*
Mary Vespa, *Ryerson University*

Finally, special thanks must go to my husband Jonathan, for loving and encouraging me no matter how many projects I take on at once, and to my multitalented daughter Rachel; every day I am awed and inspired by her curiosity, creativity, wit, and love of language.

A Final Word

English Essentials has been designed to benefit you as much as possible. Its format is inviting, its explanations are clear, and its many activities, practices, tests, and assignments will help you learn through doing. It is a book that has been created to reward effort, and if you provide that effort, you can make yourself a competent and confident writer. We wish you success.

John Langan   **Beth Johnson**   **Lisa Salem-Wiseman**

BECOMING A BETTER WRITER PART 1

OBJECTIVES

In Parts 2 to 6, this page will be filled with a list of objectives, to allow you to quickly identify the skills that you will acquire throughout the chapters. This lets you know what you can reasonably expect to have learned by the end of the unit.

PART 1   PRETEST

The list of objectives will be followed by a short list of questions designed to help you identify how far you need to travel to fulfill the objectives of the section. This pretest will let you see which skills you may already have, which skills you may need to brush up on, and which skills you may need to learn from the ground up.

Answers to the pretest questions are available on the Online Learning Centre, where you will also find additional exercises and tests to help you develop your writing skills.

ORGANIZING YOUR WRITING

The stories in this book emphasize the life and career benefits that come from improving your writing skills. So, how can you do it? What, in brief, do you need to become a better writer? You need to know the basic goals in writing and to understand the different ways you can choose to organize your writing—as explained on the pages that follow.

Two Basic Goals in Writing

When you write a paper, your two basic goals should be (1) to make a point and (2) to support that point. Look for a moment at the following cartoon:

PEANUTS reproduced by permission of United Feature Syndicate, Inc.

See if you can answer the following questions:

- What is Snoopy's point in his paper?

  _____

- What is his support for his point?

  _____

Snoopy's point, of course, is that dogs are superior to cats. But he offers no support whatsoever to back up his point! There are two jokes here. First, he is a dog and so is naturally going to believe that dogs are superior. The other joke is that his evidence ("They just are, and that's all there is to it!") is nothing but a lot of empty words. His somewhat guilty look in the last panel suggests that he knows

3

he has not proved his point. To write effectively, you must provide real support for your points and opinions.

● How might Snoopy support his point?

He might list a number of reasons that dogs are better than cats.

After writing his main point and his supporting points in an informal outline, Snoopy is ready to turn his ideas into a paragraph.

Writing Paragraphs

A paragraph is a series of sentences about one main idea, or point. A paragraph usually starts with a sentence (called the **topic sentence**) that states the main point that the writer is making, and the rest of the paragraph provides specific details to support and develop that point.

Here is what Snoopy's paragraph might look like:

Why Dogs are Better than Cats

There are three main reasons that dogs are better than cats. First of all, there is no pleasure greater than returning home after a long day at work or school, to be greeted at the front door by the enthusiastic barking and tail-wagging of your best friend. A dog will always be happy to see you, unlike a cat, who will usually not even bother to get up from its nap to see who has arrived. Besides being affectionate and loving, dogs also respond well to training and can be quite obedient. When you tell your dog to "come," he or she will come. When you tell your dog to "sit," "stay," or even "shake hands," the dog will obey. Have you ever tried to order a cat around? Trust me—it can't be done! Dogs respond to their masters, while cats are their own masters. Finally, dog owners are able to experience the pleasure of sharing daily exercise and fresh air with a faithful companion.

Walking with a dog by your side is an enjoyable way to meet your neighbours, see your neighbourhood, and spend time with your pet. While some cat owners do attempt to force their pets onto leashes, the experiment usually ends with scratches and tears. So, if you are looking for an enthusiastic and energetic friend and companion, you would do well to adopt a dog. If you wish to be ignored and abused, a cat is for you.

Patterns of Organization

In the paragraph that you have just read, Snoopy has proven his main point by contrasting dogs and cats. This paragraph pattern is called **compare and contrast.** "Compare" means to discuss the similarities between two things. "Contrast" means to discuss the differences between two things.

 There are two ways of organizing a compare and/or contrast paragraph:

- **Block format:**
  Discuss all of the features of the first thing you are comparing. Then, discuss all the features of the second.

  Dogs
  — greet owners at the front door
  — follow orders
  — go for walks

  Cats
  — don't greet owners at the front door
  — don't follow orders
  — don't go for walks

- **Point-by-point format:**
  Discuss one feature of the first, followed by the same feature of the second. Repeat for each feature.

  Greeting owners at the front door
      Dogs: yes
      Cats: no

  Following orders
      Dogs: yes
      Cats: no

  Going for walks with owners
      Dogs: yes
      Cats: no

  Which method of organization, block or point-by-point, does Snoopy use for his paragraph? _____

To be effective, the supporting material in a paragraph must be organized in a logical way. Perhaps the most common way to do so is to use a **listing order**. In other words, provide a list of three or more reasons, examples, or other details. Use transitional words and phrases such as *First of all, For one thing, Another, Secondly, Also, In addition, Last of all,* and *Finally* to mark the items in your list.

> **NOTE**   Keep your transitional words and expressions consistent. If you start with "first," you should continue with "second," not "secondly" and "third," not "thirdly."

There is more than one way to prove a point, though. Snoopy might have chosen to discuss the superiority of dogs by telling a story about an exceptional dog. This paragraph pattern is called **narration.**

Dorado: A Brave and Loyal Dog

Unlike cats, dogs have often distinguished themselves by performing incredible acts of bravery and heroism. On September 11, 2001, a computer technician named Omar Eduardo Rivera was working in his office on the 71st floor of the World Trade Center. Mr. Rivera is blind, and Dorado, his four-year-old Labrador Retriever, was lying under his desk. When the hijacked airplane struck the south tower, he heard the sound of breaking glass. Unaware that a terrorist attack was taking place, he stayed at his desk; soon, however, Dorado became quite agitated, running repeatedly into the corridor. Rather than running to safety, Dorado returned to Mr. Rivera, pushing him out of the office and leading him to an emergency exit. Then, with the help of another man, Dorado began to guide Mr. Rivera down the stairs. Although people were panicking and pushing one another, Dorado stayed by his owner's side, protecting him from the crowds. At one point, Dorado was separated from Mr. Rivera, but he returned to his side. It took more than an hour for them to make it down seventy flights of stairs. Finally, they reached street level and ran; moments later, their tower began to collapse. While Dorado's bravery and loyalty are inspiring, they are examples of the qualities shared by most members of the canine family. Many dog owners can probably imagine their companions acting in a similar manner; however, it is hard to imagine a cat behaving the same way.

 When telling a story, use **time order**; write about things in the order in which they happened. Use transition words such as "then," "soon," "next," "later," or "finally," to lead the reader through the events.

- List three transition words that Snoopy uses in this paragraph:

_____   _____   _____

Methods of Organization

There are still other ways to organize paragraphs. Here are some common methods of organization, including the two you've just read about.

Compare and contrast   Physical description
Narration   Process description
Classification   Cause and effect

The method of organization you choose will depend on the topic your instructor assigns, as well as on your own interpretation of and approach to that topic.

CLASSIFICATION

Snoopy might also have written a paragraph classifying some of the different "personality types" of dogs, such as "the baby," "the protector," and "the best friend."

Write a possible first sentence for this paragraph.

_____

List two characteristics for each type. Try brainstorming with a partner.

The Baby: _____

The Protector: _____

The Best Friend: _____

Now, write a short paragraph on this subject.

PHYSICAL DESCRIPTION

Snoopy might have decided instead to describe the physical attributes of a particular dog or breed of dog. Snoopy might begin by describing his large head, with plenty of room for his massive brain. He might then proceed to his long ears, which not only help him hear the sound of food hitting his supper dish, but also double as a scarf to keep him warm in the winter.

When writing a physical description, it is most effective to use **describing order**, moving from top to bottom, or left to right.

What would he describe next? Can you finish the description?

_____

_____

 Here is a photo of Zeus, a Bernese mountain dog.

What things would you describe about this dog? List them in order, with a short description after each. Try brainstorming with a partner.

First   _____

Second   _____

Third   _____

Fourth   _____

Keep in mind that even descriptive paragraphs should have a point. What point do you want to make about Zeus's appearance?

Write a possible first sentence for a descriptive paragraph.

_____

Now, on a separate piece of paper, write a short paragraph describing Zeus.

PROCESS DESCRIPTION

Yet another choice of organization would be to describe a process. Snoopy might have written step by step about the process of a human falling in love with a dog.

 What are three steps that he could include? Try brainstorming with a partner.

_____

_____

_____

Write a possible first sentence for this paragraph.

_____

Now, write a short paragraph on this subject.

CAUSE AND EFFECT

Finally, Snoopy could organize his paragraph according to either the causes or effects of a particular action or event. For example, he could write about the causes of a person's bond with his or her dog. Or, he could write about the positive effects that dog ownership can have on ill or elderly people.

Choose one of these topics and list some possible causes or effects. Try brainstorming with a partner.

Topic: _____

_____

_____

_____

Write a possible first sentence for this paragraph.

_____

Now, on a separate piece of paper, write a short paragraph on this subject.

 Here is a paragraph written by college student Samantha Conte. Read the paragraph and answer the questions that follow.

When I was young, my mother's friend once told me, "The Conte women are strong ones." At the time I was too young to understand what she meant by this statement, but as the years progressed and my mother shared some of her stories with me, I began to understand. When she reached adolescence in the mid-1960s, there were many temptations. My mother resisted the pressure to experiment, but she still experienced the effects of drug and alcohol abuse first-hand. Her father was an alcoholic. When her mother was ill with breast cancer and unable to work, her father was more concerned with drinking than working. This put a lot of pressure on my mother, who was the oldest of five children, and she began working at the age of twelve to support the family. Because her father's drinking caused so many problems within her parents' household, she has never taken a single drink in her lifetime. She once told me that, during her teens, she had decided that she "never wanted to be like them." Furthermore, she has never used drugs. "If I ever catch any of you doing any drugs, you will go straight to boot camp" my mother told my sisters and me. I did not know why she was being so strict until she told me about her first husband, Luigi, whom she had married right out of high school. Though originally a nice and gentle man, Luigi began to experiment with certain drugs after they were married, and he eventually became a heroin addict. Before my mother knew it, she was pregnant and had a wild husband who was selling their possessions for drug money. Shortly after their daughter was born, Luigi ended up in prison. My mother filed for divorce, but the divorce was never finalized because Luigi died from a brain aneurism the night he was released from prison, leaving my mother a widow and a single parent with a dead-end job. My mother waited until her daughter was in school, worked during the day, and attended university at night. After many years of struggling to make ends meet, my mother graduated with a university degree and became an accountant. Eventually, she remarried and tried to make a life for herself and her child. She decided she would never let anyone push her around again. She did not like the idea of not being in control of her own life. As children, my sisters and I were always told that we have to be independent. "You can marry a millionaire," my mother says, "but you still have to be in the position to leave and stand on your own two feet." My mother, Kathy Luciani Conte, has an inner beauty of wisdom and intelligence that no one can take away from her. Yet, every time I look at her weathered eyes and tired face, I wish that her problems could be lifted gently off her shoulders for someone else to bear.

- What is the method of organization?
- What main point is Samantha making about her mother?
- What examples does she use to support this point?
- Is her concluding sentence effective? Why or why not?
- What would an appropriate title be for this paragraph?

Suggested Writing Topics

It is easiest to write well about a topic that interests you. Here are some topics to choose from. Your instructor may ask you to choose from these topics for a writing assignment, or you may use these topics for prewriting and writing practice. To practise using the different patterns of organization, you may want to select one topic from each category.

Narration Topics

Tell the story of
    a. an experience that taught you to take chances
    b. an experience you would like to forget
    c. the worst vacation you ever took
    d. an incident that taught you the value of friendship
    e. an experience that changed your life (e.g. the birth of a child, the death of someone close to you, etc.)
    f. a job that changed your life

 Use **time order** to organize your support.

Compare and Contrast Topics

Compare and/or contrast
    a. the experiences of being a high school student and being a college student
    b. two people you know who have different attitudes toward life
    c. two movies or television shows that are similar in subject matter
    d. your current career goals with those you had as a child (what you wanted to be "when you grew up")
    e. life in Canada with life in another country
    f. two contemporary performers (actors, musicians, etc.)

Use **listing order** to organize your support.

Classification Topics

Write about three different types of
   a. teachers
   b. friends
   c. jobs
   d. college students
   e. reality television shows
   f. celebrities

 Use **listing order** to organize your support.

Process Description Topics

Write about the process of
   a. ending a relationship
   b. applying to college
   c. passing an English class
   d. failing an English class
   e. talking your way out of a traffic ticket
   f. falling in love

 Use **time order** to organize your support.

Physical Description Topics

Describe the physical characteristics of
   a. your first love
   b. a place that is or was important to you
   c. a photograph that means a lot to you
   d. a work of art that you love
   e. a character from your favourite movie
   f. an object that has special significance for you

Use **describing order** to organize your support.

Cause and Effect Topics

Write about the causes of or reasons for
   a. the popularity of fast-food restaurants
   b. your admiration of _____ (the person you most admire)
   c. your fear of _____ (your greatest fear)

Write about the effects of
   a. a college education
   b. your fear of _____ (your greatest fear)
   c. Canadians' reliance on over-processed or fast food

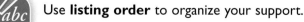 Use **listing order** to organize your support.

THE WRITING PROCESS

Even professional writers do not sit down and write a paper in a single draft. Instead, they have to work on it one step at a time. Writing a paper is a process that can be divided into the following five steps:

STEP 1 **Getting Started through Prewriting**

STEP 2 **Preparing a Scratch Outline**

STEP 3 **Writing the First Draft**

STEP 4 **Revising**

STEP 5 **Editing**

STEP 1 GETTING STARTED THROUGH PREWRITING

A student named Monique was given the assignment "Write a paragraph about the types of challenges facing college students today." Like many students, she found it difficult to get started.

Her instructor helped her by showing her a few methods to start the ideas flowing. These techniques are known as "**prewriting**" techniques, because you use them before you even try to start writing. These techniques will help you figure out both the point you want to make and the support you need for that point.

Here are four helpful prewriting techniques:

- Freewriting

- Questioning

- List making

- Mapping

 Try these techniques yourself when you find yourself staring at a blank page!

Freewriting

Freewriting is just sitting down and writing whatever comes into your mind about a topic. Do this for ten minutes or so. Write without stopping and without worrying in the slightest about spelling, grammar, and other technical concerns. Simply get down on paper all the information that occurs to you about the topic.

Below is part of the freewriting done by Monique for her paragraph.

> College is so hard for students today, teachers just don't get it. We have to work to pay crazy tuition costs, sometimes 2 or more jobs. Teachers tell us to cut down on our hours but then how are we supposed to pay for school? Teachers pile on the work and we have to juggle homework and assignments with work responsibilities. Lots of students have kids, too. Like Tonya. She has trouble making her morning classes cuz of dropping Curtis off at daycare. And when he's sick she can't come to school. And some of us don't live at home so we have to worry about paying rent and making meals and cleaning the apartment...

Notice that there are many problems with spelling, grammar, and punctuation in Monique's freewriting. Monique is not worried about such matters, nor should she be—at this stage. She is just concentrating on getting ideas and details down on paper. She knows that it is best to focus on one thing at a time. At this point, she just wants to write out thoughts as they come to her, to do some thinking on paper.

You should take the same approach when freewriting: explore your topic without worrying at all about writing "correctly." Figuring out what you want to say should have all your attention in this early stage of the writing process.

 The more you write, the better you'll get at expressing yourself in writing. Try keeping a journal or blog to get used to thinking on the page or screen. Be sure to write every day—don't worry about spelling or punctuation!

 On a sheet of paper, freewrite for at least ten minutes on the topic of "different ways of coping with stress." Don't worry about grammar, punctuation, or spelling. Try to write—without stopping—about whatever comes into your head concerning the topic.

Questioning

Questioning means that you generate details about your topic by writing down a series of questions and answers about it. Your questions can start with words like *who, what, when, where, why,* and *how.*

Here are just some of the questions that Monique might have asked while developing her paper:

- Who are the students facing the biggest challenges today?

- What challenges are they facing?

- Why is school so challenging for students today?

- What other responsibilities do students have?

- How do students balance schoolwork with other responsibilities?

- When do working students or students with children find time to study?

On a sheet of paper, answer the following questions about ways of coping with stress:

- What are some of the things that stress you out?
- Who do you talk to when you feel stressed out?
- Where do you go when you feel the effects of stress?
- What is one thing you do to cope with stress?
- Why does this method work? (Give one reason and some details that support that reason.)
- What is another thing you do to cope with stress? Why does this method work?
- Can you think of a third thing you do to cope with stress? Why does this method work?

List Making

In list making (also known as brainstorming), you make a list of ideas and details that could go into your paper. Simply list these items, one after another, without worrying about putting them in any special order. Try to accumulate as many details as you can think of. For example:

Juggling work and school

Juggling school and parenthood

I work to pay for school, but work is making it hard to do well in school!

Teachers don't understand—it was different when they were in school

It's hard to find time to do homework

Daycares that open late make it hard to get to early morning classes

Missing class when kids are sick

 On a separate piece of paper, make a list of ideas about coping with stress. Don't worry about putting them in a certain order. Just get down as many ideas as occur to you. The list can include specific methods of dealing with stress.

Mapping

Mapping, also known as "clustering," "diagramming," or "linking," is a method of gathering and organizing ideas with shapes and lines. The simple visual design makes connections easy to follow. To create a map, write your topic in the centre of your page and circle it. Next, think of a main point or idea related to your topic. Write it down and connect it to your topic with a line. Circle that idea, and then jot down any related facts or ideas, linking them to the idea with lines. Continue the process as shown below.

 In the centre of a piece of paper, write down the topic "Ways of Coping with Stress" and circle it. Now, following the instructions above, begin to fill the page with related ideas, points, facts, and examples related to your topic.

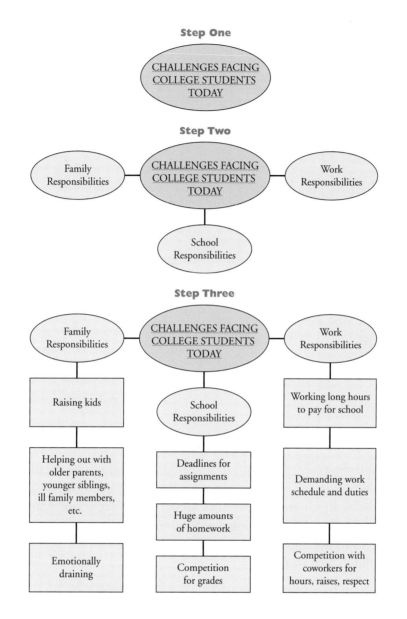

STEP 2 PREPARING A SCRATCH OUTLINE

A scratch outline is a brief plan for a paragraph. It shows at a glance the point of the paragraph and the support for that point. It is the logical framework on which the paper is built.

This rough outline may follow prewriting or it may gradually emerge in the midst of that stage. Or it may gradually emerge in the midst of these strategies. In fact, trying to outline is a good way to see if you need to do more prewriting. If a solid outline does not emerge, then you know you need to do more prewriting to clarify your main point or its support. And once you have a workable outline, you may realize, for instance, that you want to do more list making to develop one of the supporting details in the outline.

In Monique's case, as she was working on her list of details, she suddenly discovered what the plan of her paragraph could be. She realized that she could describe in turn each of three different kinds of challenges faced by college students in the twenty-first century.

Students today are faced with the challenge of juggling three sets of responsibilities:

1. Work responsibilities

2. Family responsibilities

3. School responsibilities

After all her preliminary writing, Monique sat back, pleased. She knew she had a promising paper—one with a clear point and solid support. Monique was now ready to write the first draft of her paper, using her outline as a guide.

 Using the list you have prepared, see if you can prepare a scratch outline made up of the three main ways you can think of to manage stress.

Although there is no way to completely avoid stress, there are three methods that you can learn to manage your stress.

Reason 1:_____

Reason 2:_____

Reason 3:_____

STEP 3 WRITING THE FIRST DRAFT

When you do a first draft, be prepared to put in additional thoughts and details that didn't emerge in your prewriting. And don't worry if you hit a snag. Just leave a blank space or add a comment such as "Do later" and press on to finish the paper. Also, don't worry yet about grammar, punctuation, or spelling. You don't want to take time correcting words or sentences that you may decide to remove later. Instead, make it your goal to develop the content of your paper with plenty of specific details.

Here is part of Monique's first draft.

First Draft

A lot of college students today face the challenge of juggling school work with the responsibilities of work and family. Today's students are given strict deadlines for turning in assignments and may lose marks for late work. Many college programs expect students to spend all their free time doing homework. There is a lot of competition for good grades. My friend Jessica missed out of being on the dean's list by just 3 marks and now she's worried about getting into the journalism program. Students don't only have school to worry about. Most students work outside of school. Some work crazy hours on top of going to school full time. Working long hours can leave students too tired to concentrate on their studies. Some bosses don't care that an employee is also a student. They schedule that employee for shifts that interfere with classes. The employees that only have work to focus on end up being the boss's favourite. That's not fair. They don't have to worry about school, too. Some students are also parents, or take care of other family members. This can leave you emotionally drained and make it hard to concentrate on school. Also, it can be hard when your child is sick and you have to miss classes or don't have time to finish a paper.

Now write a first draft of your paragraph about dealing with stress. Begin with a sentence stating the main idea of your paper, and then support it by discussing each of the three ways of dealing with stress. Don't worry about grammar, punctuation, or spelling. Just concentrate on getting the details down on paper.

STEP 4 REVISING

Revision (re + vision) means "to see again." This part of the process involves looking at your writing again, with fresh eyes. Put your paper aside (for a few minutes, an hour, several hours, or overnight, if possible) before looking at it again. Revising is as much a stage in the writing process as prewriting, outlining, and writing the first draft. Revising means that you rewrite a paper, building upon what has been done, to make it stronger and better. One writer has said about revision, "It's like cleaning house—getting rid of all the junk and putting things in the right order." A typical revision means writing at least one or two more drafts, adding and omitting details, organizing more clearly, and beginning to correct spelling and grammar.

Here is part of Monique's second draft.

Second Draft

Many twenty-first century college students face greater challenges than the generation before them. Not only do they have to cope with the increased demands of college programs, but many have to juggle schoolwork with the responsibilities of part-time or full-time jobs and caring for children or other family members. First of all, today's students are given strict deadlines for turning in assignments and may lose marks for late work. In addition to work done in class, many college programs expect students to spend two or three hours a night doing homework. With many students hoping to graduate with top marks, there is a lot of competition for good grades. These demands are stressful enough, but in addition to school, most of today's students work outside of school, with some working as many as thirty or more hours a week.

Notice that in redoing the draft, Monique started by making the point of her paragraph clearer. Also, she inserted transitions ("First of all" and "in addition") to clearly set off the different responsibilities. She took out the detail about her friend because it wasn't relevant to her argument, and she added more details to support her points.

Monique then went on to revise the second draft. Since she was doing her paper on a computer, she was able to print it out quickly. She double-spaced the lines, allowing room for revisions, which she added in longhand as part of her third draft, and eventually the paragraph on page 19 resulted. (Note that if you are not using a computer, you may want to skip every other line when writing out each draft. Also, write on only one side of a page, so that you can see your entire paper at one time.)

Ideally, you will have a chance to put the paper aside for a while before doing later drafts. When you revise, try to do all of the following:

- Omit any details that do not truly support your topic sentence.

- Add more details as needed, making sure you have plenty of specific support for each of your three reasons.

- If necessary, rearrange your ideas in a different, more effective order.

- Be sure to include a final sentence that rounds off the paper, bringing it to a close.

 Choose transitional words and phrases from this list to help your paragraph or essay flow more smoothly.

Transitional Words and Expressions			
Also	Further, furthermore	In the same way	Second, secondly
Although	In addition	Last, lastly	Similarly
Besides	In contrast	Next	Still
Even so, even though	Indeed	Of course	Then
Finally	In fact	On the other hand	
First, firstly	In the first place	Regardless	

STEP 5 EDITING

Editing, the final stage in the writing process, means checking a paper carefully for spelling, grammar, punctuation, and other errors. You are ready for this stage when you are satisfied that your point is clear, your supporting details are good, and your paper is well organized.

At this stage, you should read your paper out loud. Hearing how your writing sounds is an excellent way to pick up grammar and punctuation problems in your writing. Chances are that you will find a mistake at every spot where your paper does not read smoothly and clearly. For more suggestions on the editing stage, see Part 5: Proofreading.

At this point in her work, Monique read her latest draft out loud. She looked closely at all the spots where her writing did not read easily. She used a grammar handbook to deal with the problems at those spots in her paper, and she made the corrections needed so that all her sentences read smoothly. She also used her dictionary to check on the spelling of every word she was unsure about. She even took a blank sheet of paper and used it to uncover her paper one line at a time, looking for any other mistakes that might be there.

Here is Monique's final paragraph.

Final Draft

Being a Student: A Difficult Juggling Act

Many twenty-first century college students face greater challenges than the generation before them. Not only do they have to cope with the increased demands of college programs, but many have to juggle schoolwork with the responsibilities of part-time or full-time jobs and caring for children. First of all, today's students are given strict deadlines for turning in assignments and may lose marks for late work. In addition to work done in class, many college programs expect students to spend two or three hours a night doing homework. Also, with many students hoping to graduate with top marks, there is a lot of competition for good grades. These demands are stressful enough, but most of today's students have more than just school to worry about. With the cost of a college education so high, most students need to work to pay tuition and living expenses, with some working as many as thirty or more hours a week. The same job that is supposed to help a student pay for college can leave that student too tired to concentrate on his or her studies. In addition, the demands of a job create extra stress. Some bosses are not very understanding of an employee's school schedule and may interpret your inability to work certain times as a lack of loyalty to the company. This might cause you to lose out on raises, bonuses, or other rewards. Finally, if you think it's difficult to be both a student and an employee, consider how hard it is to add the role of parent. Students with children face additional challenges. They need to put their children first, which can leave little time at the end of the day for homework and studying. Instructors may not understand that you may occasionally have to miss class to care for your child. With all these extra pressures and responsibilities, it might be wise for high schools to start offering extracurricular courses in juggling.

Comment: Monique added an explanation of why many students need to work.

Comment: Examples of the "extra stress" referred to in the previous sentence.

Comment: Another transition—this one introduces Monique's final point: the added stress of being a student and a parent.

Comment: Examples of the "additional challenges" mentioned in the previous sentence.

Comment: Concluding statement. Notice how Monique incorporates the "juggling" image of the title!

When you have an almost-final draft of your paragraph on stress, edit it in the following ways:

- Read the paragraph aloud, listening for awkward wordings and places where the meaning is unclear. Make the changes needed for the paper to read smoothly and clearly. In addition, see if you can get another person to read the draft aloud to you. The spots that this person has trouble reading are spots where you may have to do some revision and correct your grammar or punctuation mistakes.

- Using your dictionary or spell-check program, check for any words that might be misspelled. However, be aware that spell-check programs miss many errors. For example, if you were to write "Their" instead of "There" in the sentence "There are many sources of stress for students," the program would accept it because "their" is an actual word, even though the word would be incorrect in this sentence.

- Finally, take a sheet of paper and cover your paper so that you can expose and carefully proofread one line at a time. Use your handbook to check any other spots where you think there might be grammar or punctuation mistakes in your writing.

GIVING YOUR WORK A TITLE

A college paper should always have a title. Calling your paper "Paper #1" is like naming your first child "Baby #1" or your dog "Dog"! Your piece of writing is unique, and its title should reflect that uniqueness.

- Choose a title that is informative and interesting, and that reflects your paper's topic, argument, and tone.

- The title should spark the reader's interest, making the reader want to read your paper.

- Centre the title at the top of the first page, and use the same font as the rest of your paper.

- Resist the urge to make the title a different colour.

- Do not use quotation marks around the title or put a period after the title.

- Capitalize each word in the title. (The only exceptions are small words such as *a, the, and, of, in,* and *for* in the middle of a title.)

- Skip a line between the title and the first sentence of the paper.

PREPARING IN-CLASS (HAND-WRITTEN) WRITING ASSIGNMENTS

Many college instructors will assign essays to be written in class. Here are some tips for formatting these assignments:

- Write on only one side of the paper.

- Write on every other line (double space).

- Use blue or black ink—never pencil or coloured ink.

- Write letters and punctuation marks as clearly as you can, taking care to distinguish between lower case and capital letters.

- Do not write in all capital letters.

- Write your name, the date, the title, and the section number of your course on the first page.

- Write your name on every page.

Writing Essays

Like a paragraph, an essay starts with a point and then goes on to provide specific details to support and develop that point. However, a paragraph is a series of sentences about one main idea or point, while an essay is a series of paragraphs about one main idea or point. Since an essay is much longer than one paragraph, it allows a writer to develop more fully a topic, adding examples and details to support the main argument.

Look at the following essay, written by Monique after she was asked to develop more fully her paragraph on the challenges facing college students.

Being a Student: A Difficult Juggling Act

It was Friday night, at ten o'clock, and Naomi had just checked on her sleeping five-year-old son after getting home from her shift at the coffee shop. She now lay on her bed, surrounded by books and papers, working on an essay for her English class. Her mother stood in the doorway, shaking her head. "When I was in college," she said, "we went out on Friday nights. We worked hard, but we still had time for fun." Naomi looked up from her books and rolled her eyes. "You don't get it, Mom," she sighed. "It was easier in your day." Naomi may be right. Twenty-first century college students may in fact face greater challenges than the generation before them. Not only do they have to cope with the increased demands of college programs, but many have to juggle schoolwork with the responsibilities of part-time or full-time jobs and caring for children.

First of all, today's students are given strict deadlines for turning in assignments and may lose marks for late work. Many programs have a strict "no late papers" policy, so a student who was not able to meet the deadline could lose anywhere from 5% to 100% of a paper's value. In addition to work done in class, many college programs expect students to spend two or three hours a night doing homework. There is a lot of competition for grades, and those students who are lucky enough to be able to devote several hours a night to reading and assignments are often those who graduate with the top marks.

Academic demands are stressful enough, but most of today's students have more than just school to worry about. With the cost of a college education so high, most students need to work to pay tuition and living expenses, with some working as many as thirty or more hours a week. The same job that is supposed to help a student pay for college can leave that student too tired to concentrate on his or her studies. In addition, the demands of a job create extra stress. Some bosses are not very understanding of an employee's school schedule and may interpret your inability to work certain times as a lack of loyalty to the company. This might cause you to lose out on raises, bonuses, or other rewards.

Finally, if you think it's difficult to be both a student and an employee, consider how hard it is to add the role of parent. Students with children face additional challenges. They need to put their children first, which can leave little time at the end of the day for homework and studying. Young children get sick frequently and require their parents' attention, which can interfere with attending classes and completing assignments. In addition, daycare spaces are expensive and difficult to find. With waiting lists of more than a year for many daycares and after-school programs, many young parents turn to less reliable forms of childcare, such as family members or friends. As a result, students with children find themselves having to miss classes frequently; this has a negative effect on their grades.

As you can see, while attending college carries with it many pressures, many of today's students are not only students, but also employees and parents. With all these extra pressures and responsibilities, it might be wise for high schools to start offering extracurricular courses in juggling.

Comment: An interesting, eye-catching opening.

Comment: Thesis statement

Comment: Notice how Monique uses more specific examples.

Comment: Monique has expanded this section with more detailed information.

Comment: Here, Monique rephrases her thesis statement.

- Which sentence in the introductory paragraph expresses the central point of the essay?

_____

- How many supporting paragraphs are provided to back up the central point?

_____

THE PARTS OF AN ESSAY

Each of the parts of an essay is explained below.

Introductory Paragraph

A well-written introductory paragraph will normally do the following:

- Gain the reader's interest by using one of several common **methods of introduction**.
- Present the **thesis statement**. The thesis statement expresses the central point of an essay, just as a topic sentence states the main idea of a paragraph. The central idea in Monique's essay is expressed in the last sentence of the introductory paragraph.

Four Common Methods of Introduction

Four common methods of introduction are (1) telling a brief story, (2) asking one or more questions, (3) shifting to the opposite, or (4) going from the broad to the narrow. Following are examples of all four.

1. **Telling a brief story.** An interesting anecdote is hard for a reader to resist. In an introduction, a story should be no more than a few sentences, and it should relate meaningfully to the central idea. The story can be an experience of your own, of someone you know, or of someone you have read about. Monique uses this method of introduction for her essay on the challenges facing students.

   > It was Friday night, at ten o'clock, and Naomi had just checked on her sleeping five-year-old son after getting home from her shift at the coffee shop. She now lay on her bed, surrounded by books and papers, working on an essay for her English class. Her mother stood in the doorway, shaking her head. "When I was in college," she said, "we went out on Friday nights. We worked hard, but we still had time for fun." Naomi looked up from her books and rolled her eyes. "You don't get it, Mom," she sighed. "It was easier in your day."

2. **Asking one or more questions.** These questions may be ones that you intend to answer in your essay, or they may indicate that your topic is relevant to readers—it is something they care about. If Monique had used this approach, here is how her introductory paragraph might have looked:

   > Are you a college student? Do you hold a part-time or full-time job? Do you have family responsibilities? Do you feel that there just aren't enough hours in the day to accomplish all that you need to do? If so, you are not alone. Twenty-first century college students face greater challenges than the generation before them. Not only do they have to cope with the increased demands of college programs, but many have to juggle schoolwork with the responsibilities of part-time or full-time jobs and caring for children.

3. **Shifting to the opposite.** Another way to gain the reader's interest is to first present an idea that is the opposite of what will be written about. Using this approach, Monique might have begun her essay like this:

> People often assume that the life of a college student is a carefree existence; no one cares if you skip classes, professors are generous with extensions, and the only obligation is showing up at pub night to unwind with your classmates. However, this picture is, sadly, false. Twenty-first century college students face greater challenges than the generation before them. Not only do they have to cope with the increased demands of college programs, but many have to juggle schoolwork with the responsibilities of part-time or full-time jobs and caring for children.

4. **Going from the broad to the narrow.** Broad, general observations can capture your reader's interest; they can also introduce your general topic and provide helpful background information. If Monique had used this method of introduction, she might have begun by writing about the general challenges of living in the twenty-first century, and then narrowed her focus down to the challenges of being a student.

> Young people who are reaching their late teens and early twenties today face an entirely new set of challenges from those faced by their parents. They have grown up in a world that has been shaped by technological, social, and economic changes that their parents could not even have imagined at their age. As a result, twenty-first century college students face greater challenges than the generation before them. Not only do they have to cope with the increased demands of college programs, but many have to juggle schoolwork with the responsibilities of part-time or full-time jobs and caring for children.

5. **Beginning with a startling statement or fact.** A shocking statement or little-known fact can grab your reader's attention, making them want to read your essay to find out more. Using this approach, Monique might have begun her essay like this:

> Twenty-first century college students face greater challenges than the generation before them. Not only do they have to cope with the increased demands of college programs, but many have to juggle schoolwork with the responsibilities of part-time or full-time jobs and caring for children.

Supporting Paragraphs

Once you have your introduction and main point, it is time to think about supporting your argument. The following cartoon illustrates a common view about essay writing.

© United Media

The boy in the cartoon is wrong! The thesis statement only **states** your main point; now you have to **prove** that point.

The number of supporting paragraphs you write will depend on your topic, the nature of the assignment, and the number of words your instructor asks for. Each supporting paragraph should have its own topic sentence stating the point to be developed in that paragraph. The point can be developed using forms of support such as facts, examples, anecdotes, and quotations.

Notice that the essay on the challenges facing students has clear topic sentences for each of the three supporting paragraphs.

Transitional Sentences

In a paragraph, transitional words like *First, Another, Also, In addition*, and *Finally* are used to help connect supporting ideas. In an essay, transitional sentences are used to help tie the supporting paragraphs together. Such transitional sentences often occur at the beginning of a supporting paragraph.

- Look at the topic sentences for the second and third supporting paragraphs in the essay on college students page 21. Explain how those sentences are also transitional sentences.

_____

_____

Concluding Paragraph

The concluding paragraph often summarizes the essay by briefly restating the thesis and, at times, the main supporting points. It may also provide a closing thought or two as a way of bringing the paper to a natural, graceful, and meaningful end.

- Look again at the concluding paragraph of the essay on challenges facing college students.

Which sentence summarizes the essay? _____

_____

What supporting points are mentioned in the conclusion? _____

_____

Which sentences provide closing thoughts? _____

_____

The conclusion has been omitted from the following essay, which was written by college student Sandeep Chahal. How would you conclude this essay? Write a concluding paragraph that restates the main argument, summarizes the supporting points, and leaves the reader with an interesting thought. Sandeep's concluding paragraph can be read on the Online Learning Centre.

Godzilla: An Ideal Citizen?

Most people are aware of Godzilla, a gigantic monster created from nuclear weapons. However, how many people realize that Godzilla is actually an ideal citizen and an excellent role model? When Godzilla was formed in 1954, he was a destructive creature who scared Japan and caused much chaos though the city. Surprisingly though, Godzilla has helped more than he has harmed. Although he was chiefly a destructive creature, Godzilla has protected humans by defeating many threatening monsters. In addition, he has taught many helpful lessons and lovingly raised two children. Despite the fact that Godzilla is chiefly a destructive monster that intends to enforce his dominance, certain characteristics of his make him an ideal, helpful, caring citizen and a role model for many.

Although Godzilla is often referred to as a "monster of mass destruction" and an "incredible, unstoppable titan of terror" (Godzilla 1954), he helps more than he harms. In Godzilla's universe, there are many other monsters that pose threats such as King Ghidorah, Biolante, and Gigan. When these monsters strike, enormous calamity results; luckily, Godzilla fights and defeats these foes. While Godzilla is likely to have been only defending his property or his own life, by defeating these monsters he saves citizens and becomes an unlikely hero. After all, it is better to oppose one monster, instead of many. Furthermore, during the Showa period (1962–1975), Godzilla was literally a hero, idolized by children for defeating terrorizing monsters to save humans. Additionally, he was also willing to sacrifice himself to defeat great enemies, and even teamed with humans and other monsters to battle threatening opponents. Even in his original form, he did his best to assist humans; as the Godzillasaurus ("Godzilla vs King Ghidorah," 1991), he prevents a Japanese squad from being massacred by Americans during World War II. In fact, he has prevented more deaths than he has caused.

Surprisingly, this supposedly terrible monster is an effective teacher, bringing vital lessons to humanity. In Godzilla vs Hedorah (1971), Godzilla taught an important lesson about our environment. In this film, images of the seas are shown, polluted with toxins and other waste; the pollution forms a giant smog monster, Hedorah, who pollutes the air and ground. Before the city is laid to waste, Godzilla arrives and defeats the smog monster before it engulfs Japan with pollutants. This promotes a realization of our polluted environment and teaches humans not to pollute the water. Not only is Godzilla an environmentalist, he teaches citizens about the dangers of nuclear technology as well. During the 1950s, Godzilla served as a warning that nuclear weapons are dangerous and can create monsters. Godzilla also promotes cooperation and stresses companionship, as he often teams with others, including Rodan in Monster Zero (1965), Jet Jaguar in Godzilla vs Megalon (1973), and Anguirus in Godzilla vs Gigan (1972), to win battles that he could not have won alone. An additional important lesson Godzilla enforces, is perseverance. Godzilla would never quit or surrender. Because Godzilla is popular, the youth listen to him. This includes his own sons.

Godzilla was actually a father; he asexually reproduced on two different occasions, creating two separate sons. His first son was Minlla, an odd-looking child with not much strength or size advantage. However, rather than give up on his child, Godzilla protected him and trained him to defeat bigger opponents on their island. He ensured that Minlla was not harmed and answered his cries for need. Godzilla also had another son, Godzilla Junior. Junior was named and raised by humans, but was protected by Godzilla, who even risked his life by raiding the human areas for the secure return of his son. Not only was Godzilla compassionate for Junior, he also really cared for his son. In *Godzilla vs Destoroyah* (1995) Godzilla went into a blind rage and even sacrificed himself after Destoroyah, one of Godzilla's strongest foes, killed his son Junior, while Junior was attempting to help his father battle Destoroyah. His son would risk his life to fight an impossible battle, just to help his father, while Godzilla would sacrifice himself to gain revenge, a truly heartbreaking story. Godzilla is evidently an ideal family man; one might argue that he is a better, more nurturing, and more compassionate father than most.

_____

_____

_____

_____

_____

_____

More Questions for Consideration

- What is the effect of the title?
- What introductory strategy does the author use?
- What is the thesis statement of this essay?
- What are the three supporting points?
- What evidence does the author give to back up each point?

A NOTE ON RESEARCH

Many college writing instructors will assign paragraphs and essays for which the support comes from your personal experience or observations. Frequently, they want you to write about what you know, without the use of any sources.

If you are asked to write a paper that requires research, your instructor may give you specific instruction as to where you may find your information. If not, the best place to start is your college library. Use the library website to locate books, magazine and journal articles, or other resources. Don't be afraid to ask a librarian for help!

If you use any secondary sources in your writing, you are required to document them using the documentation format recommended by your instructor. The most common ones are MLA (Modern Language Association) and APA (American Psychological Association).

A NOTE ON PLAGIARISM

Keep in mind that you do not want to take other people's ideas or words—that would be stealing. The formal term is *plagiarizing*—using someone else's work and presenting it as your own. Every college has a policy for dealing with plagiarism; you may end up with a grade of zero in the course, or you may end up being removed from your program.

THE BASICS

OBJECTIVES

In Part 2 you will learn the basic elements of sentence construction and discover how to recognize, avoid, and correct some of the most common errors in written English.

By the end of Part 2, you should be able to

- Distinguish between the various parts of speech;

- Understand the function of subjects and verbs;

- Use the correct past tense of regular and irregular verbs;

- Distinguish between simple, compound, and complex sentences;

- Combine pairs of simple sentences into compound and complex sentences;

- Distinguish between the various pronoun forms;

- Choose the correct pronoun form;

- Distinguish between indefinite and definite articles;

- Identify missing articles in sentences;

- Distinguish between adjectives and adverbs;

- Determine whether a sentence requires an adjective or an adverb.

The following exercise will help you determine how much you already know about the topics covered in this section.

Here are five sentences, each of which contains **two** of the types of errors covered in Part 2. Correct the errors in the spaces provided. *Answers are available on the Online Learning Centre.*

1. I be glad that my son got a "A" in math.

   _____

2. If you have any questions about the dress code, just ask Jamie or I and we'll be gladly to help.

   _____

3. Ishmael says that after the game, him and his friends will stay at the field and help clean up a garbage left behind by the spectators.

   _____

4. All the neighbours is relieved that the police catched the thief.

   _____

5. The boys laughed loud when their friend tripped over a ant.

   _____

How many errors did you catch? _____/10

PARTS OF SPEECH

Words—the building blocks of sentences—can be divided into eight parts of speech. **Parts of speech** are classifications of words according to their meaning and use in a sentence.

This chapter will explain the eight parts of speech:

nouns	**prepositions**	**conjunctions**
pronouns	**adjectives**	**interjections**
verbs	**adverbs**	

NOUNS

A noun is a word that is used to name something: a person, a place, an object, or an idea. Here are some examples of nouns:

woman	city	doughnut	freedom
Margaret Atwood	street	school	possibility
Jim Carrey	Montreal	Seneca College	mystery

Most nouns begin with a lower case (not a capital) letter and are known as **common nouns**. These nouns name general things. Some nouns, however, begin with a capital letter. They are called **proper nouns**. While a common noun refers to a person or thing in general, a proper noun names someone or something specific. For example, *woman* is a common noun—it doesn't name a particular woman. On the other hand, Margaret Atwood is a proper noun because it names a specific woman.

PRACTICE 1

Insert any appropriate noun into each of the following blanks. Answers will vary.

1. Kirpal watched in amazement as the shoplifter stuffed a large
   _____ down the front of his pants.

2. _____ kicked the soccer ball down the field.

3. On my flight to Halifax, the person behind me kept putting their
   _____ on my armrest.

4. A(n) _____ crashed through the window.

5. The snowplow left a huge pile of snow right in front of my
   _____.

Singular and Plural Nouns

Singular nouns name one person, place, object, or idea. **Plural nouns** refer to two or more persons, places, objects, or ideas. Most singular nouns can be made plural with the addition of an *s*:

Singular	Plural
computer	computers
day	days
friend	friends
truth	truths
house	houses

Some nouns have irregular plurals. You can check the plural of nouns you think may be irregular by looking up the singular form in a dictionary. Here are some common irregular plurals:

foot	feet
child	children
box	boxes
bus	buses
mouse	mice
tomato	tomatoes
knife	knives
man	men
tooth	teeth

For more information on nouns, see "Subjects and Verbs," page 41.

PRACTICE 2

Underline the three nouns in each sentence. Some are singular, and some are plural.

1. Two bats swooped over the heads of the frightened children.

2. How did you get that stain on the sleeve of your jacket?

3. The lost dog has fleas and a broken leg.

4. Mariah likes to write all her assignments in green ink.

5. Some students start studying the night before an exam.

PRONOUNS

A **pronoun** is a word that stands for a noun. Pronouns eliminate the need for constant repetition. Look at the following sentences:

- The phone rang, and Gizman answered the phone.

- Denisha met Denisha's friends in the record store at the mall. Denisha meets Denisha's friends there every Saturday.

- The server rushed over to the new customers. The new customers asked the server for menus and coffee.

Now look at how much clearer and smoother the sentences sound with pronouns.

- The phone rang, and Gizman answered **it**.
  The pronoun *it* is used to replace the word *phone*.

- Denisha met **her** friends in the mall record store. **She** meets **them** there every Saturday.
  The pronoun *her* is used to replace the word Denisha. The pronoun *she* replaces Denisha. The pronoun *them* replaces the words *Denisha's friends*.

- The server rushed over to the new customers. **They** asked **him** for menus and coffee.
  The pronoun *they* is used to replace the words *the new customers*. The pronoun *him* replaces the words *the server*.

Following is a list of commonly used pronouns known as **personal pronouns**:

I	you	he	she	it	we	they
me	your	him	her	its	us	them
my	yours	his	hers		our	their

PRACTICE 3

Fill in each blank with the appropriate personal pronoun.

1. Erasto feeds his pet lizard every day before school, and _____ also gives _____ flies in the afternoon.

2. When Alicia interviewed the striking workers, _____ told _____ about their demand for higher wages and longer breaks.

3. To make studying for the final exam easier, students should save all returned tests, and _____ should also keep _____ review sheets.

4. The pilot announced that we would fly through some air pockets, but _____ said that we should be past _____ soon.

5. I sent my instructor an e-mail last Friday, but she insists that _____ never received _____.

There are a number of types of pronouns. For convenient reference, they are described briefly in the box below.

Types of Pronouns

Personal pronouns can act as subjects, objects, or possessives in a sentence.

Singular I, me, my, mine, you, your, yours, he, him, his, she, her, hers, it, its

Plural we, us, our, ours, you, your, yours, they, them, their, theirs

Relative pronouns refer to someone or something already mentioned in the sentence.

who, whose, whom, which, that

Interrogative pronouns are used to ask questions.

who, whose, whom, which, what

Demonstrative pronouns are used to point out particular persons or things.

this, that, these, those

NOTE   Do not use *them* (as in them shoes), *this here, that there, these here,* or *those there.*

Reflexive pronouns are those that end in *-self* or *-selves*. A reflexive pronoun is used as the object of a verb (as in *Cary cut* **herself**) or the object of a preposition (as in *Jack sent a birthday card to* **himself**) when the subject of the verb is the same as the object.

Singular myself, yourself, himself, herself, itself

Plural ourselves, yourselves, themselves

Intensive pronouns have exactly the same forms as reflexive pronouns. The difference is in how they are used. Intensive pronouns are used to add emphasis. (*I* **myself** *will need to read the contract before I sign it.*)

Indefinite pronouns do not refer to a particular person or thing.

each, either, everyone, nothing, both, several, all, any, most, none

Reciprocal pronouns express shared actions or feelings.

each other (used for two), one another (used for three or more)

For more information on pronouns, see "Pronoun Forms," pages 71–82, and "Pronoun Problems," pages 83–94.

PRACTICE 4

Insert one of each of the following types of pronouns in the appropriate spaces: relative, demonstrative, reflexive, indefinite, and reciprocal.

1. Rather than hire painters, Raina has decided to paint her son's room _____.

2. Jamal and his two brothers are always fighting with _____.

3. The college offers a scholarship to students _____ get 80% or more.

4. I don't want these earrings. I would like to see _____ ones on the top shelf.

5. _____ on the bus became angry when the driver pulled over to have a cigarette.

VERBS

Every complete sentence must contain at least one verb. There are two types of verbs: **action verbs** and **linking verbs**.

Action Verbs

An **action verb** tells what is being done in a sentence. For example, look at the following sentences:

- Céline Dion **performed** in Las Vegas last year.
- Rainwater **poured** into the storm sewer.
- The dentist **drilled** into the infected tooth.

In these sentences, the verbs are *performed, poured,* and *drilled.* These words are all action verbs; they tell what is happening in each sentence.

For more about action verbs, see "Subjects and Verbs," page 41.

PRACTICE 5

Insert an appropriate word into each blank. That word will be an action verb; it will tell what is happening in the sentence. Answers will vary.

1. When Jesse's mother came into the room, he quickly _____ what he was doing.

2. The animals in the cage _____ all day.

3. I only _____ healthy food.

4. Lamia _____ her boyfriend on the phone.

5. Our instructor _____ our papers over the weekend.

Linking Verbs

Some verbs are **linking verbs**. These verbs link (or join) a noun to something that is said about it. For example, look at the following sentence:

- The clouds **are** steel grey.

In this sentence, *are* is a linking verb. It joins the noun *clouds* to words that describe it: *steel grey.* Other common linking verbs include *am/is/are, appear(s), become(s), feel(s), seem(s),* and *was/were.*

Words that refer to the senses are also linking verbs. For example: look(s), sound(s), feel(s), smell(s), taste(s).

For more about linking verbs, see "Subjects and Verbs," page 41.

PRACTICE 6

Into each slot, insert one of the following linking verbs: *am, feel, is, looks, are*. Use each linking verb once.

1. The important papers _____ in a desk drawer.

2. I _____ anxious to get my test back.

3. The economic situation for the next year _____ bad.

4. To serve customers who work late, the grocery store _____ open until 11 p.m.

5. Whenever I _____ angry, I go off by myself to calm down.

Helping Verbs

Sometimes the verb of a sentence consists of more than one word. In these cases, the main verb will be joined by one or more **helping verbs**. Look at the following sentence.

- The basketball team **will be leaving** for their game at six o'clock.
  In this sentence, the main verb is *leaving*. The helping verbs are *will* and *be*.

Other helping verbs include *can, could, do, has, have, may, might, must, should,* and *would*.

For more information about helping verbs, see "Subjects and Verbs," pages 42 and 44.

PRACTICE 7

Into each slot, insert one of the following helping verbs: *does, must, should, could,* and *has been*. Use each helping verb once.

1. _____ your boss know that you want to take next week off?

2. The victim _____ describe her attacker in great detail.

3. You _____ rinse the dishes before putting them into the dishwasher.

4. My neighbour _____ arrested for drunk driving.

5. Even though we asked him nicely, the bus driver told us that he _____ not make any extra stops.

PREPOSITIONS

A **preposition** is a word, usually indicating direction, location, or order, that connects a noun or a pronoun to another word in the sentence. For example, look at the following sentence:

- A man **on** the bus was snoring loudly.

  On is a preposition. It connects the noun *bus* to *man*.

Here is a list of common prepositions:

about	around	beneath	during	into	over	under
above	at	beside	except	like	since	up
across	before	between	for	of	through	with
after	behind	by	from	off	to	without
among	below	down	in	on	toward	

The noun or pronoun that comes after the preposition is called the **object** of the preposition. Let us look at the sentence again:

- A man **on** the **bus** was snoring loudly.

  The noun *bus* is the object of the preposition *on*. It tells you where the man was.

A group of words that begins with a preposition and ends with its object is called a **prepositional phrase**. The words *on the bus*, for example, are a prepositional phrase.

Now read the following sentences and explanations.

- A spider was crawling **up the teacher's leg**.

  The noun *leg* is the object of the preposition *up*. *Up* connects *leg* with the word *crawling*. The prepositional phrase *up the teacher's leg* describes *crawling*. It tells just where and in what direction the spider was crawling.

- The man **with the black moustache** left the restaurant quickly.

  The noun moustache is the object of the preposition *with*. The prepositional phrase *with the black moustache* describes the word *man*. It tells us exactly which man left the restaurant quickly.

- The plant **on the windowsill** was a present **from my mother**.

  The noun windowsill is the object of the preposition *on*. The prepositional phrase *on the windowsill* describes the word *plant*. It describes exactly which plant was a present, and where the plant is located.

  There is a second prepositional phrase in this sentence. The preposition is *from*, and its object is *mother*. The prepositional phrase *from my mother* explains *present*. It tells who gave the present.

For more about prepositions, see "Subjects and Verbs," page 43 and "Subject–Verb Agreement," pages 119–130.

PRACTICE 8

Into each slot, insert one of the following prepositions: *after, of, by, in,* and *without.* Use each preposition once.

1. Would you like a drive home _____ class?

2. Please put the milk back _____ the refrigerator when you are finished with it.

3. _____ giving any notice, the tenant moved out of the expensive apartment.

4. Ahmed hungrily ate three scoops _____ ice cream and an order of French fries.

5. The recycling bins _____ the back door contain glass bottles, plastic containers, and old newspapers.

ADJECTIVES

An **adjective** is a word that describes a noun (the name of a person, place, or thing). Look at the following sentence.

- The dog lay down on a mat in front of the fireplace.

Now look at this sentence when adjectives have been inserted.

- The **shaggy** dog lay down on a **worn** mat in front of the fireplace.
  The adjective *shaggy* describes the noun *dog*; the adjective *worn* describes the noun *mat.* Adjectives add spice to our writing. They also help us to identify particular people, places, or things.

Adjectives can be found in two places:

1. An adjective may come before the word it describes (a **damp** night, the **mouldy** bread, a **striped** umbrella).

2. An adjective that describes the subject of a sentence may come after a linking verb. The linking verb may be a form of the verb *be* (he is **furious**, I am **exhausted**, they are **hungry**). Other linking verbs include *feel, look, sound, smell, taste, appear, seem,* and *become* (the soup tastes **salty**, your hands feel **dry**, the girl seems **sad**).

   The words *a, an,* and *the* (called **articles**) are generally classified as adjectives.

For more information on adjectives, see "Adjectives and Adverbs," pages 104–116.

PRACTICE 9

Write any appropriate adjective in each slot. Answers will vary.

1. When Guillermo first moved to Manitoba, he found the winters to be very
   _____ and _____.

2. _____ pizza was eaten greedily by the _____ teenagers.

3. Melissa gave away the sofa because it was _____ and _____.

4. Although the alley is _____ and _____, Karen often takes
   it as a shortcut home.

5. The owner of that restaurant throws away any _____ food, but she takes any
   _____ food to a local homeless shelter.

6. When I woke up in the morning, I had a(n) _____ fever and a(n)
   _____ throat.

ADVERBS

An **adverb** is a word that describes a verb, an adjective, or another adverb. Many adverbs end in the letters *ly*. Look at the following sentence:

- The parrot squawked in the pet-store window as the children watched.

  Now look at this sentence after adverbs have been inserted.

- The parrot squawked **loudly** in the pet-store window as the children watched **silently**.

The adverbs add details to the sentence. They also allow the reader to contrast the noise the parrot is making to the silence of the children. Look at the following sentences and the explanations of how adverbs are used in each case.

- The chef yelled **angrily** at the young waiter.
  The adverb *angrily* describes the verb *yelled*.

- Carl **rarely** watches television.
  The adverb *rarely* describes the verb *watches*.

- My mother has an **extremely** busy schedule on Tuesdays.
  The adverb *extremely* describes the adjective *busy*.

- When I am nervous, I speak **very** softly.
  The adverb *very* describes the adverb *softly*.

Some adverbs do not end in *-ly*. Examples include *very, often, never, always,* and *well*.

For more information on adverbs, see "Adjectives and Adverbs," pages 104–116.

PRACTICE 10

Write any appropriate adverb in each slot. Answers will vary.

1. Screaming _____, the man slammed down the telephone.

2. Skating _____ toward the goal, the little girl prepared to score.

3. The 911 operator spoke _____ to the young child.

4. The *Canadian Idol* contestant smiled _____ after finishing her song.

5. Navneet _____ studies, so it is no surprise that she failed her final exam.

CONJUNCTIONS

Conjunctions are words that connect one idea to another within a sentence. There are two types of conjunctions, coordinating and subordinating.

Coordinating Conjunctions (Joining Words)

Coordinating conjunctions join two equal ideas. Look at the following sentence:

- Most Canadians pay both a provincial sales tax **and** the federal Goods and Services Tax (GST), **but** Alberta does not have a provincial sales tax.

  In this sentence, the coordinating conjunction *and* connects the modified nouns *provincial sales tax* and *federal Goods and Services Tax.* The coordinating conjunction *but* connects the first part of the sentence, *Most Canadians pay both a provincial sales tax **and** the federal Goods and Services Tax (GST),* to the second part, ***but** Alberta does not have a provincial sales tax.*

Following is a list of all the coordinating conjunctions. It helps to think of them as **joining words**.

and	for	or	yet
but	nor	so	

  The coordinating conjunctions can be remembered by thinking of the word "FANBOYS."

F =	for	(Serena enjoys competitive swimming, **for** it is challenging.)
A =	and	(I was nominated for an award, **and** I won!)
N =	nor	(Pavlo doesn't like spinach, **nor** does he like broccoli.)
B =	but	(Sanah had a soccer game, **but** it was cancelled due to rain.)
O =	or	(David needs to save money, **or** he will go broke.)
Y =	yet	(Priya is mad at Melissa, **yet** she invited her to the party.)
S =	so	(Vancouver is very rainy, **so** I will pack my umbrella.)

For more on coordinating conjunctions, see information on joining words in "Sentence Types," pages 61–70, and "Run-Ons and Comma Splices," pages 145–156.

PRACTICE 11

Write a coordinating conjunction in each slot. Choose from the following: *and, but, so, or*, and *nor*. Use each conjunction once.

1. Either Devlin _____ Alex scored the winning touchdown.

2. I expected roses for my birthday, _____ I received a vase of plastic tulips from the discount store.

3. The cafeteria was serving liver and onions for lunch, _____ I bought a sandwich at the corner deli.

4. Nashana brought a pack of playing cards _____ a pan of brownies to the company picnic.

5. Neither my sofa _____ my armchair matches the rug in my living room.

Subordinating Conjunctions

When a **subordinating conjunction** is added to a word group, the words can no longer stand alone as an independent sentence. They are no longer a complete thought. For example, look at the following sentence:

- Jaylin fainted in class.

  The word group *Jaylin fainted in class* is a complete thought. It can stand alone as a sentence.

See what happens when a subordinating conjunction is added to a complete thought:

- **When** Jaylin fainted in class

  Now the words cannot stand alone as a sentence. They are dependent on other words to complete the thought.

- **When** Jaylin fainted in class, we brought her some water and called the Student Health Centre.

  In this book, a word that begins a dependent word group is called a **dependent word**. Subordinating conjunctions are common dependent words.

Below are some subordinating conjunctions.

after	because	even though	though	when	wherever
although	before	if	unless	whenever	whether
as	even if	since	until	where	while

Following are some more sentences with subordinating conjunctions:

- **After** she finished her last exam, Joanne said, "Now I can relax."

  After she finished her last exam is not a complete thought. It is dependent on the rest of the words to make up a complete sentence.

- Lamont listens to books on tape **while** he drives to work.

  While he drives to work cannot stand by itself as a sentence. It depends on the rest of the sentence to make up a complete thought.

- **Since** apples were on sale, we decided to make an apple pie for dessert.

  Since apples were on sale is not a complete sentence. It depends on *we decided to make an apple pie for dessert* to complete the thought.

For more information on subordinating conjunctions, see information on dependent words in "Sentence Types," pages 61–70; "Fragments," pages 131–144; and "Run-Ons and Comma Splices," pages 145–156.

PRACTICE 12

Write a logical subordinating conjunction in each slot. Choose from the following: *even though, because, until, when,* and *before.* Use each conjunction once.

1. The bank was closed down _____ it lost more money than it earned.

2. _____ Paula wants to look mysterious, she wears dark sunglasses and a scarf.

3. _____ the restaurant was closing in fifteen minutes, customers sipped their coffee slowly and continued to talk.

4. _____ anyone else could answer it, Jordan rushed to the phone and whispered, "It's me."

5. The waiter was instructed not to serve any food _____ the guests of honour arrived.

INTERJECTIONS

Interjections are words that can stand independently and are used to express emotion. Examples are *oh, wow, ouch,* and *oops.* These words are usually not found in formal writing.

- **"Hey!"** yelled Maggie. "That's my bike."
- **Oh,** we're late for class.

 A word may function as more than one part of speech. For example, the word *dust* can be a verb or a noun, depending on its role in the sentence.

- I **dust** my bedroom once a month, whether it needs it or not. (verb)
- The top of my refrigerator is covered with an inch of **dust**. (noun)

 Choose a piece of your own writing. It could be a school assignment, a letter, an e-mail, or something else. Read through it, looking for two examples of each of the following:

Two nouns: _____   _____

Two pronouns: _____   _____

Two verbs: _____   _____

Two prepositions: _____   _____

Two adjectives: _____   _____

Two adverbs: _____   _____

Two conjunctions: _____   _____

Two interjections: _____   _____

CHAPTER 4

SUBJECTS AND VERBS

Basics about Subjects and Verbs

Every complete sentence contains a **subject** and a **verb**.

SUBJECTS

The **subject** of a sentence is the person, place, thing, or idea that the sentence is about. The subject can be called the "who or what" word. To find the subject, ask yourself, "Who or what is this sentence about?" or "Who or what is doing something in this sentence?"

For example, look at the following two sentences:

- People applauded.

- Antonietta wrote the answers on the board.

People is what the first sentence is about; they are the ones who applauded. So *people* is the subject of the first sentence. The second sentence answers the question, "Who is doing something in the sentence?" The answer is *Antonietta.* She is the person who wrote the answers on the board. So *Antonietta* is the subject of the second sentence.

A subject will always be either a noun or a pronoun. A **noun** is the name of a person, place, thing, or idea. A **pronoun** is a word—such as I, you, he, she, it, we, or they—that stands for a noun.

VERBS

Many **verbs** express action; they tell what the subject is doing. You can find an **action verb** by asking, "What does the subject do?" Look again at these sentences:

- People applauded.

- Antonietta wrote the answers on the board.

You remember that *people* is the subject of the first sentence. What did they do? They *applauded. Applauded* is the verb in the first sentence. *Antonietta* is the subject in the second sentence. What did Antonietta do? She *wrote*, so *wrote* is the verb in the second sentence.

Some verbs do not show action; they are called **linking verbs**. Linking verbs like *is, are, was*, and *were* join (or link) the subject to something that is said about the subject. For example, in the sentence *Antonietta is a teacher*, the linking verb *is* connects the subject *Antonietta* with what is said about her—that she is a teacher.

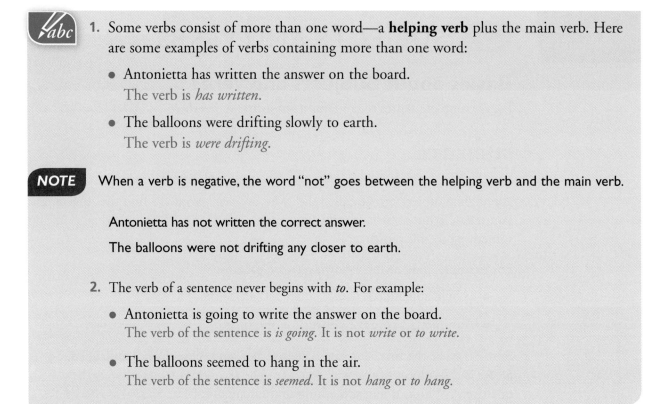

1. Some verbs consist of more than one word—a **helping verb** plus the main verb. Here are some examples of verbs containing more than one word:

   - Antonietta has written the answer on the board.
     The verb is *has written*.

   - The balloons were drifting slowly to earth.
     The verb is *were drifting*.

   NOTE   When a verb is negative, the word "not" goes between the helping verb and the main verb.

   Antonietta has not written the correct answer.

   The balloons were not drifting any closer to earth.

2. The verb of a sentence never begins with *to*. For example:

   - Antonietta is going to write the answer on the board.
     The verb of the sentence is *is going*. It is not *write* or *to write*.

   - The balloons seemed to hang in the air.
     The verb of the sentence is *seemed*. It is not *hang* or *to hang*.

Understanding Subjects and Verbs

In each sentence, underline the subject <u>once</u> and the verb <u>twice</u>. Then check your answers below.

¹Kin Sambath lives in Toronto. ²He is twenty-six years old. ³He likes to be called "Sam." ⁴Sam has lived in Canada for sixteen months. ⁵He moved here from Cambodia. ⁶His family still lives in Phnom Penh, the capital city of Cambodia. ⁷Sam takes ESL classes at York University's English Language Institute. ⁸After improving his English, Sam wants to study Finance at York. ⁹Then, he plans to return to Cambodia to help his father with his business.

Answers

¹Kin Sambath, lives; ²He, is; ³He, likes; ⁴Sam, has lived; ⁵He, moved; ⁶family, lives; ⁷Sam, takes; ⁸Sam, wants; ⁹he, plans

Check Your Understanding

Underline each subject <u>once</u> and each verb <u>twice</u>.

¹Sam knew that he would have to leave Cambodia to learn English and gain an education. ²Canada offered many opportunities to learn English, so he chose to come here. ³The biggest challenges for Sam were the loneliness and the culture shock. ⁴He was used to living with a big family—his mother, father, brother, and sister-in-law. ⁵Sam found it difficult to adjust to doing everything by himself. ⁶He shopped for his own food, cooked his own meals, and cleaned his own room. ⁷At first, shopping was tricky because he didn't know what food to buy. ⁸Cooking also confused him, as he couldn't read the instructions for cooking the food he had bought. ⁹The culture shock doesn't bother Sam anymore. ¹⁰His favourite thing about Canada is that he feels safe here.

NOTE   The subject of a sentence is never part of a prepositional phrase. A **prepositional phrase** is a group of words that begins with a preposition and ends with a noun or a pronoun. Common prepositions are *about, after, as, at, before, between, by, during, for, from, in, into, like, of, on, outside, over, through, to, toward, with,* and *without.* See Chapter 3 for more information on prepositional phrases. As you look for the subject of a sentence, it may help to cross out any prepositional phrases that you find. Here are examples:

The coffee ~~from the leaking pot~~ stained the carpet.

One ~~of my classmates~~ fell asleep ~~during class~~.

The woman ~~on that motorcycle~~ has no helmet.

The cracks and booms ~~during the thunderstorm~~ were terrifying.

PRACTICE 1

In each sentence below, cross out the prepositional phrases. Then underline the subject of each sentence <u>once</u> and the verb of each sentence <u>twice</u>.

1. Students from all over the world come to Canada to pursue their education.

2. More than 130,000 students arrive in Canada every year.

3. Canada provides educational opportunites for students from developing countries.

4. Some countries do not have the resources to support colleges and universities.

5. Canada also offers many opportunities to students wanting to learn English or French.

6. International students come from many races, countries, and cultures.

7. They bring a rich variety of knowledge and skills to our classrooms and our society.

8. Some international students hope to work in Canada after their education is complete.

9. Others return to their countries to contribute to developing economies.

10. Canada has had a long and successful history of educating international students.

NOTE   As already mentioned, many verbs consist of a main verb plus one or more helping verbs. Helping verbs are shown below:

Forms of *be*:	be, am, is, are, was, were, being, been
Forms of *have*:	have, has, had
Forms of *do*:	do, does, did
Forms of *can*:	can, could
Other helping verbs:	may, might, must, ought (to), shall, should, will, would

---

PRACTICE 2

In each sentence below, cross out the prepositional phrases. Then underline the subject of each sentence once and the verb of each sentence twice.

1. Dogs at the animal shelter wait for a good home.

2. The frozen fish on the counter defrosted quickly.

3. My computer's screen went blank without warning.

4. The man who lives next door looks like Brad Pitt.

5. A very large truck stalled on the bridge.

6. The orange in the refrigerator has purple spots.

7. Everyone cried at one point during the movie.

8. Several sad-looking puppies huddled in the small cage.

9. Two young boys from the neighbourhood were playing basketball in the schoolyard.

10. By the end of the day, we had sold between 350 and 400 tickets.

PRACTICE 3

Cross out the prepositional phrases in the paragraph below. There may be more than one prepositional phrase in each sentence. Then underline the subject of each sentence <u>once</u> and the verb of each sentence <u>twice</u>.

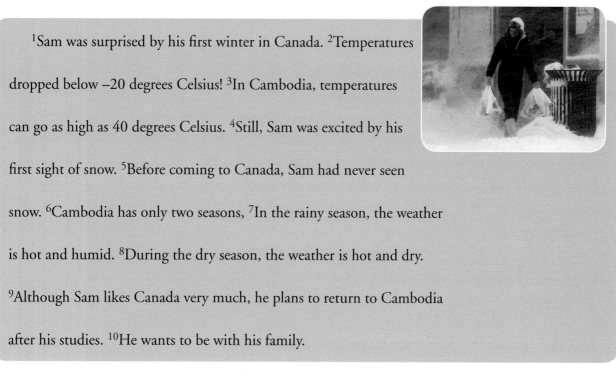

¹Sam was surprised by his first winter in Canada. ²Temperatures dropped below –20 degrees Celsius! ³In Cambodia, temperatures can go as high as 40 degrees Celsius. ⁴Still, Sam was excited by his first sight of snow. ⁵Before coming to Canada, Sam had never seen snow. ⁶Cambodia has only two seasons, ⁷In the rainy season, the weather is hot and humid. ⁸During the dry season, the weather is hot and dry. ⁹Although Sam likes Canada very much, he plans to return to Cambodia after his studies. ¹⁰He wants to be with his family.

Name: _____   Section: _____   Date: _____

Score: (Number right) _____ x 10 = _____%

Subjects and Verbs

For each sentence, cross out any prepositional phrases. Then underline the subject <u>once</u> and the verb <u>twice</u>. Remember to include any helping verb(s).

1. A family of mice scurried across the basement floor.

2. Ramona loves to exchange e-mails with her friends.

3. Many park visitors have complained about the new regulations limiting the number of campfires and barbecues.

4. The pot of vegetable soup simmered gently on the stove.

5. My digital camera takes very clear pictures in all kinds of locations.

6. After the party, we went to a doughnut shop and drank coffee until 3 a.m.

7. The summer concert was cancelled with only one day's notice.

8. The coffee from the leaking pot left a large brown stain on the white carpet.

9. A German shepherd waited patiently outside the drugstore.

10. The curious child stared silently at the man in the Santa Claus suit in July.

> **TEST 2**   Name: _____   Section: _____   Date: _____
>
> Score: (Number right) _____ x 10 = _____ %

Subjects and Verbs

For each sentence, cross out any prepositional phrases. Then underline the subject <u>once</u> and the verb <u>twice</u>. Remember to include any helping verb(s).

1. The hallway of Clayton's apartment building smells like garbage.

2. The people in my family speak three different languages fluently.

3. A man in the subway car offered his seat to the pregnant woman.

4. Without a word, Kadian raced out of the house and into the front yard.

5. Groups of voters lined up at the entrance to the gym.

6. Dave's girlfriend is good at fixing cars.

7. To earn money to pay for school, I work at the computer lab between classes.

8. Huge mounds of dirt surround the construction site, causing the neighbours to complain.

9. The tiles on the bathroom floor look grey in the dim light.

10. Movies about serial killers always seem popular with audiences.

Subjects and Verbs

For each sentence, cross out any prepositional phrases. Then underline the subject <u>once</u> and the verb <u>twice</u>. Remember to include any helping verb(s).

1. The movie audience shrieked in terror and glee at the sight of the bloodthirsty zombie.

2. A solution to the problem suddenly popped into my head.

3. During the long bus trip from Winnipeg to Vancouver, many passengers fell asleep.

4. For his birthday dinner, Santo had a pizza with pepperoni, mushrooms, and onions.

5. After my final exam, I can forget about school for a week.

6. During the hot, dry summer, the farmers worried about their crops.

7. Drops of icy rain began to fall on the soccer players.

8. As a result of my father's illness, the past two months have been a nightmare for my family.

9. To catch the bus to school, Domenic awakens before sunrise.

10. Shalina has been sending romantic e-mails to her boyfriend during computer lab.

TEST 4   Name: _____   Section: _____   Date: _____

Score: (Number right) _____ x 5 = _____ %

Subjects and Verbs

For each sentence, cross out any prepositional phrases. Then underline the subject <u>once</u> and the verb <u>twice</u>. Remember to include any helping verb(s).

[1]The social networking website Facebook was launched on February 4, 2004 by a Harvard University student named Mark Zuckerberg. [2]The membership of Facebook was expanded to include first students from certain American universities, then students from colleges and universities across the globe, and finally, anyone thirteen years or older. [3]The site has more than 60 million active users, with over 2 million Canadian users. [4]Users create profiles containing educational background, personal and professional information, and photographs. [5]They can join groups of friends and exchange both private and public messages. [6]The site's name refers to the paper facebooks containing photographs of members of the campus community that some colleges and universities give to incoming students as a way to get to know other people on campus. [7]Facebook is the number one site for photos in the United States with over 60 million photos uploaded weekly. [8]One interesting phenomenon is the use of Facebook to mourn for and memorialize a deceased individual. [9]Memorial pages have been created for murder victims, including a 14-year-old girl stabbed in January, 2008, and an 18-year-old girl shot at Montreal's Dawson College in September 2006. [10]These sites allow people to share their memories of the deceased, to express their anger at the victim's death, and to comfort one another.

⬤ IRREGULAR VERBS

Basics about Irregular Verbs

Most English verbs are **regular**. That is, they form their past tense and past participle by adding *-ed* or *-d* to the basic form, as shown here:

Basic Form	Past Tense	Past Participle
ask	asked	asked
raise	raised	raised

Some English verbs are **irregular.** They do not form their past tense and past participle by adding *-ed* or *-d* to the basic form of the verb. Instead, their past tenses and past participles are formed in other ways. Here are some of the most common irregular verbs.

Basic Form	Past Tense	Past Participle	Basic Form	Past Tense	Past Participle
become	became	become	grow	grew	grown
begin	began	begun	have	had	had
break	broke	broken	hide	hid	hidden
bring	brought	brought	is	was	been
build	built	built	keep	kept	kept
catch	caught	caught	know	knew	known
choose	chose	chosen	leave	left	left
come	came	come	lay	laid	laid
do	did	done	lie	lay	lain
drink	drank	drunk	read	read	read
drive	drove	driven	see	saw	seen
eat	ate	eaten	shake	shook	shaken
feel	felt	felt	spend	spent	spent
find	found	found	take	took	taken
forget	forgot	forgotten	tell	told	told
get	got	got, gotten	write	wrote	written
give	gave	given			
go	went	gone			

Since irregular verbs are used more frequently in English than regular verbs, it is important to be familiar with them. Because there are no consistent rules for the forms of irregular verbs, it is a good idea to memorize the different forms for the most common verbs. Make a list of the most common verbs and their forms.

A word about past participles

The past participle is used in the following ways:

1. To describe something that happened in the faraway past (known as the past perfect tense):

   I broke my roommate's DVD player. (past tense)
   I told my roommate that I **had broken** his DVD player. (past perfect tense)

   The DVD player was broken before *the speaker told his roommate.*

2. To form the passive voice:

   The DVD player **was broken**.
   The DVD player **has been broken**.

   In this sentence, the DVD player is the subject, while in the first sentence, the pronoun "I" is the subject.

3. To modify a noun:

   I took the **broken** DVD player to a repair shop.

A word about helping verbs

Sometimes the verb of a sentence consists of more than one word. In these cases, the main verb will be joined by one or more **helping verbs**. Look at the following sentences:

I **went** to bed late last night.

I **have gone** to bed early every night this week.

I **should have gone** to bed earlier last night.

In this sentence, the main verb is *gone*. The helping verb in the second sentence is *have*. The helping verbs in the third sentence are *should* and *have*. Other common helping verbs include *be, can, could, do, has, may, must, will,* and *would*.

 If you think a verb is irregular, and it is not in the list on the previous page, look it up in your dictionary. If it is irregular, the principal parts will be listed.

Understanding Irregular Verbs

In the following passage about Jasleen Kaur, a student at Dawson College in Montreal, **five** mistakes in irregular verbs are underlined. The correct forms of the verbs are then shown in the spaces below.

¹During her first semester at college, Jasleen <u>becomes</u> discouraged. ²The workload nearly <u>driving</u> her crazy! ³She had always <u>did</u> well in high school. ⁴But at college, everything <u>feel</u> like it is happening all at once. ⁵She worried that she had <u>choose</u> courses that were too hard.

1. <u>became</u>
2. <u>drove</u>
3. <u>done</u>
4. <u>felt</u>
5. <u>chosen</u>

Check Your Understanding

Write the correct form of the **five** verbs in the spaces provided.

¹Jasleen _____ (to find) that she was unable to sleep. ²She _____ (to lose) weight and catch a cold. ³She wanted to do something before her health suffered any more. ⁴She went to see her instructors, to see if they could help. ⁵She _____ (to tell) them where she was having problems, and they gave her advice. ⁴She_____ (to buy) an organizer and keep careful track of her classes and activities. ⁵She formed study groups with other students on her residence floor. ⁶By the end of her first year, she felt she had _____ (to begin) to win at the college game.

Three Problem Verbs

Three common irregular verbs that confuse many writers are *be*, *do*, and *have*. Here are the correct present tense, past tense, and past participle forms of these three problem verbs.

	Present Tense	Past Tense	Past Participle
Be	I am he, she, it **is** you, we, they **are**	I was he, she, it **was** you, we, they **were**	I have **been** he, she, it has **been** you, we, they have **been**
Do	I **do** he, she, it **does** you, we, they **do**	I did he, she, it **did** you, we, they **did**	I have **done** he, she, it has **done** you, we, they have **done**
Have	I have he, she, it **has** you, we, they **have**	I had he, she, it **had** you, we, they **had**	I have **had** he, she, it has **had** you, we, they have **had**

PRACTICE 1

Write the correct form of the **ten** verbs in the spaces provided.

¹Last semester, Jasleen _____ (to take) a literature class that she liked very much. ²As her reading skills _____ (to grow) stronger, Jasleen _____ (to become) more and more confident. ³She _____ (to find) that she loved to discover new worlds through reading. ⁴While she was taking the class, she _____ (to spend) hours in the library, looking for books to take back to her room. ⁵One afternoon, she _____ (to choose) *Romeo and Juliet*. ⁶At first, the language was difficult to understand, but she _____ (to keep) reading. ⁷Her teacher suggested that Jasleen rent a DVD of a production of the play. ⁸Seeing the story acted out by professionals, Jasleen _____ (to begin) to understand the language. ⁹She _____ (to tell) her friend Zahra the story of the two doomed lovers, and one night Zahra _____ (to come) over to Jasleen's room to watch the DVD. ¹⁰Now, the two girls plan to save their money so they can go see a play at Stratford in the summer.

PRACTICE 2

For each sentence below, fill in the correct form of the verb in the space provided.

broke, broken   **1.** When I _____ my leg, my friends scribbled cheerful messages on the cast.

spend, spent   **2.** Nathan _____ most of his teenage years dressed in black and alone in his bedroom.

catch, caught   **3.** The kindergarten teacher _____ chicken pox from one of her students.

went, gone   **4.** The sign on the door of the clothing store said "I have _____ to lunch. I'll be back at 2 p.m."

wrote, write   **5.** Before he was famous, the horror author Stephen King taught high school English and _____ short stories and novels at night.

done, did   **6.** When my little sister broke the living-room lamp, she told my parents that I had _____ it.

bring, brought   **7.** Seven people _____ potato salad to the picnic, and only one person made a dessert.

chose, choose   **8.** Although she was close to winning $100,000, the game-show contestant lost it all when she _____ the wrong answer to the final question.

drove, drive   **9.** On Canada Day, Julie and her friends _____ to Ottawa for the celebrations.

eaten, ate   **10.** My friend stuck to his diet for six days. Then he _____ ate an entire chocolate cake in fifteen minutes.

PRACTICE 3

Write the correct form of the **ten** verbs in the spaces provided.

¹Before coming to college, Jasleen _____ (to read) and _____ (to write) a lot in high school. ²Once she _____ (to come) to Dawson, she _____ (to find) that reading and writing were even more important in college. ³She also learned that living with her aunt and uncle could be difficult. ⁴Family members often _____ (to come) by to visit her when she needed to be working. ⁵At other times, she _____ (to grow) bored of looking at the four walls of her room. ⁶She even _____ (to catch) herself falling asleep. ⁷She _____ (to know) that she needed to find other places to do her school work. ⁸She _____ (to take) her books to the library and tried studying there. ⁹The library quickly _____ (to become) one of her favourite places. ¹⁰It was beautiful and quiet. ¹¹Now, you can often find Jasleen hard at work in the library.

PRACTICE 4

Each of the items below contains **two** errors in irregular verbs. Find the errors and cross them out. Then, in the spaces provided, write the correct forms of the verbs.

NOTE   To help you master irregular verbs, explanations are given for two of the sentences.

1. Once I seen a hawk dive from the top of a tall tree to capture a field mouse. The bird catch the tiny creature in its claws and flew back to its perch.

   a. _____

   b. _____

   Use the past tense of the irregular verb *see* for the first correction needed.

2. I always have gave my little children household chores. This month, my son sets the table, and my daughter does some dusting. Last month, they both done some weeding in the backyard.

   a. _____

   b. _____

   Use the past participle of the irregular verb *give* for the first correction needed.

3. My aunt be a big fan of Céline Dion. Every time she hears "My Heart Must Go On," she becomes misty-eyed. Last year, she and my uncle gone on a trip to Las Vegas, to see Céline in concert. While there, she bought bottles of Céline's new perfume, "Enchanting," for herself and all her friends.

   a. _____

   b. _____

4. It is dangerous to shake a baby. Many babies who have been shook have suffered brain injuries. The adults who done this seldom meant to cause such harm.

   a. _____

   b. _____

5. I was determined not to forget anything I needed at the store. I sat down and write a long shopping list. Feeling proud of myself, I went to the store. Then I realized I had forgot the list.

   a. _____

   b. _____

TEST 1   Name: _____   Section: _____   Date: _____

Score: (Number right) _____ x 20 = _____ %

Irregular Verbs

Fill in the blanks with the correct form of the verb in brackets.

1. It really can be more fun to give than to receive. Yesterday I _____ (to give) my sister a ring of mine that she has always loved.

2. In the winter, I drink about a litre of orange juice a week. But last week when it was so hot, I _____ (to drink) that much in one day.

3. I was angry that my friend took the money that was lying on the dresser. She didn't know it was mine, but she _____ (to know) it wasn't hers.

4. Last summer, Navneet and her family _____ (to drive) all day to see the giant goose in Wawa, Ontario. They were disappointed to find that it wasn't a real goose.

5. Three people had _____ (to see) the shooting take place, but no one could be sure what the shooter looked like.

TEST 2   Name: _____   Section: _____   Date: _____

Score: (Number right) _____ x 10 = _____%

Irregular Verbs

For each sentence, fill in the correct form of the verb shown in brackets in the space provided.

¹Think of a time when you _____ (to begin) something new in your life. ²Maybe you switched to a new school, _____ (to take) a new job, or even _____ (to leave) a relationship that was not working. ³Try to remember how you _____ (to feel) at first. ⁴Were you nervous? ⁵Or were you confident you _____ (to know) what you were doing? ⁶Many students find the adjustment to college very difficult, even if they _____ (to do) very well in high school and always _____ (to get) good grades. ⁷Jasleen _____ (to find) college difficult at first, but now she feels much more confident and strong. ⁸She has even found the strength to make a very difficult decision. ⁹She has _____ (to choose) to move out of her aunt and uncle's house next year. ¹⁰She and two of her friends _____ (to find) an affordable apartment on Kent Avenue near the college. ¹¹Jasleen is looking forward to the adventure!

TEST 3   Name: _____   Section: _____   Date: _____

Score: (Number right) _____ x 10 = _____%

Irregular Verbs

Read each sentence below. Then choose an appropriate irregular verb and write the correct form in the space provided. Answers may vary.

1. Sandy has _____ to a counsellor every week since her parents' divorce.

2. My grandmother has _____ our family history.

3. Our neighbours _____ us crazy when they first moved in, but now we're good friends.

4. How long have you and Stephanie _____ each other?

5. The lucky woman who _____ the home run ball got it autographed by Blue Jays' player Frank Thomas.

6. In the middle of dinner, Claudia gasped, "I _____ I was supposed to babysit tonight!"

7. Trying to avoid catching a cold, everyone in the family _____ extra vitamin C every day last winter.

8. Glenroy _____ his textbook at home.

9. The boss_____ everyone to plan to work late Thursday night.

10. Only the people who had _____ the first movie understood the sequel.

Name: _____ Section: _____ Date: _____

Score: (Number right) _____ x 10 = _____%

Irregular Verbs

Read each sentence below. Then choose an appropriate irregular verb and write the correct form in the space provided. Answers may vary.

1. Last July, Ivan _____ a Canadian citizen.

2. The tiny, cute puppy has _____ a forty-kilogram monster.

3. Last night, Natalia _____ nearly four hours shovelling snow.

4. While visiting Niagara Falls, Zamil _____ a fifty-dollar bill on the ground.

5. My father has _____ everything he can to keep our car in good shape.

6. I had _____ to do the assignment.

7. Franklin's sisters had _____ the whole pie before he got home.

8. The eccentric billionaire _____ all his money to his dog.

9. The city of Vancouver was _____ to host the 2010 Olympic Winter Games.

10. Pakistan's Tarbela Dam was _____ between 1968 and 1974. It is the world's largest earth-filled dam and a major source of Pakistan's hydroelectric power.

SENTENCE TYPES

Basics about Sentence Types

There are three basic kinds of sentences in English:

SIMPLE SENTENCES

A **simple sentence** has only one subject–verb combination and expresses one complete thought.

- Our daughter cooked dinner tonight.
  Daughter is the subject, and *cooked* is the verb.

A simple sentence may have more than one subject or more than one verb:

- Our son and daughter are cooking dinner tonight.
  Son and *daughter* are the two subjects; *are cooking* is the verb.

- Our children pushed and shoved each other angrily in the kitchen.
  Children is the subject; *pushed* and *shoved* are the two verbs.

COMPOUND SENTENCES

A **compound sentence** is made up of two or more complete thoughts, joined with a coordinating conjunction (joining word). See page 38 for more on coordinating conjunctions.

Following are two complete thoughts, joined to form a compound sentence:

- Rose wants chilli for dinner, but she forgot to buy beans.

By using a comma and a coordinating conjunction such as *but*, we can combine what would otherwise be two simple sentences (*Rose wants chilli for dinner* and *She forgot to buy beans*) into one compound sentence. In addition to *but*, the words *and* and *so* are the coordinating conjunctions most often used to connect two complete thoughts. Here are examples using *and* and *so*:

- The driver failed to signal, and he went through a stop sign.

- The meal was not hot, so we sent it back to the kitchen.

COMPLEX SENTENCES

A **complex sentence** is made up of one complete thought and a thought that begins with a subordinating conjunction (dependent word) like *after, although, as, because, before, if, since, unless, until, when, where,* and *while*. The dependent statement can either begin a sentence or finish a sentence. For more about subordinating conjunctions, see page 39.

A comma is placed after a dependent statement when it starts a sentence.

- **Although I had a free ticket to the game**, I was too tired to go.

- I set my alarm for 5 a.m. **because I wanted to finish a paper.**

- **After the test was over,** we got something to eat.

When you write, try to make your sentences varied and interesting. Using all three kinds of sentences will both help you express more complex thoughts and give your writing a lively style.

Understanding Sentence Types

Notice the different sentence types used in this passage about Jessica Lambert, a student at Humber College in Toronto.

[1]Jessica is a student at Humber College. [2]She has graduated from the General Arts and Sciences program, and she is now a student in the Occupational Therapist/Physiotherapist Assistant program. [3]Although Jessica was born in Moscow, she lived in Israel for ten years. [4]She moved to Canada in 2001. [5]When she first arrived in Toronto, she was not sure what she wanted to do. [6]Her parents wanted her to continue her education, but she didn't know what program to choose.

Sentences 1 and 4 are simple sentences. Sentences 2 and 6 are compound sentences. Sentences 3 and 5 are complex sentences.

 Look at a piece of writing (for example, a school assignment, a letter, an e-mail, a newspaper or magazine article). Can you find two simple sentences? Two compound sentences? Two complex sentences?

Check Your Understanding

Combine each group of simple sentences below into a compound or a complex sentence using the words *after*, *because*, *before*, *but*, and *so*. Write your answers in the spaces provided.

1. Jessica had learned English in Israel. She found it very difficult to understand the English that she heard spoken in Toronto.

   _____

   _____

   _____

2. She was afraid to speak to anybody. She was not confident about her English skills.

   _____

   _____

   _____

3. Jessica was nervous about entering college. She decided to ease into the new experience.

   _____

   _____

   _____

4. She started full-time studies. Jessica enrolled in a summer course that met twice a week.

   _____

   _____

   _____

5. She had taken a part-time course. Jessica found it much less frightening to start school in the fall.

   _____

   _____

   _____

PRACTICE 1

Combine each group of simple sentences below into a compound or a complex sentence. Write your sentences in the spaces provided.

1. Jessica started the General Arts and Sciences program. She learned that she would be taking courses in math, literature, critical thinking, composition, and college skills.

2. Math is her favourite course. There is no language difference to overcome.

3. At first the classes seemed very large. All the students seemed much younger than Jessica.

4. Eventually, she discovered that all the students were as nervous as she was. They seemed young and confident.

5. Someone asked Jessica if she would recommend returning to school as a mature student. She would tell that person to "go for it!"

6. Jessica applied to both the paramedic and occupational therapist/physiotherapist assistant programs. Both careers appealed to her.

7. She was disappointed. She was not accepted into the paramedic program.

8. She had been interested in a career as a paramedic. She now realizes that it is a very demanding profession.

9. She wants a rewarding, fulfilling career. She also wants to have a family someday.

10. Jessica likes to get to know people. An occupational therapist/physiotherapist assistant has much more opportunity to spend time getting to know the patients.

1. _____

   _____

2. _____

   _____

3. _____

   _____

4. _____

   _____

5. _____

   _____

6. _____

   _____

7. _____

   _____

8. _____

   _____

9. _____

   _____

10. _____

   _____

PRACTICE 2

A. Use a comma and a logical joining word to combine the following pairs of simple sentences into a compound sentence. Choose an appropriate word from the list of coordinating conjunctions (*and, but, for, or, nor, so, yet*). Place a comma before the coordinating conjunction.

   1. Kwan is quite attractive. She sees herself as ugly.

_____

   2. Jared struggles with math. He got a good mark in the class.

_____

   3. I lost my watch. I don't know what time it is.

_____

   4. The book is four hundred pages long. The print is very small.

_____

   5. The night air was chilly. I put on a sweater.

_____

B. Use a suitable subordinating conjunction to combine the following pairs of simple sentences into complex sentences. Choose from *although, because, since,* and *when*. Place a comma after a dependent statement when it starts a sentence.

   6. Strawberries are expensive. I don't often buy them.

_____

   7. An elephant's skin is very thick. It is also very sensitive.

_____

   8. The city pools have been crowded. The weather turned hot.

_____

   9. I quickly called the police. I heard a scream outside.

_____

  10. Danielle seems unfriendly. She is really just shy.

_____

TEST 1   Name: _____   Section: _____   Date: _____

Score: (Number right) _____ x 10 = _____ %

Sentence Types

A. Use a comma and a suitable coordinating conjunction to combine the following pairs of simple sentences into compound sentences.

1. The coffee is cold. It is also too strong.

   _____

2. Our car runs well. Its body is dented and rusty.

   _____

3. The book was very expensive. I didn't buy it.

   _____

4. Gene laughed throughout the movie. His date didn't laugh once.

   _____

5. The electricity was out. We had no candles.

   _____

B. Use a suitable subordinating conjunction to combine the following pairs of simple sentences into complex sentences. Place a comma after a dependent statement when it starts a sentence.

6. The ball game was postponed. It began to rain heavily.

   _____

7. Sam practises his saxophone. The dog howls.

   _____

8. The house looks beautiful. It seems cold and unfriendly to me.

   _____

9. She doesn't drive. Mia must walk or take the bus to work.

   _____

10. The beautiful fireworks exploded. The audience gasped and applauded.

   _____

TEST 2   Name: _____   Section: _____ Date: _____

Score: (Number right) _____ x 10 = _____%

Sentence Types

A. Use a comma and a suitable coordinating conjunction to combine the following pairs of simple sentences into compound sentences.

1. Eddie was tired of his appearance. He shaved all the hair off his head.

   _____

2. Eddie bought new clothing in bright colours. He added an earring as well.

   _____

3. Twenty students were enrolled in the class. Only eight were present on the day of the snowstorm.

   _____

4. Thirty percent of M&M's are brown. Twenty percent of them are red.

   _____

5. The coffee stain did not wash out of my white pants. I dyed the pants tan.

   _____

B. Use a suitable subordinating conjunction to combine the following pairs of simple sentences into complex sentences. Place a comma after a dependent statement when it starts a sentence.

6. I need to improve my grades. I will start taking more notes in class.

   _____

7. There used to be many small stores downtown. They are gone now.

   _____

8. The bus came into sight. Connie shouted "Goodbye!" and rushed out the door.

   _____

9. Very little is understood about mental illness. It has always frightened people.

   _____

10. I'm allergic to most animals. Reptiles don't bother me.

    _____

| TEST 3 | Name: _____ | Section: _____ | Date: _____ |

Score: (Number right) _____ x 10 = _____ %

Sentence Types

Combine each group of simple sentences into compound or complex sentences. Combine the first two sentences into one sentence, and combine the last two sentences into another sentence. Use any appropriate coordinating or subordinating conjunctions.

> **Two comma hints**
>
> 1. Use a comma between two complete thoughts joined by a coordinating conjunction.
>
> 2. Place a comma after a dependent statement when it starts a sentence.

1. It had rained for three days. The sun finally came out.
   We wanted to have a picnic. The ground was too wet.

   _____

   _____

2. Roy saw a bright rainbow. He ran to get his camera.
   He rushed back to take a picture. The rainbow had gone.

   _____

   _____

3. My nosy neighbour was at my door. I pretended not to be home.
   I didn't want to talk to her. I find her very annoying.

   _____

   _____

4. Nadine hates her job. She won't leave it.
   She likes the pension plan. She will stay until retirement.

   _____

   _____

5. I had to meet my girlfriend's mother. I was very nervous.
   I was afraid of her opinion of me. She was very warm and friendly.

   _____

   _____

Sentence Types

Combine each pair of sentences in the most clear and logical way, using either coordinating or subordinating conjunctions. Answers will vary.

1. Ernesto and Maria are quite short. Their children are all quite tall.

   _____

2. My cousin was falling behind in math class. He decided to hire a peer tutor.

   _____

3. The thunderstorm rattled the windows. The dog hid in the closet.

   _____

4. The movie turned out to be too scary. I took the children home.

   _____

5. Jakub hates flying. He flew to Poland over the summer to visit his family.

   _____

6. Nobody was very hungry Christmas Eve. We ate cereal for dinner.

   _____

7. The mechanic called about our car. He didn't have good news.

   _____

8. Amir is limping badly. He twisted his ankle playing basketball.

   _____

9. I met my new neighbour. I had never been friends with a blind person.

   _____

10. Hiking the West Coast Trail. I feel ready to take on any challenge.

    _____

 PRONOUN FORMS

Basics about Pronouns

A **pronoun** is a word that can be used in place of a noun.

- André scrubbed the potatoes. Then **he** peeled some carrots. In the second sentence above, the word *he* is a pronoun that is used in place of the noun *André*.

For more information on pronouns, see "Parts of Speech," pages 29–40.

This chapter explains how to choose the correct pronoun to use in a sentence. It covers the following four areas:

1. Personal pronouns as subjects and objects

2. Pronouns with *and* or *or*

3. Pronouns in comparisons

4. *Who* and *whom*

PERSONAL PRONOUNS AS SUBJECTS, OBJECTS, AND POSSESSIVES

Pronouns have different forms, or cases, depending on their use in a sentence. As explained below, they may serve as **subjects, objects,** or **possessives.**

SUBJECT PRONOUNS

Subject pronouns act as the subjects of verbs. Here are the subject forms of personal pronouns:

	First Person	**Second Person**	**Third Person**
Singular	I	you	he, she, it
Plural	we	you	they

- **I** have an itch.
  I is the subject of the verb *have*.

- **She** always remembers her nieces' birthdays.
  She is the subject of the verb *remembers*.

- **They** agreed to the deal and shook hands.
  They is the subject of the verbs *agreed* and *shook*.

71

OBJECT PRONOUNS

Object pronouns act as the objects of verbs or of prepositions. Here is a list of the object forms of personal pronouns:

	First Person	**Second Person**	**Third Person**
Singular	me	you	him, her, it
Plural	us	you	them

When a pronoun receives the action of a verb, an object pronoun should be used.

- Sara pinched **him**.
  Him receives the action of the verb *pinched*. *Him* tells who was pinched.

- Jeff is addicted to Coca-Cola. He drinks **it** for breakfast.
  It receives the action of the verb *drinks*. *It* tells what Jeff drinks for breakfast.

When a pronoun is the object of a preposition, an object pronoun should be used. Prepositions are words such as *to, for, with,* and *from*. (A longer list of prepositions is on page 35.)

- My sister tossed the car keys to **me**.
  Me is the object of the preposition *to*.

- Because it was her husband's birthday, Rita threw a party for **him**.
  Him is the object of the preposition *for*.

When the preposition *to* or *for* is understood, an object pronoun must still be used.

- My sister tossed **me** the car keys.
  The preposition *to* is implied before the pronoun *me*.

- Rita threw **him** a party.
  The preposition *for* is implied before the pronoun *him*. The party was thrown in *his* honour.

 Choose a piece of your own writing and circle all the pronouns. Now, draw an arrow from each pronoun to the noun it replaces.

POSSESSIVE PRONOUNS

Possessive pronouns show that something is owned, or possessed. Here are possessive forms of personal pronouns:

	First Person	**Second Person**	**Third Person**
Singular	my, mine	your, yours	his, her, hers, its
Plural	our, ours	your, yours	their, theirs

- If Meghan needs a sweater, she can borrow **mine**.
  Mine means *my sweater* or *the sweater belonging to me.*

- The tree lost most of **its** branches during the ice storm.
  Its branches means *the tree's branches* or *the branches belonging to the tree.*

- Tim and Emily saw many of **their** friends at the party.
  Their friends means *the friends belonging to Tim and Emily.*

 Possessive pronouns never contain an apostrophe.

- The chameleon changes the colour of its skin to match its surroundings.
  It's means **it is**. Whenever you write **it's**, try substituting **it is**.

- The chameleon changes the colour of **it's** skin to match **it's** surroundings

- The chameleon changes the colour of **it is** skin to match **it is** surroundings.

If it doesn't make sense, remove the apostrophe!

PRACTICE 1

Each sentence contains one pronoun. Underline each pronoun. Then, in the space in the margin, identify the pronoun by writing **S** for a subject pronoun, **O** for an object pronoun, and **P** for a possessive pronoun. The first item is done for you as an example.

_____**O**_____ 1. The concert gave <u>me</u> a headache.

_____ 2. Your father is very friendly.

_____ 3. They once lived in Sri Lanka.

_____ 4. Read the letter out loud to us.

_____ 5. Apparently she is somebody famous.

_____ 6. The door on my closet has a broken hinge.

_____ 7. A stone almost hit me in the eye.

_____ 8. Their second-hand car gave them nothing but trouble.

_____ 9. I often forget to bring a calculator to math class.

_____ 10. Next Friday, our brother will be twenty-eight.

PRACTICE 2

Fill in each blank with the appropriate pronoun in the margin. Before making your choice, decide if you need a subject, an object, or a possessive pronoun.

her, she   **1.** Over the summer, Kiran changed _____ hair colour, job, and boyfriend.

Me, I   **2.** _____ will treat you to lunch today.

our, us   **3.** Over the last ten years, twenty-three foster children have lived with _____.

your, you   **4.** You should iron _____ shirt before going to the job interview.

we, us   **5.** Will you join _____ at the movies Friday night?

They, Them   **6.** _____ cannot find an apartment they like in this neighbourhood.

I, me   **7.** Richard can give _____ a ride to school tomorrow.

him, his   **8.** When he died at the age of ninety-six, Grandpa still had all of _____ teeth.

he, him   **9.** Jill spotted her son on the playground and brought _____ a sandwich.

We, Us   **10.** _____ held a family meeting to decide how to split up household chores.

PRONOUNS WITH *AND* AND *OR*

Deciding which pronoun to use may become confusing when there are two subjects or two objects joined by *and* or *or*. However, the rules remain the same: Use a subject pronoun for the subject of a verb; use an object pronoun for the object of a verb or preposition.

- My brother and **I** loved the *Harry Potter* books when we were younger.

  I is a subject of the verb loved. *Brother is also a subject of* loved.

- Our parents often read the books to my brother and **me**.

  Me is an object of the preposition to. *Brother is also an object of* to.

You can figure out which pronoun to use by mentally leaving out the other word that goes with *and* or *or*. For instance, in the first example above, omitting the words *my brother and* makes it clear that *I* is the correct pronoun to use: . . . **I** loved the *Harry Potter* books. (You would never say "**Me** loved the *Harry Potter* books.")

Try mentally omitting words in the following sentences. Then fill in each blank with the correct pronoun in parentheses.

- The prom was so long ago, I can't remember all of the details. Either Gene or *(I, me)* _____ drove. Furthermore, I can't remember whether Katie Davis went with him or *(I, me)* _____.

The correct choice for the first blank becomes clear when the words "Either Gene or" are omitted: *I drove. I* is a subject of the verb *drove.*

The correct choice for the second blank becomes clear when the words "him or" are omitted: *I can't remember whether Katie Davis went with . . . me. Me* is an object of the preposition *with.*

PRACTICE 3

In each sentence, a choice of a subject or an object pronoun is given in parentheses. In the blank space, write the correct pronoun.

1. Is that package addressed to my brother or *(I, me)* _____?

2. According to Jess, either *(he, him)* _____ or his roommate will fix the broken window.

3. The piano is too heavy for Maya and *(she, her)* _____ to move on their own.

4. Hiroshi and *(he, him)* _____ first met when they were in grade four.

5. In the TV series *Little Mosque on the Prairie*, Layla is a Muslim teenager; there are many differences of opinion between her conservative father and _____ *(she, her)*.

6. My mother heard that the new position of floor manager will go either to her coworker Ken or *(she, her)* _____.

7. For many years, *(we, us)* _____ and Keishon have sat next to each other at football games.

8. That strong coffee kept Dad and *(we, us)* _____ awake for hours.

9. Nabil and *(I, me)* _____ had been arguing loudly when our teacher walked into the room.

10. She simply frowned at Nabil and *(I, me)* _____ and left.

PRONOUNS IN COMPARISONS

When pronouns are used in comparisons, they often follow the word *than* or *as.*

*   My best friend, Matt, is a better athlete than **I** am.
    I is the subject of the verb *am.*

*   Rhonda's behaviour puzzled you as much as it puzzles **me.**
    Me is the object of the verb *puzzled.*

 To avoid repetition, the verb "puzzled" may be replaced by "does" or omitted entirely.

*   Rhonda's behaviour puzzled you as much as it does **me.**

*   Rhonda's behaviour puzzled you as much as **me.**

Now try to fill in the correct pronouns in the following comparisons:

- Sari is upset that her little sister gets better grades than _____ (*she, her*) does.

- Your behaviour disappoints your father as much as it disappoints _____ (*I, me*).

In the first blank above, you should have written the subject form of the pronoun, *she*. *She* is the subject of the verb *does*.

In the second blank above, you should have written the object form of the pronoun, *me*. *Me* is the object of the verb *disappoints*.

PRACTICE 4

In each sentence, a choice of a subject or an object pronoun is given in parentheses. In the blank space, write the correct pronoun.

1. Della has been in the choir longer than *(we, us)* _____ have.

2. Our argument bothers you as much as it bothers *(I, me)* _____.

3. Omar told his teammates he runs faster than *(they, them)* _____ do.

4. My little brother is five inches taller than *(I, me)* _____ am.

5. The math final worries me more than it worries *(she, her)* _____; she is hardly studying for it.

6. We don't give parties as often as *(them, they)* _____ do.

7. As a child, I had a pet collie; there was no relative I loved as much as I loved *(he, him)* _____.

8. My friends all had the flu at the same time as I did, but I wasn't as sick as *(they, them)* _____ were.

9. Julius bats the ball farther than his sister, but she runs the bases faster than *(he, him)* _____ does.

10. That buzzing noise in the lamp annoys Dad more than it annoys *(we, us)* _____; he has to leave the room.

WHO, WHOM

Who is a subject pronoun, and *whom* is an object pronoun

- The person **who** owns the expensive car won't let anybody else park it.
  Who owns the expensive car is a dependent word group. *Who* is the subject of the verb *owns*.

- The babysitter **whom** they trust cannot work tonight.
  Whom they trust is a dependent word group. *Whom* is the object of the verb *trust*. The subject of *trust* is *they*.

As a general rule, to know whether to use *who* or *whom*, find the first verb after *who* or *whom*. Decide whether that verb already has a subject. If it doesn't have a subject, use the subject pronoun *who*. If it does have a subject, use the object pronoun *whom*.

See if you can fill in the right pronoun in the following sentences.

- The arrested person is a man *(who, whom)* _____ my sister once dated.

- The man and woman *(who, whom)* _____ live next door argue constantly.

In the first sentence above, look at the verb *dated*. Does it have a subject? Yes, the subject is *sister*. Therefore the object pronoun *whom* is the correct choice: *The arrested person is a man whom my sister once dated. Whom* is the object of the verb *dated*.

In the second sentence above, look at the verb *live*. Does it have a subject? No. Therefore the subject pronoun *who* is the correct choice: *The man and woman who live next door argue constantly. Who* is the subject of the verb *live*.

> **NOTE**   In informal speech and writing, *who* is often substituted for *whom*.

- The babysitter who they trust cannot work tonight.

In formal writing, however, *whom* is generally used. In the practices and tests in this chapter, use the formal approach.

PRACTICE 5

In each blank space, write the correct choice of pronoun.

1. The company hired a secretary *(who, whom)* _____ can speak French.

2. Chen's first boss was a man *(who, whom)* _____ he could not please.

3. I admire a man *(who, whom)* _____ cries at movies.

4. John Abbott is a prime minister *(who, whom)* _____ few Canadians remember.

5. Students *(who, whom)* _____ cheated on the test were suspended.

WHO AND WHOM IN QUESTIONS

In questions, *who* is a subject pronoun, and *whom* is an object pronoun. You can often decide whether to use *who* or *whom* in a question in the same way you decide whether to use *who* or *whom* in a statement.

- **Who** should go?

  The verb after *who* is *should go*, which does not have another subject. Therefore use the subject form of the pronoun, *who*.

- **Whom** should I send?

  I is the subject of the verb *should send*, so use the object form of the pronoun, *whom*.

PRACTICE 6

Fill in each blank with either *who* or *whom*.

1. *(Who, Whom)* _____ will do the dishes tonight?

2. *(Who, Whom)* _____ were you expecting?

3. *(Who, Whom)* _____ woke up in the middle of the night?

4. *(Who, Whom)* _____ is making all that racket?

5. *(Who, Whom)* _____ did you just call on the phone?

TEST 1 Name: _____ Section: _____ Date: _____

Score: (Number right) _____ x 10 = _____%

Pronoun Forms

Fill in each blank with the appropriate pronoun from the margin.

She, Her **1.** _____ got the highest grade on the midterm test.

who, whom **2.** I don't know _____ to trust anymore.

we, us **3.** We are sure that getting married is the right thing for _____.

they, them **4.** Since my aunt and uncle enjoy basketball more than I do, I gave the tickets to _____.

I, me **5.** She and _____ have been friends since we were little children.

he, him **6.** I don't know whether to believe you or _____.

she, her **7.** John and his sister both speak some Mandarin, but John is more fluent than _____.

he, him **8.** We enjoyed no teacher as much as _____; he was always interesting.

who, whom **9.** Our mayor is a former nun _____ decided to enter politics.

who, whom **10.** The principal is a young man _____ has earned the community's respect.

TEST 2   Name: _____   Section: _____   Date: _____

Score: (Number right) _____ x 10 = _____ %

Pronoun Forms

Fill in each blank with the appropriate pronoun from the margin.

we, us   1. You are welcome to drive to the meeting with _____.

they, them   2. This summer, my aunt and uncle asked me to go camping with _____ in Algonquin Park.

I, me   3. My mother changes her mind more frequently than _____.

who, whom   4. The man _____ the car hit is my uncle.

we, us   5. Next weekend you and _____ should go to a movie together.

I, me   6. My dog and _____ often hike in the woods for hours at a time.

she, her   7. Cymone's boss said there was no employee he valued as much as _____.

he, him   8. Does that red sports car belong to his parents or _____?

who, whom   9. The mechanic _____ usually works on our car is on vacation.

he, him   10. When the captain's boat capsized, _____ and his crew had a dangerous adventure.

TEST 3   Name: _____   Section: _____   Date: _____

Score: (Number right) _____ x 20 = _____%

Pronoun Forms

The following paragraph about Keifer Sutherland contains **five** pronoun errors. Correct them as you rewrite the paragraph in the space below. There may be more than one error in a sentence.

[1]Kiefer Sutherland is the son of Donald Sutherland and Shirley Douglas, both of who are famous actors. [2]Kiefer is the grandson of Canadian politician Tommy Douglas, whom was named "The Greatest Canadian" by CBC viewers in 2004. [3]Kiefer and his twin sister Rachel were born in London where his parents were working at the time. [4]Kiefer and his family moved to Los Angeles soon after, but when his parents divorced in 1970, him and his mother moved to Toronto. [5]He didn't even know his father was famous until he was eighteen because him and his sister didn't have a close relationship with he.

_____

_____

_____

_____

_____

_____

_____

_____

_____

TEST 4   Name: _____   Section: _____   Date: _____

Score: (Number right) _____ x 20 = _____ %

Pronoun Forms

The following paragraph about Keifer Sutherland contains **five** pronoun errors. Correct them as you rewrite the paragraph in the space below. There may be more than one error in a sentence.

¹Kiefer started acting at the age of nine, but his first film role was in *Max Dugan Returns* when he was 17. ²The movie features both his father and he. ³After winning a Genie Award for his performance in *The Bay Boy* (1984), him and some friends moved to New York City to pursue acting. ⁴He has starred in more than fifty movies and television shows, but he is best known as the star of the hit series *24*. ⁵Many Canadian actors have guest-starred on *24*, and Kiefer's support of Canadian talent has been instrumental in getting they involved in the show. ⁶In September, 2007, The Alliance of Canadian Cinema, Television and Radio Artists gave he the Award of Excellence, calling Sutherland a great Canadian success story. ⁷The president of ACTRA stated that them were "proud of him for strong support of other Canadian actors in Hollywood, while building one of the most successful careers in the industry." ⁸As famous as he is, Sutherland still enjoys such normal activities as playing pool, riding horses, playing guitar, and cooking. ⁹He also plays hockey in a celebrity league.

_____

_____

_____

_____

_____

_____

_____

_____

_____

_____

_____

CHAPTER 8

 PRONOUN PROBLEMS

Three Common Pronoun Problems

1. **Pronoun shifts in number** A pronoun must agree in number with the noun it refers to.

Incorrect	Either Paola or her sister left **their** backpack at my house.
Correct	Either Paola or her sister left **her** backpack at my house.

The subject in this case is "either." Think of it as meaning "either **this one** or **that one.**"

Incorrect	Each of the candidates for premier has **their** strengths.
Correct	Each of the candidates for premier has **his or her** strengths.

The subject in this case is "each." Think of it as meaning "each **one.**"

> **NOTE** Because it is not stated whether the candidates are male or female, "his or her" is the correct wording.

2. **Pronoun shifts in person** Pronouns must be consistent in person. Unnecessary shifts in person (for example, from *I* to *one*) confuse readers.

Incorrect	**One's** patience runs thin when I am faced with a slow-moving line at the bank. ("One" is a formal way of saying "people in general.")
Correct	**My** patience runs thin when I am faced with a slow-moving line at the bank.
Correct	**One's** patience runs thin when **one** is faced with a slow-moving line at the bank.

3. **Unclear pronoun reference** A pronoun must clearly refer to the noun it stands for.

Incorrect	Michael gave Ming **his** car keys. (Does *his* refer to Michael or Ming?)
Correct	Michael gave **his** car keys to Ming.

PRONOUN SHIFTS IN NUMBER

A pronoun must agree in number with the noun it refers to, which is called the pronoun's **antecedent**. Singular nouns require singular pronouns; plural nouns require plural pronouns.

   In the following examples, pronouns are printed in **boldface type**; the antecedents are printed in *italic* type.

- In the fall, the *tree* outside my window loses all **its** leaves.
  The antecedent *tree* is singular, so the pronoun must be singular: *its*.

- When *Vic* went away to college, **his** little brother wrote to **him** almost every day.
  The antecedent *Vic* is singular, so the pronouns must be singular: *his* and *him*.

- Do the *neighbours* know that **their** dog is loose?
  The antecedent *neighbours* is plural, so the pronoun must be plural: *their*.

- *Sarah and Greg* act like newlyweds, but **they** have been married for years.
  The antecedent *Sarah and Greg* is plural, so the pronoun must be plural: *they*.

PRACTICE 1

In each blank space, write the noun or nouns that the given pronoun refers to.

Example   The ridges on our fingertips have a function. They help fingers to grasp things.

   They refers to _____ridges_____.

1. The photographer realized she had left her camera on the subway train. *She* refers to
   _____.

2. The movie had its strengths, but it also had a lot of weaknesses. *Its* refers to _____.

3. Jon and Anjelica don't get along with their stepfather. *Their* refers to _____.

4. Guillermo never drinks coffee in the evening. It keeps him awake all night. *It* refers to
   _____.

5. Nora is a year older than her brother, but they are both in grade six. *They* refers to
   _____.

PRACTICE 2

In the spaces provided for each sentence, write **(a)** the pronoun used and **(b)** the noun or nouns that the pronoun refers to.

1. The movie started late, and it was badly out of focus. The pronoun _____
   refers to _____.

2. Marlene buys most of her clothing at thrift shops. The pronoun _____ refers
   to _____.

3. As the horse neared the finish line, his energy ran out. The pronoun _____
   refers to _____.

4. A man was at the door a minute ago, but now he is gone. The pronoun
_____ refers to _____.

5. Carla and Vicki are twins, but they don't look alike. The pronoun _____
refers to _____.

Indefinite Pronouns

Most pronouns refer to one or more particular persons or things. However, **indefinite pronouns** do not refer to particular persons or things. The following indefinite pronouns are always singular:

anybody	either	neither	one
anyone	everybody	no one	somebody
anything	everyone	nobody	someone
each	everything	nothing	something

- *Something* has left **its** muddy footprints on the hood of the car.
- *One* of my sisters has lost **her** job.
- *Everybody* is entitled to change **his or her** mind.
  The indefinite pronouns *something, one,* and *everybody* are singular. The personal pronouns that refer to them must also be singular: *its, her,* and *his or her.*

NOTE   Choose a pronoun that agrees in gender with the noun it refers to. Because *one of my sisters* is clearly feminine, use *her.* But *everybody* includes males and females, so use *his or her.* If *his or her* seems awkward in a sentence, try rewriting the sentence with a plural subject.

- People are entitled to change **their** minds.

The following indefinite pronouns are always plural:

both	many	several
few	other	

- *Both* of my brothers worked **their** way through college.
  Both, the subject of this sentence, is plural, so the plural pronoun *their* is used.

The following indefinite pronouns are singular or plural, depending on their context:

all	more	none
any	most	some

- *Some* of the pie is fine, but its crust is burnt.

  Some here refers to one thing—the pie, so the singular pronoun *its* is used.

- *Some* of the students forgot their books.

  Some here refers to several students, so the plural pronoun *their* is used.

PRACTICE 3

In the spaces provided for each sentence, write **(a)** the pronoun or pronouns needed and **(b)** the word that the pronoun or pronouns refer to.

Example   Neither of the boys has had (*his/their*) measles shot yet.

The pronoun needed is _____ **his** _____. The word it refers to is _____ **neither (which means neither one)** _____.

1. Everything in the office has (*its/their*) own place. The pronoun needed is
   _____. The word it refers to is _____.

2. Neither of my uncles has ever smoked in (*his/their*) life. The pronoun needed is
   _____. The word it refers to is _____.

3. Many restaurants in town post (*its/their*) menus in the window. The pronoun needed is
   _____. The word it refers to is _____.

4. Don't eat any of those grapes until you've washed (*it/them*). The pronoun needed is
   _____. The word it refers to is _____.

5. Is anyone brave enough to read (*their/his or her*) essay aloud to the class? The pronoun needed is
   _____. The word it refers to is _____.

6. Both of the girls invited (*her mother/their mothers*) to the mother–daughter luncheon. The
   pronoun needed is _____. The word it refers to is
   _____.

7. Everybody loses (*their/his or her*) temper occasionally. The pronoun needed is
   _____. The word it refers to is _____.

8. Nobody can enter that plant without (*their/his or her*) security badge. The pronoun needed is
   _____. The word it refers to is _____.

9. Most of the room has been painted, and (*it is/they are*) almost dry. The pronoun needed is
   _____. The word it refers to is _____.

10. Most of the invitations have been addressed, but (*it/they*) still have to be stamped. The pronoun
    needed is _____. The word it refers to is _____.

> **NOTE** A **collective noun** refers to a group of persons or things considered to be a unit. Collective nouns are usually singular. For a list of examples, see Chapter 11, p. 123.

- The *committee* submitted *its* decision in writing.
  Committee refers to a single unit, so the singular pronoun *its* is used.

PRONOUN SHIFTS IN PERSON

A pronoun that refers to the person who is speaking is called a **first-person pronoun**. Examples of first-person pronouns are *I, me,* and *our.* A pronoun that refers to someone being spoken to, such as *you,* is a **second-person pronoun**. And a pronoun that refers to another person or thing, such as *he, she,* or *it,* is a **third-person pronoun**.

Following are the personal pronouns in first-, second-, and third-person groupings:

	First Person	**Second Person**	**Third Person**
Singular	I, me, my, mine	you, your, yours	he, him, his; she, her, hers; it, its
Plural	we, us, our, ours	you, your, yours	they, them, their, theirs

When a writer makes unnecessary shifts in person, the writing may become less clear. The sentences below, for example, show some needless shifts in person. (The words that show the shifts are **boldfaced**.)

- The worst thing about **my** not writing letters is that **you** never get any back.
  The writer begins with the first-person pronoun *my,* but then shifts to the second-person pronoun *you.*

- Though **we** like most of **our** neighbours, there are a few **you** can't get along with.
  The writer begins with the first-person pronouns *we* and *our,* but then shifts to the second-person pronoun *you.*

These sentences can be improved by eliminating the shifts in person:

- The worst thing about **my** not writing letters is that **I** never get any back.

- Though **we** like most of **our** neighbours, there are a few **we** can't get along with.

Write the correct pronoun in each space provided.

they, we   **1.** Whenever students are under a great deal of stress, _____ often stop studying.

one, you   **2.** If you want to do well in this course, _____ should plan on doing all the assignments on time.

you, me   **3.** When I took a summer job as a waitress, I was surprised at how rude some customers were to _____.

I, you   **4.** I hate speaking in front of large groups because _____ always turn red and start to stammer.

I, one   **5.** When I dropped my son off at school this morning, _____ was disgusted by the amount of garbage in the schoolyard.

I, you   **6.** Although I like visiting my Aunt Rita, _____ always feel as if my visit has disrupted her life.

we, you   **7.** When we answer the telephone at work, _____ are supposed to say the company name.

I, one   **8.** I would like to go to a school where _____ can meet many people who are different from me.

you, they   **9.** Dog owners should put tags on their dogs in case _____ lose their pets.

we, they   **10.** People often take a first-aid course so that _____ can learn how to help choking and heart-attack victims

UNCLEAR PRONOUN REFERENCE

A pronoun must refer clearly to its antecedent—the word it stands for. If it is unclear which word a pronoun refers to, the sentence will be confusing. As shown below, some pronouns are unclear because they have two possible antecedents. Others are unclear because they have no antecedent.

Two Possible Antecedents

A pronoun's reference will not be clear if there are two possible antecedents.

- Eva told her mother that she had received a postcard from Japan.
  Who received the postcard, Eva or her mother?

- I wrote a to-do list with my purple pen, and now I can't find it.
  What can't the writer find, the list or the pen?

An unclear sentence with two antecedents can sometimes be corrected by using the speaker's exact words.

- Eva told her mother, "**I** received (or: "**You** received) a postcard from Japan."

For an explanation of how to use quotation marks, see pages 199–207 in "Quotation Marks."

In some cases, the best solution is to replace the pronoun with the word it was meant to refer to.

- I wrote a to-do list with my purple pen, and now I can't find **the list** (*or:* **the pen**).

No Antecedent

A pronoun's reference will not be clear if there is no antecedent.

- I just received our cable TV bill. **They** said The Movie Network is providing a free preview next month.
  Who said there's a free preview? We don't know because *they* has no word to refer to.

- My older brother is a chemist, but **that** doesn't interest me.
  What doesn't interest the writer? Is the writer not interested in the fact that his brother is a chemist? The pronoun *that* doesn't refer clearly to any word in the sentence.

To correct an unclear reference in which a pronoun has no antecedent, replace the pronoun with the word or words it is meant to refer to.

- I just received our cable TV bill. **The cable company** said The Movie Network is providing a free preview next month.

- My older brother is a chemist, but **chemistry** doesn't interest me.

PRACTICE 5

In each sentence below, underline the correct word or words in parentheses.

1. At a local deli, *(they / the owners)* provide each table with a free bowl of pickles.

2. Joan said the cordless phone is under the red pillow, but I can't find *(it / the phone)*.

3. Rita asked Paula *(if she could help with the dishes. / , "Can I help with the dishes?")*

4. On the radio, *(they / the announcers)* said that all public schools are closed today due to the snowstorm.

5. When my cousins arrived with the homemade pakoras, *(my cousins / they)* were very welcome.

PRACTICE 6

Revise each sentence to eliminate the unclear pronoun reference.

1. When Nick questioned the repairman, he became very upset.

   _____

   _____

2. My parents are expert poker players, but I've never become any good at it.

   _____

   _____

3. Alisha told her sister that her boyfriend was moving to another province.

   _____

   _____

4. I bought a treadmill that has a timer, but I never use it.

   _____

   _____

5. I went to the hardware store for 100-watt light bulbs, but they didn't have any.

   _____

   _____

TEST 1   Name: _____   Section: _____   Date: _____

Score: (Number right) _____ x 10 = _____ %

Pronoun Problems

A. In each blank space, write the pronoun that agrees in number with the word or words it refers to.

its, their   **1.** The school has computers in many of _____ classrooms.

her, their   **2.** My mother and her sister often share _____ clothing and jewellery.

his or her, their   **3.** No one in the class remembered _____ textbook.

her, their   **4.** Neither of the little girls wants to share _____ toys.

B. For each sentence, cross out the pronoun that makes a shift in person. Then, in the space provided, write a pronoun that corrects the shift in person.

_____   **5.** We work at a store where the owners don't provide you with any health insurance.

_____   **6.** I wanted to see the movie star, but one couldn't get past her security guard.

_____   **7.** Young people who join gangs often say that the gang becomes like your family.

C. In each sentence below, choose the correct word or words and write them in the space provided.

8. Jamal stopped at the post office and asked _____ to hold his mail while he was on vacation.

   a. a postal worker

   b. them

9. Carrie told Linda _____

   a. that she had gotten four phone calls that afternoon.

   b. , "You got four phone calls this afternoon."

10. Andrea could be a cafeteria server again next semester, but she really hates _____

   a. it.

   b. working in the cafeteria.

TEST 2   Name: _____   Section: _____   Date: _____

Score: (Number right) _____ x 10 = _____%

Pronoun Problems

Rewrite each sentence, correcting any mistakes in pronouns. Mark any correct sentences with a *C*.

1. On the radio, it says that the temperature will go down to –35 degrees Celsius by tonight.

   _____

2. The newspaper carrier didn't realize that you would have to deliver papers at 5 a.m.

   _____

3. One of my friends has left their backpack on the kitchen floor.

   _____

4. Everybody in our apartment building was told to lock his or her door in the evening.

   _____

5. In this letter from the bank, they say my account is overdrawn.

   _____

6. Each of my brothers has their own television.

   _____

7. Some of the businesses in town have a daycare centre for the children of their employees.

   _____

8. My mother always uses coupons at the grocery store, but I can't find the time for it.

   _____

9. Mohammed told his father he was late for his doctor's appointment.

   _____

10. If people want something from the kitchen, you have to go and get it.

    _____

TEST 3   Name: _____   Section: _____   Date: _____

Score: (Number right) _____ × 20 = _____ %

Pronoun Problems

Rewrite the following profile of Hong Kong-born chef Susur Lee, correcting the **five** errors. Some sentences are correct.

[1]For ordinary people who aren't born with wealth and advantages, following your dreams might seem impossible. [2]Celebrity chef Susur Lee is someone who has become world-famous in their field, in spite of his humble beginnings. [3]Lee was born in Hong Kong in 1958, the youngest of four brothers and sisters. [4]His family made their home in a poor part of the city. [5]At the age of 14, a local restaurant hired him to wash their woks. [6]At fifteen, he went to work at Hong Kong's famous Peninsula Hotel, where they hired him to make sauces.

_____

_____

_____

_____

_____

_____

_____

_____

_____

_____

Pronoun Problems

Complete the following profile of Hong Kong-born chef Susur Lee by writing the correct pronoun in the space provided. If the pronoun reference is unclear, replace the pronoun with a noun.

[1]In 1978, Susur Lee immigrated to Canada, where _____ quickly gained a reputation for blending the cooking traditions of China with those of France and other countries. [2]In 1987 _____ opened Lotus, a 12-table restaurant in Toronto's Little Italy. [3]Lotus closed _____ doors in 1997, and Lee moved to Singapore to head up Club Chinoise. [4]Lee returned three years later and opened Susur, a chic downtown restaurant famous for _____ backwards-tasting menu, in which the small courses move from heaviest to lightest.

[5]Susur Lee has become one of the best-known chefs in Canada. [6]_____ has been regularly praised in *Toronto Life* magazine, which repeatedly rates Susur as one of the top restaurants in the city. [7]The Zagat restaurant guide, called _____ "a culinary genius." [8]Whenever anyone famous visits the Toronto area, _____ are sure to visit Susur, or at least to try to get a reservation. [9]In 2004, Lee opened a second restaurant, Lee, next door to Susur. [10]Each of the two restaurants has _____ own focus: Susur is fine dining, while Lee is more casual fare.

[11]In 2006, Lee faced Bobby Flay in an episode of Food Network's *Iron Chef America*. [12]After sneaking a taste of one of Lee's dishes during the judging, Flay told reporters that he was sure _____ was going to win because the dish was so good. [13]The contest ended in a tie.

[14]It's hard to believe that a 14-year-old boy who got his start washing woks in Hong Kong has become one of the most celebrated chefs in the world. [15]However, it shows that if you follow your passion, _____ can achieve almost anything. [16]Susur Lee and his wife live in Toronto with their three sons, who love to eat all kinds of food, including McDonald's hamburgers.

CHAPTER 9

ARTICLES

An article is a word that refers to a noun, providing information about the noun. There are only three articles in English:

a	an	the

INDEFINITE ARTICLES

A and **an** are **indefinite articles.**

Use **a** or **an** if the noun that follows

a. is singular, *or*

b. refers to something that can be counted (one friend, two bananas, three cities), *or*

c. signals a nonspecific person, place, or thing.

- Judy is **a** friend of mine.
  She is just one of a number of friends.

- I read **a** novel for English class.
  It is just one, ordinary novel.

- James lives in **a** large city.
  The city is not specified.

An is used when the noun that follows begins with a vowel sound

- Judy is **an** honest woman.
  Honest *begins with a vowel sound.*

- I wrote **an** essay on Margaret Laurence's *The Stone Angel* for English class.
  Essay *begins with a vowel sound.*

- James lives in **an** average-sized city.
  Average *begins with a vowel sound.*

PRACTICE 1

Insert the appropriate indefinite article into each of the following blanks.

1. Jonathan is waiting for _____ important letter.

2. Felix got into _____ good college near his parents' home.

3. Would you like _____ pickle with your sandwich?

4. My cousin wants to be _____ astronaut when she grows up.

5. I'll be with you in _____ hour or two.

Do *not* use **a** or **an** if the noun that follows refers to something that cannot be counted.

Examples of uncountable nouns:

Abstract nouns:	happiness, confidence, magic, success
Food and drink:	water, wine, pasta, cheese
Activities:	hockey, poker, soccer, work

- After **school**, Jenna walks to **work** with her best friend.

- I'm not very good at **soccer**. I think I'll play **baseball** this summer instead.

- Greg is a good student, but his teachers say he lacks **confidence**.

NOTE   To express a specific amount of an uncountable noun, you can use a word such as "some," "any," "much," or "more," or add a countable noun to the uncountable noun.

- I wish you **much happiness.**
  Not "I wish you a happiness."

- Joe ordered **a glass of wine** and **a plate of pasta.**
  Not "Joe ordered a wine and a pasta."

- Rachel played **a game of poker** with her father.
  Not "Rachel played a poker with her father."

PRACTICE 2

Underline the uncountable noun in each sentence.

1. My brother is studying philosophy.

2. Would you like some pie?

3. The door was made of steel.

4. On weekends, Jay plays hockey with his friends.

5. Their eyes met across the room, as if by magic.

DEFINITE ARTICLES

The is a definite article.

Use **the** if the noun that follows signals a specific person, place, or thing.

- Ryan is **the boy** that I like.
  He is the one, specific boy.

- This is **the street** where I live.
  It is the one, specific street.

- I have a box full of all **the love letters** I have ever received.
  These aren't just any letters; they are the ones I have received.

The should also be used when the noun has already been mentioned.

- The bride wore **a beautiful** Vera Wang dress (*one of many beautiful Vera Wang dresses*). **The dress** (*the specific dress that the bride wore*) cost more than my car.

The is also used to refer to menu items offered by a restaurant.

- The spaghetti (*the specific spaghetti dish prepared by that particular kitchen*) sounds delicious, but I think I'll have the steak (*the specific steak prepared by that particular kitchen*).

PRACTICE 3

Fill in each blank with the appropriate definite (*the*) or indefinite (*a, an*) article.

1. Are you going to _____ dance at the community centre?

2. Steve drove up in _____ apple-red sports car.

3. When Tyler doesn't get his way, he throws _____ tantrum.

4. Neetha has a red dress and a black dress. She has decided to wear _____ black one tonight.

5. How was_____ movie you saw last night?

SUPERLATIVES

A *superlative* is a word that denotes the highest degree of comparison and requires the use of **the** to indicate this.

> When he died, Kenneth Thomson was **the richest** man in Canada.
> Of all the sisters, Louise is **the nicest**.

PRACTICE 4

Underline the superlative in each of the following sentences.

1. That was the worst movie I have ever seen.

2. Of all my allergies, my allergy to cats is the worst.

3. My biology exam was the hardest exam I've ever written.

4. For Marwan's birthday, his mother baked him the best chocolate cake he had ever eaten.

5. Malina chose the hardest-working student in the class to be her partner.

ARTICLES WITH PROPER NOUNS

Do *not* use **the** with most proper nouns.

- I live in Toronto.

- Jason goes to Capilano College.

- Carl took Ellen to Tim Horton's for their first date.

- It is not advisable to go swimming in Lake Ontario.

The following types of proper nouns are exceptions:

Proper nouns that follow the pattern "the _____ of _____":

- the Art Gallery of Ontario

- the University of Alberta

- the prime minister of Canada

Proper nouns that refer to a collective organization:

- the Canadian Opera Company

- the Toronto Blue Jays

- the Royal Canadian Mounted Police

Proper nouns that refer to newspaper titles:

- the *Calgary Herald*

- the *Globe and Mail*

- the *New York Times*

Some proper nouns that refer to geographical features:

- the Rocky Mountains

- the West Coast

- the Himalayas

Some proper nouns that refer to oceans, seas, or rivers:

- the Pacific Ocean

- the Yangtze River

- the Red Sea

Proper nouns that refer to countries and regions with plural names:

- the Philippines

- the West Indies

- the Netherlands

TEST 1   Name: _____   Section: _____   Date: _____

Score: (Number right) _____ x 10 = _____ %

In each sentence below, write the correct article in the spaces provided.

1. When he was _____ prime minister of Canada, Jean Chretien was hit in the face with _____ cream pie while visiting Prince Edward Island.

2. _____ *Halifax Gazette* is _____ oldest newspaper in Canada.

3. On our holiday, we plan to drive across Canada, starting with _____ swim in the Atlantic Ocean and ending with a swim in _____ Pacific Ocean.

4. Su Mi's sister attends _____ University of Cape Breton, where she is studying to be _____ nurse.

5. _____ Hockey Hall of Fame is located at _____ northwest corner of Yonge St. and Front St. in downtown Toronto.

TEST 2   Name: _____   Section: _____   Date: _____

Score: (Number right) _____ x 10 = _____ %

In each sentence below, write the correct article (*a, an,* or *the*) in the spaces provided. If no article is needed, place an *X* in the space.

1. When Kirpal returned to _____ car, he was shocked to discover that the front left tire had _____ puncture.

2. _____ University of King's College is one of _____ the oldest universities in Canada, and also one of the smallest.

3. Jason says that the movie *The Departed* is _____ best movie he's ever seen. I wonder if he knows that it's _____ remake of *Internal Affairs,* a movie made in Hong Kong in 2002.

4. On Christmas morning, Jeff hoped that _____ large, square present under the tree was _____ new computer.

5. When Delia was in Vancouver, she visited Stanley Park, _____ Art Gallery of Vancouver, and _____ Vancouver Aquarium.

TEST 3   Name: _____   Section: _____   Date: _____

Score: (Number right) _____ x 5 = _____ %

In the following paragraphs about Canadian hockey player Sidney Crosby, fill in the blanks with the missing articles.

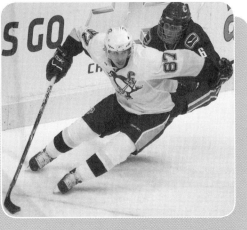

[1]Sidney Crosby is considered by many to be _____ most talented hockey player in _____ world. [2]He was born in Halifax, Nova Scotia to parents Tina and Troy Crosby in 1987. [3]He first showed interest in _____ sport of hockey at the age of two, shooting pucks at the dryer in his family's basement. [4]He received his first pair of skates _____ year later, and quickly went on to become _____ national sensation before he had even reached his teens.

[5]_____ following year, he was _____only player under eighteen to play for Canada in the 2003 World Junior Championships. [6]He scored _____ goal against Switzerland, making him— at sixteen— _____ youngest player ever to score for Canada. [7]The following year, he joined the QMJHL (Quebec Major Junior Hockey League) and won both the scoring title and the award for _____ most valuable player.

[8]At _____ age of 18, he was _____ first pick of the 2005 NHL entry draft. [9]He was drafted by _____ Pittsburgh Penguins and went on to become one of _____ leading NHL scorers that season. [10]In _____ 2006–07 season, he became the only athlete to win _____ scoring title in any major North American sports league while still _____ teenager. [11]That same year, he also won _____three highest individual honours for an NHL forward: the Hart Trophy, the Art Ross Trophy, and the Lester B. Pearson Award. [12]He is only _____ seventh player in NHL history to win all three in _____ same season.

TEST 4   Name: _____   Section: _____   Date: _____

Score: (Number right) _____ x 10 = _____ %

In each sentence below, there are two missing articles. Rewrite the sentences with the correct articles in the spaces provided.

1. Shelley finds money everywhere. Last week she found loonie while crossing street in front of her house. _____

   _____

2. The three qualities I want in a husband are honesty, sense of humour, and full head of hair.

   _____

   _____

3. For dinner, I think I will have daily special and glass of wine.

   _____

   _____

4. On first Wednesday of every month, Josie babysits little boy who lives next door.

   _____

   _____

5. In June, my assistant will start new job with Department of Parks and Recreation.

   _____

   _____

ADJECTIVES AND ADVERBS

Identifying Adjectives and Adverbs

Adjectives

An **adjective** describes a noun or pronoun. It generally answers such questions as "What kind of? Which one? How many?"

An adjective may come before the noun it describes.

- The **weary** hikers shuffled down the **dusty** road.

  The adjective *weary* describes the noun *hikers*; it tells what kind of hikers. The adjective *dusty* describes the noun *road*; it tells what kind of road.

- The **brick** house on the corner has **five** bedrooms.

  The adjective *brick* tells what material the house is built of. The adjective *five* tells how many bedrooms there are in the house.

> **NOTE** Words that describe nationality or type are also adjectives. These adjectives are capitalized. **For more information on capitalization, see Chapter 25.**

- In 2008, three **Canadian** actors were nominated for **Academy** Awards.

  The adjective *Canadian* refers to the nationality or origin of the actors; the adjective *Academy* tells which awards they were nominated for.

An adjective that describes the subject of a sentence may also come after a linking verb (such as *be, is, seem,* and *were*).

- I forgot to wear sunscreen this afternoon at the beach; my skin is red and sore.

  The adjectives *red* and *sore* describe the noun *skin*. They follow the linking verb *is*.

- After Fahira stayed up all night studying, she was **tired** and **cranky**.

  The adjectives *tired* and *cranky* describe the pronoun *she*. They follow the linking verb *was*.

For more information on linking verbs, see "Subjects and Verbs," page 41.

PRACTICE I

Complete each sentence with an appropriate adjective. Then underline the noun or pronoun that the adjective describes. Answers will vary.

Examples   My _____favourite_____ <u>sweater</u> had shrunk in the wash.

The school <u>principal</u> was _____**strict**_____ .

1. This _____ weather really bothers me.

2. I'm in the mood for a(n) _____ movie.

3. I've never read such a(n) _____ book.

4. A(n) _____ person makes a poor boss.

5. My aunt has an unusually _____ voice.

6. The dance at school last night was _____ .

7. Talia's friends all think her boyfriend is _____ .

8. It's too bad that you are so _____ .

9. I can't believe you put _____ sauce on your hamburger!

10. Sylvia wrote her sister a(n) _____ letter.

Types of Adjectives

Adjectives can refer to impression, appearance, origin, material, or purpose.

When you use more than one adjective to describe the same word, there is a specific order to follow:

Opinion	Description	Origin	Material	Purpose or type
What you think of someone or something (*beautiful, sad, difficult, delicious*).	The size, shape, colour, or age of someone or something (*huge, rectangular, orange, old*).	The place or period that someone or something comes from (*Vietnamese, Italian, prehistoric, northern, western*).	What something is made of (*brick, paper, wooden, metal, chocolate*).	What something is, does, or is used for (*washing* machine, *writing* desk, *workout* clothes, *swimming* lessons).

I often plan my route to work so that I can drive past that *beautiful old Victorian rooming* house.

> *beautiful* describes an opinion about the house
>
> *old* describes the age of the house
>
> *Victorian* describes the period of the house's construction
>
> *rooming* describes the function of the house.

PRACTICE 2

Fill in each blank with the appropriate adjective.

famous, voice, Canadian
1. As a teenager, the _____ _____ soprano Measha Brueggergosman took _____ lessons in Fredericton, New Brunswick.

new, national, marketing
2. My _____ _____ professor used to work for a _____ corporation.

second, tax, Canadian
3. My _____ cousin is an expert in _____ _____ law.

cake, metal, chocolate
4. I'm making a _____ cake. Have you seen my _____ _____ pan?

math, bedroom, difficult
5. Sonja sat for hours on her _____ floor, struggling with a _____ _____ problem.

 Adjectives can be formed by two words joined with a hyphen. These are called compound adjectives.

- On her *twenty-third* birthday, Ling flew to Toronto to visit her *English-speaking* friends.
  Twenty-third is a compound adjective that tells which birthday Ling is celebrating. *English-speaking* is a compound adjective that tells what language Ling's friends speak.

- The *Vancouver-born* actor, Seth Rogen, became quite *well-known* after starring in the movie "Knocked Up."
  Vancouver-born and *well-known* are compound adjectives that describe where the actor was born and how many people know who he is.

Adverbs

An **adverb** is a word that describes a verb, an adjective, or another adverb. Many adverbs end in *-ly*. Adverbs generally answer such questions as "How? When? Where? How much?"

How?

- The chef **carefully** spread raspberry frosting over the cake.

  The adverb *carefully* describes the verb *spread. Carefully* tells how the chef spread the frosting.

When?

- Mohammed broke his leg **yesterday** when he fell down the stairs.

  The adverb *yesterday* describes the verb *broke. Yesterday* tells when Mohammed broke his leg.

Where?

- After going to every club in the city, we went **home.**

  The adverb *home* describes the verb *went. Home* tells where we went.

How much?

- Ann was **extremely** embarrassed when she stumbled on stage.

  The adverb *extremely* describes the adjective *embarrassed.* It tells how much Ann was embarrassed.

- That lamp shines **very brightly.**

  The adverb *very* describes the adverb *brightly.* Very tells how *brightly* the lamp shines. The adverb *brightly* describes the verb *shines*; it tells how the lamp shines.

Adverbs with Action Verbs

Action verbs are verbs that describe an action, including actions that can't be seen, such as "thinking." Be careful to use an adverb—not an adjective—with an action verb. Compare the following:

Incorrect	Correct
The student snored loud during the lecture. *Loud* is an adjective.	The student snored **loudly** during the lecture.
The graduates marched proud. *Proud* is an adjective.	The graduates marched **proudly.**
The batter swung wild at all the pitches. *Wild* is an adjective.	The batter swung **wildly** at all the pitches.

 Look at a piece of your own writing (for example, a school assignment, a letter, an e-mail). Underline three adjectives, drawing arrows linking the adjectives to the nouns or pronouns they describe. Now, circle three adverbs, drawing arrows linking the adverbs to the verbs they describe.

PRACTICE 3

Complete each sentence with the adverb form of the adjective in the margin. (Change each adjective in the margin to an adverb by adding -ly.)

Example   *quick*   Sandra read the book too _____ **quickly** _____ .

bright   1. The car shone _____ after we washed it.

helpless   2. The family watched _____ as their house burned.

hurried   3. The two teachers spoke _____ between classes.

shy   4. The little girl peeked _____ at her new neighbour.

honest   5. A good businessperson deals _____ with everyone.

quiet   6. The old woman hummed _____ as she did her shopping.

longing   7. The cat stared _____ at the leftover tuna casserole.

frequent   8. Premium TV channels _____ show the same movie ten or more times in one month.

kind   9. Our neighbour _____ offered to feed our pets while we were gone.

serious   10. Many teenagers complain that their parents don't take them _____ .

PRACTICE 4

Complete each sentence correctly with either the adverb or adjective in the margin.

rapid, rapidly   1. Felipe spoke _____ in Spanish to his grandfather.

rapid, rapidly   2. Their _____ conversation was difficult for me to follow.

quiet, quietly   3. My son will only sleep if the room is totally _____ .

quiet, quietly   4. The audience sat _____ through the first act of the show.

patient, patiently   5. Ravi waited _____ for the elevator to arrive.

patient, patiently   6. The mother is _____ with her youngster.

prompt, promptly   7. The invitation asks for a _____ response.

prompt, promptly   8. It is important to arrive _____ for a job interview.

cheerful, cheerfully   9. Olga smiled _____ at the customer.

cheerful, cheerfully   10. Her _____ smile warmed the room.

USING ADJECTIVES AND ADVERBS IN COMPARISONS

Comparing Two Things

In general, to compare two things, add *-er* to adjectives and adverbs of one syllable.

- Grilling food is **faster** than roasting.

  The adjective *faster* is used to compare two methods: grilling and roasting.

- My mother works **longer** each day than my father.

  The adverb *longer* is used to compare how long two people work each day.

For two-syllable words ending in one or more consonants followed by a y (such as lazy, angry, or crazy), change the *y* to an *i* and add *–er*

- The sky today is even **hazier** than it was yesterday.

  The adjective *hazier* is used to compare today's sky to yesterday's sky.

- Jay threw a party while his parents were away. His father was angry, but his mother was even **angrier.**

  The adjective *angrier* is used to compare Jay's father's state of mind to his mother's.

For longer adjectives and adverbs, do not add *-er*. Instead, add the word *more* when comparing two things.

- I think the Canadian electoral process is **more complicated** than the American electoral process.

  The words *more complicated* describe the subject *Canadian electoral process*; they are being used to compare two things, the Canadian and American electoral processes.

- Maria sings **more sweetly** than I do.

  The words *more sweetly* describe the verb sings; they compare the ways two people sing.

PRACTICE 5

Write in the correct form of the word in the margin by adding either *-er* or *more*, or changing a *y* to an *i* and adding *–er*.

Examples	*tall*	Anjelica is _____**taller**_____ than her twin sister.
	carefully	I prefer to ride with Dan. He drives _____**more carefully**_____ than you.

full **1.** This bag of potato chips is _____ than that one.

affectionate **2.** My dog is _____ than my boyfriend.

wrinkled **3.** This shirt looks _____ than it did before I ironed it.

lazy **4.** Raisa's brother is even _____ than she is.

annoying **5.** There are few sounds _____ than fingernails scratching a board

Comparing Three Things

In general, to compare three or more things, add *-est* to adjectives and adverbs of one syllable.

- Grilling food is faster than roasting, but microwaving is **fastest** of all.

  The adjective *fastest* is used to compare three methods: grilling, roasting, and microwaving. It indicates that microwaving is faster than the other two.

- My mother works longer each day than my father, but in my family, I work the **longest.**

  The adverb *longest* is used to compare how long three or more people work each day. It indicates that of the three, I work the most number of hours.

For longer adjectives and adverbs, do not add *-est*. Instead, add the word most when comparing three or more things.

- My dog is more intelligent than my cat, but my parrot is the **most intelligent** pet I have ever had.

  Most intelligent is used to compare three animals. It shows which one is the smartest.

- Among the couples I know, my brother and sister-in-law are the **most happily** married of all.

  Most happily is used to compare how happy many married couples are. It indicates that my brother and sister-in-law are more happily married than any of the other couples I know.

PRACTICE 6

Write in the correct form of the word in the margin by adding either *-est* or most.

Examples   *cold*   The _____**coldest**_____ day on record in Nunavut was –92 degrees Celsius!

   delightful   Every parent thinks his or her child is the _____**most delightful**_____ child in the world.

young   1. Cody is the _____ of eight children.

important   2. The _____ thing in Julia's life is clothes.

fresh   3. The farmer's market in the park has the _____ vegetables in town.

artistic   4. Of the eighteen students in my class, Monique is the _____.

difficult   5. My brother enjoys playing the _____ video games he can find.

> **NOTES**
>
> **1.** Do not use both an -*er* ending and *more*, or an -*est* ending and *most*.
>
> | | |
> |---|---|
> | Incorrect | My father's eyelashes are **more longer** than my mother's. |
> | Correct | My father's eyelashes are **longer** than my mother's. |
>
> **2.** Certain short adjectives and adverbs have irregular forms:
>
> | | Comparing two | Comparing three or more |
> |---|---|---|
> | **bad, badly** | worse | worst |
> | **good, well** | better | best |
> | **little** | less | least |
> | **much, many** | more | most |

- The grape cough syrup tastes **better** than the orange syrup, but the lemon cough drops taste the **best.**

- Sid is doing **badly** in speech class, but I'm doing even **worse.**

USING TWO TROUBLESOME PAIRS: *GOOD* AND *WELL, BAD* AND *BADLY*

Good is an adjective that often means "enjoyable," "talented," or "positive."

- I had a **good** day.

- Sue is a **good** skier.

- Think **good** thoughts.

As an adverb, *well* often means "skillfully" or "successfully."

- Sue skis **well.**

- The schedule worked **well.**

- Jiao interacts **well** with others.

As an adjective, *well* means "healthy."

- The patient is **well** once again.

Bad is an adjective. *Badly* is an adverb.

- I look **bad**.

  Bad is an adjective that comes after the linking verb *look*. It describes the appearance of the subject of the sentence, *I*.

- I need sleep **badly.**

  Badly is an adverb that describes the verb *need*. It explains how much the sleep is needed.

PRACTICE 7

Complete the sentence with the correct word from the margin.

good, well   **1.** Natasha dances really _____.

good, well   **2.** Did you have a _____ day at school?

bad, badly   **3.** I need a haircut _____.

bad, badly   **4.** My mother has a really _____ headache.

good, well   **5.** No student did very _____ on the math test.

bad, badly   **6.** Luckily, no one was _____ hurt in the accident.

good, well   **7.** This machine bakes bread very _____.

bad, badly   **8.** After a week on a liquids-only diet, Ben looks really _____.

good, well   **9.** Keep taking the antibiotic until it's gone, even if you think you are completely _____.

good, well   **10.** Working in a nursing home was a _____ experience for me.

 In standard English, it is incorrect to express a negative idea by pairing one negative with another. This is called a **double negative**. Common negative words include *not, nothing, never, nowhere, nobody,* and *neither.* To correct a double negative, either eliminate one of the negative words or replace a negative with a positive word.

Incorrect	I **shouldn't** go **nowhere** this weekend.
Correct	I **should** go **nowhere** this weekend.
Correct	I **shouldn't** go **anywhere** this weekend.

Shouldn't means *should not,* so the first sentence above contains two negatives: *not* and *nowhere.* In the first correct sentence, *not* has been eliminated. In the second correct sentence, *nowhere* has been replaced with a positive word.

The words *hardly, scarcely,* and *barely* are also negatives. They should not be paired with other negatives such as *never* and *not.* Correct a double negative containing *hardly, scarcely,* or *barely* by eliminating the other negative word.

Incorrect	I **couldn't scarcely** recognize you.
Correct	I **could scarcely** recognize you.

TEST 1

Name: _____   Section: _____   Date: _____

Score: (Number right) _____ x 10 = _____ %

Adjectives and Adverbs

In the following paragraph, **ten** adjectives or adverbs are missing. Fill in each blank with the correct adjective or adverb from the following list. <u>Adjectives:</u> *public, secret, emergency-room, busy, thirty-two, Chinese, grateful.* <u>Adverbs:</u> *softly, confidently, recently.*

[1]Vincent Lam, whose family comes from Vietnam's _____ community, was born _____ years ago in London, Ontario, and grew up in Ottawa. [2]He now works as an _____ doctor in a _____ hospital in Toronto. [3]However, Lam, who speaks _____ yet _____, has had a _____ life that his _____ patients knew nothing about. [4]_____, though, that life has become very _____.

TEST 2   Name: _____   Section: _____   Date: _____

Score: (Number right) _____ × 10 = _____%

Adjectives and Adverbs

In the following paragraph, **ten** adjectives or adverbs are missing. Fill in each blank with the correct adjective or adverb from the following list: *emergency, one, short, young, important, first, exciting, spare, award-winning, good.*

[1]Vincent Lam is the author of an _____ book of _____ stories, entitled *Bloodletting & Miraculous Cures*, which was published in 2005. [2]Lam has wanted to be a writer ever since he was a _____ child, but he chose _____ medicine because he was _____ at working with his hands and he thought it would be an _____ career. [3]However, he continued to write in his _____ time. [4]*Bloodletting & Miraculous Cures* is Lam's _____ book, and he was as surprised as anyone when it was included on the list of nominees for _____ of Canada's most _____ literary awards, The Giller Prize.

TEST 3   Name: _____   Section: _____   Date: _____

Score: (Number right) _____ × 10 = _____ %

Adjectives and Adverbs

In the following paragraph, **ten** adjectives or adverbs are missing. Fill in each blank with the correct adjective or adverb from the following list: *many, successfully, honestly, astonishing, realistically, first-time, generously, skilfully, miserably, humorously.*

[1]*Bloodletting & Miraculous Cures* is considered to be an _____ achievement for a _____ author. [2]Readers and reviewers praised the book _____, saying that it portrayed the medical profession _____ and _____. [3]The novel follows four medical students and doctors—Fitz, Ming, Chen, and Sri—as they cope with the _____ challenges of applying to medical school, practicing medicine, and maintaining relationships with family members, friends, and lovers. [4]Sometimes they cope _____, but sometimes they fail _____. [5]All of this is handled _____ and _____ by Lam.

TEST 4

Name: _____   Section: _____   Date: _____

Score: (Number right) _____ x 10 = _____%

Adjectives and Adverbs

In the following paragraph, **ten** adjectives or adverbs are missing. Fill in each blank with the correct adjective or adverb from the following list: *long, greatly, well, increased, tough, suddenly, next, full-time, $40,000, harder.*

¹In January, 2007, Lam was awarded the Giller Prize for his book of stories. Since winning the award, the book has been selling _____. ²However, the _____ sales and the _____ prize money have not _____ changed Lam's life. ³He still keeps a _____ schedule as an emergency room doctor at Toronto East General Hospital. ⁴In fact, he says that writing is _____ than practicing medicine, because it demands _____ days of "slogging and beating my fists against the page until _____ something works." ⁵He is now hard at work on his _____ book—a novel. ⁶After a _____ day of writing, he says, "it's a great relief to go to the hospital."

BEYOND THE BASICS

OBJECTIVES

In Part 3, you will build on the basic skills you developed in Part 2, learning about the most common grammar errors and how to correct them.

By the end of Part 3, you should be able to:

- Choose a verb form that agrees with the subject of a sentence;

- Identify and correct sentence fragments;

- Identify and correct run-on sentences and comma splices;

- Identify and correct misplaced and dangling modifiers;

- Identify and correct faulty parallelism.

PART 3   PRETEST

Each of the following examples contains one of the types of errors covered in Part 3. Correct the sentences in the space provided.

1. During the summer, I spent my days swimming at the public pool, playing soccer in the park, and I also hung out with my friends.

   _____

2. While writing her Chemistry exam, Jessie's phone rang.

   _____

3. One of my friends are meeting me at the coffee shop.

   _____

4. If you have any questions, ask Doreen or myself.

   _____

5. At the age of five, Celia's mother threw her a princess-themed birthday party.

   _____

6. At the party, the children ate cake, played games, and then they opened the presents.

   _____

7. Today my whole school did the Terry Fox Run we raised over $1,000.

   _____

8. Everyone in my family are very proud of me for completing the run.

   _____

9. Dana has no free time, she goes to school, looks after her little brother, and works 40 hours a week.

   _____

10. Of all the seasons, I like fall the best. Because the leaves are such beautiful colours.

    _____

How many errors did you catch? _____/10

CHAPTER 11

SUBJECT–VERB AGREEMENT

Basics about Subject–Verb Agreement

In a correctly written sentence, the subject and verb agree (match) in number. Singular subjects have singular verbs, and plural subjects have plural verbs.

In simple sentences of few words, it's not difficult to make the subject and verb agree:

- Our *baby* **sleeps** more than ten hours a day. Some *babies* **sleep** even longer.

  The subject *baby* is singular, so it takes the singular verb *sleeps*.
  The subject *babies* is plural, so it takes the plural verb *sleep*.

- This *winter* **is** very cold. In Winnipeg, most *winters* **are** very cold.

  The subject *winter* is singular, so it takes the singular verb *is*.
  The subject *winters* is plural, so it takes the plural verb *are*.

However, not all sentences are as straightforward as the above examples. Here are two situations that can cause problems with subject–verb agreement.

WORDS BETWEEN THE SUBJECT AND VERB

A verb often comes right after its subject, as in this example:

- The sealed *boxes* **belong** to my brother.

> **NOTE** Here and in the rest of the chapter, the *subject* is shown in *italic type*, and the **verb** is shown in **boldface type**.

However, at times the subject and verb are separated by a **prepositional phrase**. A prepositional phrase is a group of words that begins with a preposition and ends with a noun or pronoun. *By, for, from, in, of, on*, and *to* are common prepositions. (A longer list of prepositions is on page 35.) Look at the following sentences:

- A small *bag* of potato chips **contains** 440 calories.

  In this sentence, the subject and verb are separated by the prepositional phrase *of potato chips*. The verb must agree with the singular subject *bag*—not with a word in the prepositional phrase.

- The *tomatoes* in this salad **are** brown and mushy.

  Because the subject, *tomatoes*, is plural, the verb must also be plural. The prepositional phrase *in this salad* has no effect on subject–verb agreement.

- *Books* about reptiles **fill** my daughter's room.

  The plural subject *books* takes the plural verb *fill*. *About reptiles* is a prepositional phrase.

119

COMPOUND SUBJECTS

A **compound subject** is made up of two nouns connected by a joining word. Subjects joined by *and* generally take a plural verb.

- *Running* and *lifting* weights **are** good ways to keep in shape.

- *Fear* and *ignorance* **have** a lot to do with hatred.

Understanding Subject–Verb Agreement

The following passage contains **five** mistakes in subject–verb agreement. See if you can identify them before checking the correct answer below.

¹David Simpson is waiting tables at his parents' restaurant in Calgary. ²David and his brother and sister works in the restaurant full time. ³His brother Chris helps in the kitchen, while David and his sister Sylvia serves tables in the dining room. ⁴Some parts of the job is rewarding. ⁵For example, getting to know the regular customers give him a feeling of connection to his community. ⁶Still, David does not want to work in a restaurant forever. ⁷The customers in the dining room doesn't know that this is David's last shift until next summer. ⁸David will be taking time off to study Social Work at Mount Royal College.

1. David and his brother and sister work in the restaurant full time.
2. His brother Chris helps in the kitchen, while David and his sister Sylvia serve tables in the dining room.
3. Some parts of the job are rewarding.
4. For example, getting to know the regular customers gives him a feeling of connection to his community.
5. The customers in the dining room don't know that this is David's last shift until next summer.

Check Your Understanding

The following passage has **five** errors in subject–verb agreement. Underline the errors. Then write the correct subject and verb in the space provided. Some sentences are correct.

¹When David graduated from high school four years ago, he decided not to go to college or university. ²Money, independence, and freedom was more important to him than continuing his education. ³He chose to help his parents in the family restaurant. ⁴At first, his friends from school was jealous. ⁵Books, living expenses, and tuition is very expensive. ⁶They would be spending money, while David would be making money. ⁷Now, David's friends are graduating and going on to interesting, fulfilling careers. ⁸When they have time to visit David, their stories about their experiences at school makes David wish he had made a different choice. ⁹The three years he spent out of college seems like a waste of time to him now.

1. _____

2. _____

3. _____

4. _____

5. _____

There are five other situations that affect subject–verb agreement: verb coming before the subject; compound subjects with *or nor*; collective nouns; indefinite pronoun subjects; and relative pronoun subjects. Each situation is discussed more fully below.

VERB COMING BEFORE THE SUBJECT

In most sentences, the verb follows the subject.

- *Hector* **passed** the course.
- The *plane* **roared** overhead.

However, in some sentences, the verb comes *before* the subject. To make the subject and verb agree in such cases, look for the subject after the verb. Then decide if the verb should be singular or plural. Look for the following types of sentences:

Questions:

- What **was** your *score* on the test?

   The verb *was* is singular. It agrees with the singular subject *score*. *On the test* is a prepositional phrase. The subject of a sentence is never in a prepositional phrase. (See page 43.)

● What **are** your parents going to do about your little brother's behaviour?

  The verb *are* is plural. It agrees with the plural subject *parents*. *About your little brother's behaviour* is a prepositional phrase.

Sentences that begin with such words as there is or here are:

● There **are** *mice* in my basement. The verb of this sentence is the plural verb *are*, so the subject should be plural as well.

  You can find the subject by asking, "What are in the basement?" The answer, *mice*, is the subject.

● On that shelf **are** the *reports* for this year.

  The sentence begins with the prepositional phrase *on that shelf*, which is followed by the plural verb *are*. You can find the subject by asking, "What are on that shelf?" The answer is the subject of the sentence: *reports*. The subject and verb agree—they are both plural.

Here's another helpful way to find the subject when the verb comes first: Try to rearrange the sentence so that the subject comes first. The subject may be easier to find when the sentence is in the normal order. For the sentences on the previous page, you would then get:

● Your *score* on the test **was** what?

● Your *parents* **are** going to do what about your little brother's behaviour?

● *Mice* **are** in the basement.

● The *reports* for this year **are** on that shelf.

> **PRACTICE 1**

Underline the subject of each sentence. Then, in the space provided, write the form of the verb that agrees with the subject.

1. What _____ (is, are) the capital of Burma?

2. Sandeep opened the front door, and there _____ (was, were) his mother-in-law, with a suitcase in her hand.

3. Although Canada is a wealthy country, there _____ (is, are) many hungry people in Canada's cities.

4. What _____ (was, were) your reasons for leaving?

5. Who _____ (is, are) that attractive man standing by the window?

COMPOUND SUBJECTS WITH *OR* AND *NOR*

As explained earlier in this chapter, a **compound subject** is made up of two nouns connected by a joining word. Subjects joined by *and* generally take a plural verb.

However, when a compound subject is connected by *or, nor, either . . . or*, or *neither . . . nor*, the verb must agree with the part of the subject that is closer to it.

- My *aunts* or my *mother* usually **hosts** our family gatherings.

  The singular noun *mother* is closer to the verb, so the singular verb *hosts* is used.

- Either *he* or *his parents* **were** home that night.

- Either *his parents* or *he* **was** home that night.

  In the first sentence, the plural noun *parents* is closer to the verb, so the verb is plural. In the second sentence, the singular noun *he* is closer to the verb, so the verb must be singular.

- Neither the *teacher* nor the *students* **are** to blame for the shortage of textbooks.

  The plural noun *students* is closer to the verb, so the verb is plural.

PRACTICE 2

Underline the subject of each sentence. Then, in the space provided, write the form of the verb that agrees with the subject.

1. Neither the children nor their father _____ (was, were) aware that someone was at the door.

2. In my English class, either a novel or a play _____ (is, are) assigned every week.

3. I find winters very long because neither snowboarding nor skating _____ (appeal, appeals) to me.

4. Neither those jeans nor that sweater _____ (fit, fits) you very well anymore.

5. I hope that either you or your replacement _____ (is, are) on the way to the office right now!

COLLECTIVE NOUNS

A **collective noun** refers to a group of persons or things that are thought of as one unit. Collective nouns are usually considered singular.

Common Collective Nouns

army	company	minority
association	corporation	political party
audience	council	public
board	department	school
class	family	society
club	group	team
committee	jury	
community	majority	

Following are some examples.

- My **family** *lives* on Russell Avenue.

    Family refers to a single unit, so the singular verb *lives* is used. However, if a collective noun refers to the individual members of the group, a plural verb is used.

- My **family** *live* in Toronto, Vancouver, Calgary, and Regina.

    Since one unit cannot live in four different places, *family* in this sentence clearly refers to the individual members of the group, so the plural verb *live* is used. To emphasize the individuals, some writers would use a subject that is clearly plural:

- The **members** of my family *live* in Toronto, Vancouver, Calgary, and Regina.

PRACTICE 3

Underline the subject of each sentence. Then, in the space provided, write the form of the verb that agrees with the subject.

1. The Caribbean Students' Association _____ (is, are) hosting a performance by a steel pan drum player later this month.

2. Members of the community _____ (was, were) upset about the number of home invasions in recent months.

3. The Conservative Party _____ (has, have) been in power in Canada since 2006.

4. The Safe Schools committee _____ (meet, meets) on the first Tuesday of every month.

5. I surveyed my classmates, and the majority _____ (agree, agrees) that the math exam was too difficult.

INDEFINITE PRONOUN SUBJECTS

Indefinite pronouns are pronouns that do not refer to a specific person or thing. The ones in the box below are always singular:

anybody	either	neither	one
anyone	everybody	no one	somebody
anything	everyone	nobody	someone
each	everything	nothing	something

In the following sentences, the subjects are singular indefinite pronouns. Each of the verbs is therefore also singular.

- *Each* of the puppies **is** cute in its own way.

- *Neither* of the boys **wants** to walk the dog.

- Despite the rules, nearly *everyone* in my apartment building **owns** a pet.

The following indefinite pronouns are exceptions:

both   most

Note that the indefinite pronoun *both* is always plural:

- *Both* of the puppies **are** cute in their own ways.

The definite pronoun *most* is singular or plural, depending on its context:

- *Most* of his outfit **is** white. *Most* here refers to one thing—the outfit, so the singular verb *is* is used.

- *Most* of the salespeople **are** friendly. *Most* here refers to several salespeople, so the plural verb *are* is used.

PRACTICE 4

Underline the subject of each sentence. Then, in the space provided, write the form of the verb that agrees with the subject.

1. No one _____ (know, knows) how long the snowstorm will last.

2. Someone in the apartment upstairs _____ (was, were) playing a bass guitar late at night.

3. Thank goodness most of this job _____ (is, are) already done.

4. Most of my friends _____ (like, likes) to go salsa dancing.

5. In Canada, each province _____ (has, have) a lieutenant-governor, as well as a premier.

RELATIVE PRONOUN SUBJECTS

The following are relative pronouns:

who   which   that

They are singular when they refer to a singular noun. They are plural when they refer to a plural noun.

- I met a woman *who* **is** from China:

- I met two women *who* **are** from China.
  In the first sentence above, *who* refers to the singular word *woman*, so the verb is singular too. In the second sentence, *who* refers to the plural word *women*, so the verb must be plural.

- Our car, *which* **is** only a year old, already needs a new battery.
  Which refers to *car*, a singular noun, so the singular verb *is* is used.

- My boss collects old wind-up toys *that* still **work.**
  That refers to the plural noun *toys*, so the plural verb *work* is used.

For more information on relative pronouns, see "Parts of Speech," page 32.

PRACTICE 5

Underline the subject of each sentence. Then, in the space provided, write the form of the verb that agrees with the subject.

1. The mayor of my town is a woman who _____ (know, knows) how to make things happen.

2. My friends like to listen to hip hop, which _____ (is, are) not my favourite type of music.

3. Domenico's neighbours are people who _____ (like, likes) their privacy.

4. My son's new best friend is a little boy who _____ (speak, speaks) Portuguese.

5. Ameel likes books that _____ (has, have) some action in them.

TEST 1   Name: _____   Section: _____   Date: _____

Score: (Number right) _____ x 10 = _____ %

Subject–Verb Agreement

Complete the passages below by filling in each blank with the correct form of the verb.

[1]David is very excited about going to college, but he is worried that he will be the only person in his classes who _____(is, are) returning after time away from school. [2]His friends try to make him feel better by telling him that there _____ (is, are) many older students returning to college now. [3]In fact, his friend Mary had a sixty-three-year-old man in her English class last year! [4]They finally convinced him that nobody _____ (is, are) even going to notice that he is older than the students who are right out of high school. [5]David is excited, but he will miss all the money he used to make at the restaurant. [6] He needs a new laptop, and the books for his math class alone _____ (costs, cost) $165! [7]There _____ (is, are) many sacrifices he will have to make to get an education, but he knows it will be worth it.

[1]David's friends and family _____ (is, are) throwing him a back-to-school party in the restaurant. [2]Everyone _____ (is, are) very happy for him. [3]His parents present him with a cake, and each of his friends _____ (wishes, wish) him luck in his new life as a student. [4]He is surprised when his mother and father _____ (hands, hand) him a large box. [5]He guesses that either a new backpack or some books _____ (is, are) inside. [6]He is shocked and grateful to find that his friends and family members all joined together to buy him a new laptop computer.

TEST 2   Name: _____   Section: _____   Date: _____

Score: (Number right) _____ x 10 = _____%

Subject–Verb Agreement

For each sentence below, choose the correct form of the verb from the words in the brackets, and write it in the space provided.

1. I've always thought that bananas and peanut butter _____ (taste, tastes) good together.

2. My counsellor and my English instructor _____ (has, have) agreed to write recommendations for me.

3. Kara and her two children _____ (live, lives) in a shelter.

4. Most people in this neighbourhood _____ (speak, speaks) Mandarin.

5. Shantell and Justin both _____ (see, sees) better with contact lenses than they did with glasses.

6. Isaiah was nervous about starting college, but everyone in his classes _____ (seem, seems) friendly.

7. Everything in that box _____ (go, goes) to the neighbourhood garage sale.

8. In Marc's neighbourhood, drugs and crime _____ (is, are) everywhere you look.

9. Once a month, a group of my college friends _____ (get, gets) together once a month to play poker.

10. There _____ (is, are) several good reasons for Qien to take that job.

TEST 3   Name: _____   Section: _____   Date: _____

Score: (Number right) _____ × 10 = _____ %

Subject–Verb Agreement

For each sentence below, choose the correct form of the verb from the words in the brackets, and write it in the space provided.

1. Neither the fish nor the vegetables _____ (taste, tastes) fresh in this restaurant.

2. Both of my children _____ (is, are) allergic to peanuts.

3. Here _____ (is, are) the drinks you ordered.

4. What _____ (was, were) the reasons for the workers' strike?

5. Why _____ (was, were) your assignments late?

6. I am aware that there _____ (was, were) no excuse for my behaviour.

7. Shalina was very sad when the house that she grew up in _____ (was, were) sold.

8. Where in the world _____ (is, are) those children?

9. Most of the candidates for leader _____ (has, have) good communication skills.

10. Everybody on the bus _____ (was, were) shocked when a young girl refused to give her seat to an elderly man with a cane.

Subject–Verb Agreement

Complete the following paragaph about actress Sarah Polley by filling in each blank with the correct form of the verb.

¹When somebody works at a number of different occupations, people often _____ (says, say) that person "wears a lot of different hats." ²Consider the well-known Canadian actor Sarah Polley. ³Her many fans _____ (knows, know) her as a successful writer, actor, director, singer, and political activist. ⁴Polley, who has been acting since the age of four, _____ (lists, list) over 21 film and television roles on her résumé. ⁵In 1990, she won the starring role in the CBC's television series *Road to Avonlea*, eventually earning the unofficial title of "Canada's Sweetheart." ⁶After the show was picked up by the Disney Channel, everybody in Canada _____ (was, were) surprised when she left the show, claiming that it had become too Americanized. ⁷She _____ (has, have) remained politically active throughout her career. ⁸In 1995, she lost several teeth when a riot broke out during a protest against the Ontario Progressive Conservative government. ⁹There _____ (is, are) evidence of her commitment to Canadian filmmaking throughout her career: in 2000, she dropped out of the big-budget Hollywood movie *Almost Famous* to make the low-budget Canadian movie *The Law of Enclosures*. ¹⁰Within the film industry, she _____ (has, have) not limited herself to acting. ¹¹She performed three songs on the soundtrack to the 1997 film *The Sweet Hereafter*, in which she also starred. ¹²In 2007, she directed her first feature film, *Away from Her*, which _____ (was, were) widely praised by critics. ¹³Polley herself adapted the screenplay from a short story by Canadian writer Alice Munro, and she _____ (was, were) nominated for an Academy Award for Best Adapted Screenplay. ¹⁴Award-winning actor, committed activist, admired singer, award-nominated writer, critically acclaimed director: _____ (is, are) there anything this young woman can't do?

CHAPTER 12

FRAGMENTS

Basics about Fragments

To be a complete sentence, a group of words must contain a subject and a verb. It must also express a complete thought. If it lacks a subject, verb, or a complete thought, it is a **fragment.**

> Because it was raining.
>
> Ran a marathon.
>
> Going to the movies.
>
> For example chocolate cake.

Here are three common types of fragments:

FRAGMENTS WITHOUT A SUBJECT

Some fragments do have a verb, but lack a subject.

- Joe Davis lowered himself from the van into his wheelchair. And then rolled up the sidewalk ramp.
  The second word group lacks a subject, so it is a fragment. You can often fix such a fragment by adding it to the sentence that comes before it.

- Joe Davis lowered himself from the van into his **wheelchair and** then rolled up the sidewalk ramp.

-*ING* AND *TO* FRAGMENTS

When a word ending with -*ing* appears at or near the beginning of a word group, a fragment may result.

- Hoping to furnish their new home cheaply. The newlyweds go to garage sales.
  The first word group lacks both a subject and a verb, so it is a fragment.

A fragment may also result when a word group begins with *to* followed by a verb:

- Leo jogged through the park. To clear his mind before the midterm.
  The second word group is a fragment that lacks both a subject and a complete verb. (A word that follows *to* cannot be the verb of a sentence.)

You can often fix such fragments by attaching them to the sentence that comes before or after.

- Hoping to furnish their new home **cheaply, the** newlyweds go to garage sales.

- Leo jogged through the **park to** clear his mind before the midterm.

 When an -*ing* or *to* word group starts a sentence, follow it with a comma.

EXAMPLE FRAGMENTS

Word groups that begin with words like *including, such as, especially,* and *for example* are sometimes fragments.

- For class, we had to read several books. Including *The Diary of Anne Frank*.
- My grandfather has many interests. For example, playing poker and watching old cowboy movies.

You can often fix such fragments by attaching them to the sentence that comes before, or by adding a subject and a verb.

- For class we had to read several **books, including** *The Diary of Anne Frank*.
- My grandfather has many interests. For example, **he plays** poker and **watches** old cowboy movies.

 Create sentences out of the following fragments:

For example, King Kong and Godzilla.

Running for the bus.

To study for her chemistry exam.

Including skiing, snowboarding, and ice skating.

Or a slice of pizza in the cafeteria.

SUBORDINATE FRAGMENTS

Another common kind of fragment is the **subordinate fragment,** which has a subject and verb but begins with a subordinate conjunction.

Some common subordinate conjunctions are:

after	even though	unless	wherever
although	even when	until	whether
as	if	what	which
because	since	when	while
before	that	whenever	who
even if	though	where	

A subordinate conjunction makes the word group it appears in unable to stand on its own. For example:

- Laura was tired.
  This is a complete sentence.

But add the subordinate conjunction *because* and suddenly the sentence is meaningless:

- Because Laura was tired.

Although this word group contains a subject (*Laura*) and a verb (*was*), it is an incomplete thought. The reader wants to know **what happened** because Laura was tired. A word group that begins with *because* or another dependent word cannot stand alone; another idea is needed to complete the thought. For example, we could correct the above fragment like this:

- Because Laura was tired, **she took a nap.**

  The words *she took a nap* complete the thought.

When you begin a sentence with a subordinate conjunction, place a comma between the two word groups:

- Because the movie was so violent.

- Some people left the theatre.

- Because the movie was so violent, some people left the theatre.

NOTE   When the subordinate conjunction does not begin the sentence, no comma is needed.

- Some people left the theatre because the movie was so violent.

 Write five sentences beginning with subordinate conjunctions (use the list on the previous page). Don't forget to use a comma after each subordinate clause. Now, change the word order, so that the subordinate conjunction is in the middle of the sentence.

Check Your Understanding

The passage below contains **five** dependent-word fragments. Underline each fragment. Then correct it in the space provided. The answers appear on the next page.

¹Although most college students are in their teens or twenties. ²Many are a good deal older. ³Such people are often called "nontraditional students." ⁴When they were younger. ⁵They may have been too busy raising children to attend college. ⁶Some may have decided that going to college would be good for their careers. ⁷Going to school as a "nontraditional" student has its own challenges. ⁸Which often include juggling school responsibilities with a job and family duties. ⁹However, older adults generally do very well in school. ¹⁰Because they have experience with goal-setting, prioritizing, and managing their time and resources. ¹¹Even if it means making personal sacrifices. ¹²They are willing to do whatever it takes to get an education.

1. _____

2. _____

3. _____

4. _____

5. _____

1. Although most college students are in their teens or twenties, many are a good deal older.

2. When they were younger, they may have been too busy raising children to attend college.

3. Going to school as a "nontraditional" student has its own challenges, which often include juggling school responsibilities with a job and family duties.

4. However older adults generally do very well in school because they have experience with goal-setting, prioritizing, and managing their time and resources.

5. Even if it means making personal sacrifices, they are willing to do whatever it takes to get an education.

Understanding Fragments

The following passage about Janelle Hurst, a parent and student living in Cape Breton, Nova Scotia, contains **five** fragments. See if you can find and underline the fragments. Then look at how they are corrected.

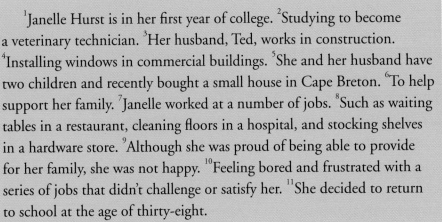

[1]Janelle Hurst is in her first year of college. [2]Studying to become a veterinary technician. [3]Her husband, Ted, works in construction. [4]Installing windows in commercial buildings. [5]She and her husband have two children and recently bought a small house in Cape Breton. [6]To help support her family. [7]Janelle worked at a number of jobs. [8]Such as waiting tables in a restaurant, cleaning floors in a hospital, and stocking shelves in a hardware store. [9]Although she was proud of being able to provide for her family, she was not happy. [10]Feeling bored and frustrated with a series of jobs that didn't challenge or satisfy her. [11]She decided to return to school at the age of thirty-eight.

1. Janelle Hurst is in her first year of college, studying to become a veterinary technician.

2. Her husband, Ted, works in construction, installing windows in commercial buildings.

3. To help support her family, Janelle worked at a number of jobs.

4. To help support her family, Janelle worked at a number of jobs, such as waiting tables in a restaurant, cleaning floors in a hospital, and stocking shelves in a hardware store.

5. Feeling bored and frustrated with a series of jobs that didn't challenge or satisfy her, she decided to return to school at the age of thirty-eight.

Check Your Understanding

Underline the **five** fragments in the following passage. Then correct them in the spaces provided.

¹The decision to return to school was a difficult one for Janelle. ²She worried about many things. ³Such as the expense of classes and textbooks, the loss of income when she left her full-time job, and the reactions of her classmates to a thirty-eight-year-old student. ⁴She also worried about her children, sixteen-year-old Nikki and thirteen-year-old David. ⁵She was afraid that juggling school, part-time work, and housework would not leave her with enough time or energy. ⁶To be the sort of mother she wanted to be. ⁷After struggling with the decision, both Janelle and Ted realized that it was important. ⁸To set a good example for their son and daughter. ⁹By pursuing her goal of becoming a veterinary technician, she would also be teaching them the value of hard work, perseverance, and belief in oneself. ¹⁰Now, David and Nikki help out with the household responsibilities. ¹¹Such as cleaning up after meals, taking out the garbage and recycling, and shovelling the driveway in the winter. ¹²Since Nikki turned sixteen, she has also been able to help her mother by doing some of the driving. ¹³Including taking her brother to his hockey and soccer practices. ¹⁴Both teenagers are proud of their mother and are happy to help her achieve her goal.

1. _____

_____

2. _____

_____

3. _____

_____

4. _____

_____

5. _____

_____

PRACTICE 1

Each of the passages that follow contains **five** fragments. Underline the fragments and then correct each in the space provided.

¹Feeling nervous about being older than the other students. ²Janelle did not participate very much in her classes at first. ³Soon, realizing that she was not the only mature student in her program. ⁴She relaxed and began to feel more comfortable. ⁶Her instructors also helped to put her at ease, and soon she was confident enough. ⁷To put her hand up and answer questions. ⁸She found that the other students were very friendly towards her, and now she is comfortable. ⁹Talking to her classmates. ¹⁰She was even invited to join a group of women in her class who have formed a study group. ¹¹They help each other meet the challenges of their course load. ¹²Sharing notes from classes, studying together at the library, and chatting online about upcoming tests and assignments.

1. _____

_____

2. _____

_____

3. _____

_____

4. _____

_____

5. _____

_____

¹Some days, remembering her past school experiences. ²Janelle can't believe that she is back in school. ³She had a difficult time with her classes in high school. ⁴Especially math class, which she found very hard. ⁵She was worried when she read the college calendar. ⁶And found that math was a required course in the first semester of her program. ⁷Now that she is taking it, she is discovering that it is not as difficult as she had feared. ⁸She has learned strategies for overcoming her "math phobia." ⁹Such as reviewing her notes after every class, visiting her college's Math Centre for extra help, and meeting her study group before tests. ¹⁰On her last test, Janelle received 80%. ¹¹She had never received such a good mark on a math test. ¹²She was thrilled. ¹³And went out to celebrate with the students from her study group.

1. _____

   _____

2. _____

   _____

3. _____

   _____

4. _____

   _____

5. _____

   _____

PRACTICE 2

Underline the fragment in each item that follows.

1. Jan is talking out loud in her bedroom. Practicing a speech for her English class.

2. Lying on the couch in front of the TV. Claudia told her roommate, "You really should get more exercise."

3. Naima hung her dress in the bathroom as the shower ran. To steam out the wrinkles.

4. Ticking loudly. The clock reminded me how little time I had to get ready.

5. Sunil spent an hour flipping through channels on his television. But couldn't find anything to watch.

6. Tony stays home on Saturday nights. To watch *Hockey Night in Canada*.

7. Staring at me with an icy look on her face. The clerk refused to answer my question.

8. I eat only healthy snacks. Such as ice cream made with natural ingredients.

9. When Deveeka heard that a movie crew was filming in her town, she spent a whole day walking the streets. Hoping to see someone famous.

10. To get to school on time. I keep the clock in my room set ten minutes ahead.

PRACTICE 3

The short passage below contains **five** fragments. Underline the fragments and then correct each in the space provided.

> [1] Balancing school, work, and family is very stressful, so Janelle makes sure she allows herself time for doing the things that she loves. [2] For example, singing in her church choir, working in her garden, and taking care of her animals. [3] Janelle and her family keep a number of animals. [4] Including a dog, two cats, a lizard, a parrot, and a tank of tropical fish. [5] She loves animals. [6] Especially dogs. [7] She found her border collie, Destiny, wandering on the side of a highway and took her to the local animal shelter. [8] Feeling sorry for the dog. [9] Janelle visited the shelter every day to see how she was doing. [10] Finally, she adopted Destiny. [11] She now volunteers at the shelter four hours a week. [12] Working at the shelter inspired her. [13] To return to school and become a veterinary technician.

1. _____

   _____

2. _____

   _____

3. _____

   _____

4. _____

   _____

5. _____

   _____

PRACTICE 4

Underline the fragment in each of the following items. Then correct it by rewriting the sentence in the space provided. Add a comma after a dependent-word group that begins a sentence.

1. Although the sign said "No Parking." I left my car there while I ran into the store.

   _____

   _____

2. I'll never be ready for the test tomorrow. Even if I study all night.

   _____

   _____

3. Sam was helpful to his mother all afternoon. Hoping to borrow her car that night.

_____

_____

4. I wasn't able to sleep. Until I found out how the book ended.

_____

_____

5. Sipping her hot chocolate at the bottom of the hill. Julie said, "I want to be a ski instructor."

_____

_____

6. After running a block to catch his bus. Mack missed it by seconds.

_____

_____

7. Many towns in Canada have interesting names. Such as Moose Jaw, Saskatchewan; Flin Flon, Manitoba; Meat Cove, Nova Scotia; and Wawa, Ontario.

_____

_____

8. You won't enjoy dinner at my aunt's. Unless you like burned chicken and soggy beans.

_____

_____

9. If the weather is bad tomorrow. We'll have to reschedule the barbecue.

_____

_____

10. Certain dogs are well suited to be guide dogs. Including German shepherds and golden retrievers.

_____

_____

TEST 1   Name: _____   Section: _____   Date: _____

Score: (Number right) _____ x 10 = _____%

Fragments

Underline the fragment in each of the following items. Then correct it in the space provided. Don't forget to add a comma after a dependent-word group that begins a sentence.

1. Because we have smoke detectors. We survived the fire.

   _____

   _____

2. Glancing at his watch frequently. The man seemed anxious to leave.

   _____

   _____

3. To keep his bike from being stolen. Damian never leaves it outside.

   _____

   _____

4. Before the game even started. I could tell team morale was low.

   _____

   _____

5. I wouldn't go out with him again. If he begged me on his knees.

   _____

   _____

6. Many Canadian performers leave Canada to pursue their careers. Some examples, Jim Carrey, Mike Myers, Keanu Reeves, and Pamela Anderson.

   _____

   _____

7. Ottawa is a beautiful place to visit. Especially in the spring, during the annual Tulip Festival.

   _____

   _____

8. After this rain stops. The children can play outside.

   _____

   _____

9. A crowd showed up to meet the author. Who had written a best-selling novel at the age of nineteen.

   _____

   _____

10. Until the tornado warning ended. Everyone stayed in the basement.

   _____

   _____

TEST 2	Name: _____ Section: _____ Date: _____

Score: (Number right) _____ x 10 = _____%

Fragments

Underline the fragment in each item that follows. Then correct the fragment in the space provided.

1. Walking is excellent exercise. Especially when you walk at a brisk pace.

_____

_____

2. Letitia sat down with her boyfriend. Then gently said, "I can't marry you."

_____

_____

3. To get her brother's attention. Véronique stood up on the stands and waved.

_____

_____

4. Sweating from the workout. Dave grabbed his water bottle and drank deeply.

_____

_____

5. Mother elephants devote much of their time to childcare. Nursing their babies up to eight years.

_____

_____

6. Named after the city of Nanaimo B.C., the Nanaimo bar is a no-bake dessert square, consisting of a layer of graham cracker crumbs topped by a light custard. And covered in soft chocolate.

_____

_____

7. A mouse popped out from under our sofa. Then scurried back quickly.

_____

_____

8. Although some Inuit still use igloos for temporary shelter on hunting trips. Most now live in regular houses during the year.

_____

_____

9. I look terrible in certain colours. Such as baby blue and pale yellow.

_____

_____

10. We do what we can to save money. For example, renting a DVD instead of going to the movie theatre.

_____

_____

Fragments

The passage that follows contains **five** fragments. Underline the fragments and then correct them in the spaces provided.

[1]On December 26, 2004, a massive earthquake off the western coast of northern Sumatra triggered a series of giant waves or "tsunamis." [2]Flooding coastal areas in countries around the Indian Ocean rim. [3]Because tsunami waves of this magnitude are rare in this region, people were not prepared for a disaster of these proportions. [4]Approximately 230,000 people were killed by the tsunami. [5]Including 168,000 in Indonesia alone. [6]The disaster prompted a huge worldwide effort to help victims of the tragedy, with billions of dollars being raised. [7]To assist people who were affected by the disaster. [8]In the three months after the tsunami, the Canadian Red Cross delivered more than one million kilograms of relief items. [9]Such as water containers, thermal blankets, hygiene kits, infant care kits, and construction materials.

[10]Although the tsunami left behind much devastation. It also brought many incredible tales of survival. [11]For example, in Banda Aceh, Indonesia, a boat still sits on the roof of a building in the centre of town, where it landed after being swept huge distances by the tsunami.

1. _____

_____

2. _____

_____

3. _____

_____

4. _____

_____

5. _____

_____

TEST 4   Name: _____   Section: _____ Date: _____

Score: (Number right) _____ x 20 = _____%

Fragments

Read each group below. Then circle the letter of the item in each group that contains a fragment.

1.

   a. Terry Fox decided to run across Canada to raise money for cancer research. He was forced to stop running outside Thunder Bay, Ontario, when he discovered that cancer had spread to his lungs.

   b. Terry Fox decided to run across Canada. To raise money for cancer research. He was forced to stop running outside Thunder Bay, Ontario, when he discovered that cancer had spread to his lungs.

   c. To raise money for cancer research, Terry Fox decided to run across Canada. He was forced to stop running outside Thunder Bay, Ontario, when he discovered that cancer had spread to his lungs.

2.

   a. Calling every half-hour, the man seemed extremely anxious to reach my father. "I have to talk to him," he kept saying.

   b. The man who called every half-hour seemed extremely anxious to reach my father. "I have to talk to him," he kept saying.

   c. Calling every half-hour. The man seemed extremely anxious to reach my father. "I have to talk to him," he kept saying.

3.

   a. People who can't read well run into constant problems. For example, when filling out a job application, they are often too embarrassed to admit they can't read it.

   b. People who can't read well run into constant problems. For example, they may have problems filling out a job application. They are often too embarrassed to admit they can't read it.

   c. People who can't read well run into constant problems. For example, filling out a job application. They are often too embarrassed to admit they can't read it.

4.

   a. Many internationally successful businesses were started in Canada, including Waterloo-based Research in Motion, the developer of the BlackBerry handheld communication device.

   b. Many internationally successful businesses were started in Canada. Including Waterloo-based Research in Motion, the developer of the BlackBerry handheld communication device.

   c. Waterloo-based Research in Motion is just one of many internationally successful businesses that were started in Canada. They developed the BlackBerry handheld communication device.

5.

   a. Large numbers of dinosaur remains have been discovered in Drumheller, Alberta. The first was the skull of what is now known as the Albertasaurus, which was discovered by J.B. Tyrrell in 1884.

   b. Large numbers of dinosaur remains have been discovered in Drumheller, Alberta, beginning with the skull of what is now known as the Albertasaurus, which was discovered by J.B. Tyrrell in 1884.

   c. Large numbers of dinosaur remains have been discovered in Drumheller, Alberta. Beginning with the skull of what is now known as the Albertasaurus, which was discovered by J.B. Tyrrell in 1884.

RUN-ONS AND COMMA SPLICES

Basics about Run-Ons and Comma Splices

A **run-on or fused sentence** is made up of two complete thoughts that are incorrectly run together without a connection between them. Here is an example of a run-on:

- Dolphins have killed sharks they never attack humans.

  The complete thoughts are *dolphins have killed sharks* and *they never attack humans.*

A **comma splice** is made up of two complete thoughts that are incorrectly joined (or spliced) together with only a comma. A comma alone is not enough to connect two complete thoughts. Here's an example of a comma splice:

- Dolphins have killed sharks, they never attack humans.

How to Correct Run-Ons and Comma Splices

There are two common ways to correct run-ons and comma splices.

- **METHOD 1   Use a Period and a Capital Letter**

Put each complete thought into its own sentence.

Run-on	Nunavut is Canada's newest territory it was created officially on April 1, 1999, with the "Nunavut Act."
Comma splice	Nunavut is Canada's newest territory, it was created officially on April 1, 1999, with the "Nunavut Act."
Correct version	Nunavut is Canada's newest territory. It was created officially on April 1, 1999, with the "Nunavut Act."

- **METHOD 2   Use a Comma and a Coordinating Conjunction**

Connect two complete thoughts into one sentence with a comma and a coordinating conjunction (*for, and, nor, but, or, yet,* and *so)*. This method allows the reader to see the connection between ideas.

Run-on	I was nervous about having surgery on my foot the surgeon carefully explained the procedure to me.
Comma splice	I was nervous about having surgery on my foot, the surgeon carefully explained the procedure to me.
Correct version	I was nervous about having surgery on my foot, but the surgeon carefully explained the procedure to me.
Run-on	The garden is overgrown the fence is falling down.
Comma splice	The garden is overgrown, the fence is falling down.

Correct version	The garden is **overgrown, and the** fence is falling down.
Run-on	The little boy appeared to be lost several women stopped to help him.
Comma splice	The little boy appeared to be lost, several women stopped to help him.
Correct version	The little boy appeared to be **lost, so** several women stopped to help him.

Understanding Run-Ons and Comma Splices

In this paragraph about Kinda Rodrigues, see if you can find and put a line (|) between the two complete thoughts in each run-on or comma splice.

[1]This is Kinda Rodrigues she is in her first semester at Humber College's School of Social and Community Services. [2]She has always wanted to help people, she is studying to be a Social Service Worker. [3]Kinda's daughter Shanielle is in grade two they do their homework together in the evenings.

● *Run-on:*	"This is Kinda Rodrigues" and "she is in her first semester at Humber College's School of Social and Community Services" are both complete thoughts. To correct the run-on, put each complete thought into its own sentence.
Correct	This is Kinda **Rodrigues. She** is in her first semester at Humber College's School of Social and Community Services.
● *Comma splice:*	"She has always wanted to help people" and "she is studying to be a Social Service Worker" are both complete thoughts. To correct the comma splice, use the coordinating conjunction *so*, which means "as a result."
Correct	She has always wanted to help **people, so** she is studying to be a Social Service Worker.
● *Run-on:*	"Kinda's daughter Shanielle is in grade two" and "they do their homework together in the evenings" are both complete thoughts. To correct the run-on, use a comma and the coordinating conjunction *and*.
Correct	Kinda's daughter Shanielle is in **grade two,** and they do their homework together in the evenings.

Check Your Understanding

Put a line (|) between the two complete thoughts in each run-on or comma splice in the following passage. Then correct the errors in the spaces provided. There may be more than one correct answer.

¹Kinda and Shanielle both love to read they read together every night. ²Kinda finds it difficult to juggle school and motherhood she knows that she is doing the right thing for herself. ³She is also setting a good example for her daughter, she is showing her that an education is worth the effort.

1. _____

2. _____

3. _____

PRACTICE 1

Draw a line (|) between the two complete thoughts in each of the run-ons and comma splices that follow. Then rewrite each sentence. Correct it in one of two ways:

a. Use a period and a capital letter to create two sentences.

b. Use a comma and a coordinating conjunction to connect the two complete thoughts.

1. Some people are morning people my family can tell you that I'm not one of them.

   _____

2. This morning I was out of jelly I spread strawberry yogurt on my toast.

   _____

3. My neighbours across the street shovelled snow from their driveway into the middle of the road, cars were getting stuck in front of our house.

   _____

4. The sun was shining brightly, I didn't bring a jacket.

   _____

5. Someone unplugged the freezer all the ice cream has melted.

   _____

6. The little girl climbed to the top of the slide she was afraid to slide down.

   _____

7. Rain fell steadily outside, it was a good day to stay indoors.

_____

8. My brother runs like a rabbit at track meets he moves like a turtle at home.

_____

9. Fast-food restaurants are changing they now offer healthier food choices.

_____

10. The button fell off the waist of my pants I fastened them with a safety pin.

_____

PRACTICE 2

Put a line (|) between the two complete thoughts in each of the following run-ons or comma splices. Then rewrite the sentences, using either **(a)** a period and a capital letter or **(b)** a comma and a coordinating conjunction.

1. The sun was going down the air was growing chilly.

_____

2. My alarm didn't go off this morning, I slept through my first class.

_____

3. My throat is very sore a bowl of ice cream will relieve it.

_____

4. The plumber repaired the water heater, the family can shower again.

_____

5. Saturday is the worst day of the week to shop, people fill up many of the stores.

_____

6. The phone rang someone knocked on the door at the same time.

_____

7. The movie was boring at first it suddenly became interesting.

_____

8. A burglar alarm went off three men raced away from the store.

_____

9. The bear looked at me hungrily, I decided not to photograph him.

_____

10. We decided to leave the restaurant, we were tired of waiting in line.

_____

Another Way to Correct Run-Ons and Comma Splices

A third way of fixing run-ons and comma splices is to add a **subordinating conjunction** to one of the complete thoughts. The sentence will then include one thought that depends upon the remaining complete thought for its full meaning. Here are some common subordinating conjunctions:

after	because	since	when
although	before	unless	where
as	if, even if	until	while

Below are run-ons or comma splices that have been corrected by adding subordinating conjunctions. In each case, a subordinating conjunction that logically connects the two thoughts has been chosen.

Run-on	The roads are covered with ice school has been cancelled.
Corrected	**Because** the roads are covered with ice, school has been cancelled.
Corrected	School has been cancelled **because** the roads are covered with ice.
Comma splice	The water began to boil, I added ears of corn.
Corrected	**After** the water began to boil, I added ears of corn.
Corrected	I added ears of corn **after** the water began to boil.
Run-on	The fish was served with its head on Carlo quickly lost his appetite.
Corrected	**When** the fish was served with its head on, Carlo quickly lost his appetite.
Corrected	Carlo quickly lost his appetite **when** the fish was served with its head on.
Comma splice	Our house is very crowded, four generations of my family live together under one roof.
Corrected	Our house is very crowded **since** four generations of my family live together under one roof.
Corrected	**Since** four generations of my family live together under one roof, our house is very crowded.

 Although either a coordinating conjunction (for, and, nor, but, or, yet, so) or a subordinating conjunction (although, because, since, etc.) can be used to join independent clauses, do not use both in the same sentence:

Correct:	Although he was tired, he didn't get home until after midnight.
Correct:	He was tired, but he didn't get home until after midnight.
Incorrect:	Although he was tired, but he didn't get home until after midnight.

PRACTICE 3

Draw a line (|) between the two complete thoughts in each of the **four** run-ons or comma splices that follow. Then correct each sentence by adding a subordinating conjunction to one of the complete thoughts. Choose from these words: *because, although, when, since.*

¹Kinda was sixteen years old she became pregnant. ²She did not want to drop out of high school, she transferred to Humewood House for her first semester of grade 12. ³Humewood House is a live-in facility in Toronto that offers high school courses, counselling, training, and daycare for young pregnant or parenting women. ⁴Students weren't allowed to take advanced-level courses, the school made an exception for Kinda. ⁵She took an advanced English class and received 80%. ⁶Humewood only provides one semester of schooling Kinda finished grade 12 at Weston Collegiate. ⁷She graduated with honours. ⁸Kinda is grateful for all the support that the Ontario government provides for young people with children, including publicly funded parenting classes and visits by public health nurses.

1. _____

2. _____

3. _____

4. _____

PRACTICE 4

Correct each run-on or comma splice by adding the subordinating conjunction shown to one of the complete thoughts. Include a comma if the subordinating conjunction starts the sentence.

1. *(although)* These boots are supposed to be waterproof my feet are soaked.

   _____

2. *(when)* The driver jumped out quickly the car burst into flames.

   _____

3. *(when)* We waded into the lake leeches attached themselves to our shins.

_____

4. *(if)* You need to make a call you can borrow my cell phone.

_____

5. *(since)* Ricardo was late to school, he had briefly lost his contact lens.

_____

6. *(while)* It was still raining, a beautiful rainbow appeared in the west.

_____

7. *(until)* The wet paint on the woodwork dries, you should not touch it.

_____

8. *(after)* The players looked depressed the team lost the game.

_____

9. *(as)* The sky darkened bats began to appear in the air.

_____

10. *(because)* That medication has serious side effects you should take it only when needed.

_____

PRACTICE 5

Draw a line (|) between the two complete thoughts in each of the **seven** run-ons or comma splices that follow. Then correct each sentence by adding a subordinating conjunction to one of the complete thoughts. Choose from these words: *when, where, although, after, because, even though, since.*

[1]She graduated from high school Kinda took two years off and worked at a grocery store. [2]It was nice to earn a regular paycheque, Kinda felt that she was wasting time. [3]She knew that she needed to go back to school, as she says, "if you don't have your education, you have nothing." [4]Kinda visited Humber College she heard about the General Arts and Science University Transfer Program. [5]She completed this program, she transferred

to Social Services. [6]Going to school as a single parent is difficult, it is worth the struggle. [7]Her babysitter didn't arrive until 8 a.m., Kinda found it very hard to get to her early morning classes. [8]Her professors were very understanding and allowed her to make up the few assignments she missed due to childcare issues. [9]Kinda advises other young people to go back to school, no matter how challenging it might be. [10]When Shanielle says "I'm proud of you, Mommy," Kinda knows all the hard work is worth it.

1. _____

   _____

2. _____

   _____

3. _____

   _____

4. _____

   _____

5. _____

   _____

6. _____

   _____

7. _____

   _____

TEST 1 Name: _____ Section: _____ Date: _____

Score: (Number right) _____ x 10 = _____ %

Run-Ons and Comma Splices

Put a line (|) between the two complete thoughts in each of the following run-ons or comma splices. Then rewrite the sentences, correcting each one by adding a logical subordinating conjunction to one of the thoughts. Include a comma if the subordinating conjunction starts the sentence.

1. Nuts are high in protein they are a healthier snack than chips.

_____

2. Many people are afraid of spiders, most spiders are quite harmless.

_____

3. It starts to rain, bring in the clothes hanging on the line.

_____

4. The dishes were done we relaxed by watching some TV.

_____

5. Precious laid down the sleeping baby, she tiptoed out of the room.

_____

6. You will be late to the party, let the host know ahead of time.

_____

7. I haven't spent much time outdoors, it has been very cold.

_____

8. Geneva apologized for yelling at Ameel, she felt better.

_____

9. You win the contest, what will you do with the prize money?

_____

10. I could not open the childproof bottle, I was following the directions carefully.

_____

Name: _____ Section: _____ Date: _____

Score: (Number right) _____ x 10 = _____%

Run-Ons and Comma Splices

Correct each run-on or comma splice by adding the subordinating conjunction shown to one of the complete thoughts. Include a comma if the subordinating conjunction starts the sentence.

1. *(because)* I let the phone ring and ring, but nobody answered it the whole family had gone to bed early.

   _____

2. *(although)* Mrs. Hunter is not an easy teacher her students love her.

   _____

3. *(after)* Debbi took a self-defence course, she felt more strong and confident when she took the bus home at night after work.

   _____

4. *(because)* My brother was tired of worrying how his hair looked, he shaved his head.

   _____

5. *(although)* Garlic tastes delicious, if you eat too much of it, you will find that people begin to avoid you.

   _____

6. *(after)* I finished watching the sad movie my eyes were red for hours, and people kept asking me what was wrong.

   _____

7. *(if)* You want to be a rock star, you'd better have a second career plan just in case.

   _____

8. *(because)* I am more alert in the morning, early classes are better for me.

   _____

9. *(before)* The party ended at 3 a.m., so we had only three hours to clean up the house, my parents were due home at 6 a.m.

   _____

10. *(before)* To improve your score on tests, you start answering a multiple-choice question, read every one of the possible answers.

    _____

TEST 3   Name: _____   Section: _____   Date: _____

Score: (Number right) _____ x 10 = _____ %

Run-Ons and Comma Splices

Rewrite each sentence below, correcting the run-on or comma splice.

1. Friends had told us the restaurant was very good, we had a dreadful meal.
   _____
   _____

2. Rebecca Hardy won the 2007 season of the reality show "Canada's Next Top Model," she signed a modelling contract with Sutherland models and a $100,000 beauty contract with Procter & Gamble.
   _____
   _____
   _____

3. The movie was scary, I turned on all the lights in the house and slept with a knife under my pillow.
   _____
   _____

4. Whitehorse, Yellowknife, and Quebec City have a 100 percent chance of having a "white Christmas," Vancouver has only an 11 percent chance.
   _____
   _____

5. Kristen came back from her blind date, she turned to her roommates and said, "Never, ever, ever again."
   _____
   _____

6. Follow the instructions carefully the computer will be set up and working in no time.
   _____
   _____

7. The two brothers seldom speak they had an argument ten years ago.
   _____
   _____

8. You are afraid of snakes, you might not want to go on the hike with us.
   _____
   _____

9. Ming wants to help her community, she works as a volunteer translator.
   _____
   _____

10. When the neighbours saw a police car pull up outside, they turned off their lights and watched through the window.
    _____
    _____

TEST 4	Name: _____	Section: _____ Date: _____
		Score: (Number right) _____ x 20 = _____%

Run-Ons and Comma Splices

Draw a line (|) between the two complete thoughts in each of the **five** run-ons or comma splices in the following paragraph. Then correct each sentence by adding a subordinating conjunction to one of the complete thoughts. Use each of the following subordinating conjunctions once: *after, although, because, if, when.*

[1]How much do you know about your own family history? [2]Gathering family stories, photos, and keepsakes can be a fascinating hobby, and it can bring your whole family closer together. [3]Young people may not be interested in such things, they may regret their lack of knowledge later. [4]People reach middle age, they often begin to wish they knew more about their family history. [5]That's why it is a great idea to get an early start on your own family's stories. [6]Probably the best way to begin is to interview older relatives, they're such good sources of information. [7]Chances are you'll have a good time doing it. [8]You're concerned about bothering people, you probably shouldn't worry. [9]Elderly family members are usually pleased and surprised when younger relatives ask questions about the past. [10]The questions don't have to be complicated ones. [11]You might start by asking things like, "Where were you born? [12]Where did your parents come from? [13]What kind of work did they do? [14]What kind of school did you go to?" [15]You do a few such interviews, you'll be on your way to becoming the family historian.

1. _____

_____

2. _____

_____

3. _____

_____

4. _____

_____

5. _____

_____

MISPLACED AND DANGLING MODIFIERS

Modifiers

A **modifier** is one or more words that describe another word or word group.

An **adjective** is a modifier that describes a noun.

- Raj was very **angry** with the man who sold him the tickets.
  Angry describes Raj.

- **Standing at the counter,** Raj yelled angrily at the ticket-seller.
  Standing at the counter describes Raj.

An **adverb** is a modifier that describes a verb.

- "You're cheating me!" Raj yelled **angrily.**
  Angrily describes the way Raj yelled.

- "You're cheating me!" Raj yelled, **with anger dripping from every word.**
  With anger dripping from every word describes the way Raj yelled.

HUMOROUS EXAMPLES

Modifier errors often lead to unintentionally humorous sentences. Consider these two real-life examples of signs.

In the lobby of a Moscow hotel across from a cemetery:

> You are welcome to visit the cemetery where famous Russian and Soviet composers, artists and writers are buried **daily except Thursday.**
> *In this sentence, **daily except Thursday** describes the verb **buried**. What should it describe? Rewrite the sentence below.*

_____

_____

In a Tokyo bar:

> Special cocktails for the ladies **with nuts.**
> *In this phrase, **with nuts** describes the noun **ladies.** What should it describe? Rewrite the phrase below.*

And then there's the old Groucho Marx joke:

> While hunting in Africa, I shot an elephant in my pajamas. How an elephant got into my pajamas I'll never know.
> *What is wrong with this, and how would you correct it?*

_____

_____

Basics about Misplaced and Dangling Modifiers

This chapter explains two common modifier problems:

1. Misplaced modifiers

Incorrect   The man bought a shirt at the department store **with yellow and blue stripes.**

Correct   The man bought **a shirt with yellow and blue stripes** at the department store.

The **shirt** has yellow and blue stripes . . . not the department store.

2. Dangling modifiers

Incorrect   **Biting my lip,** not laughing was difficult.

Correct   **Biting my lip, I found it difficult** not to laugh.

Who was **biting my lip**? Add the subject **I.**

MISPLACED MODIFIERS

A **misplaced modifier** is a modifier that is incorrectly separated from the word or words that it describes. Misplaced modifiers seem to describe words that the author did not intend them to describe. When modifiers are misplaced, the reader may misunderstand the sentence. Generally, the solution is to place the modifier after—and as close as possible to—the word or words it describes. Look at the following examples.

> **NOTE**   In this chapter, the *modifier* is shown in **boldface type** and the word it modifies is underlined.

Misplaced modifier   Sam bought a used car from a local dealer with a rusted undercarriage.

Corrected version   Sam bought a used <u>car</u> **with a rusted undercarriage** from a local dealer.

In the first sentence above, the modifier *with a rusted undercarriage* is misplaced. Its unintentional meaning is that the local dealer has a rusted undercarriage. To avoid this meaning, place the modifier next to the word that it describes, *car*.

Misplaced modifier   The robin built a nest at the back of our house of grass and string.

Corrected version   The robin built a <u>nest</u> **of grass and string** at the back of our house.

In the first sentence above, the words *of grass and string* are misplaced. Because they are near the word *house*, the reader might think that the house is made of grass and string. To avoid this meaning, place the modifier next to the word that it describes, *nest*.

Misplaced modifier   Take the note to Mr. Henderson's office which Kim wrote.

Corrected version   Take the <u>note</u> **which Kim wrote** to Mr. Henderson's office.

In the first sentence above, the words *which Kim wrote* are misplaced. The words must be placed next to *note*, the word that they are clearly meant to describe.

Following is another example of a sentence with a misplaced modifier. See if you can correct it by putting the modifier in another place in the sentence. Write your revision on the lines below.

Misplaced modifier   I am going to Quebec City to visit my aunt on a train.

_____

_____

The original version of the sentence seems to say that the speaker will visit with his aunt on the train. However, the modifier *on a train* is meant to tell how the speaker is going to Quebec City. To make that meaning clear, the modifier needs to be placed closer to the words <u>am going</u>: "I <u>*am going*</u> **on a train** to Quebec City to visit my aunt."

PRACTICE 1

Underline the misplaced words in each sentence. Then rewrite the sentence in the space provided, placing the modifier where its meaning will be clear.

1. I'm returning the shirt to the store that is too small.

_____

_____

2. The plants by the lamp with small purple blossoms are violets.

_____

_____

3. We watched as our house burned to the ground with helpless anger.

_____

_____

4. This morning I saw an accident walking down the street.

_____

_____

5. The bracelet on Xiao Hong's arm made of gold links belongs to her mother.

_____

_____

Certain Single-Word Modifiers

Certain single-word modifiers—such as *almost, only, nearly,* and *even*—limit the words they modify. Such single-word modifiers must generally be placed before the word they limit.

Misplaced modifier	Cristina almost sneezed fifteen times last evening.
Corrected version	Cristina sneezed **almost** <u>fifteen</u> times last evening.

Because the word *almost is* misplaced in the first sentence, readers might think Cristina *almost sneezed fifteen times,* but in fact did not sneeze at all. To prevent this confusion, put *almost* in front of the word it modifies, *fifteen.* Then it becomes clear that Cristina must have sneezed a number of times.

> PRACTICE 2

Underline the misplaced words in each sentence. Then rewrite the sentence in the space provided, placing the modifier where its meaning will be clear.

1. My little sister nearly has one hundred stuffed animals.

   _____

   _____

2. Suha almost cried through the whole sad movie.

   _____

   _____

3. I didn't even make one mistake on the midterm test.

   _____

   _____

4. The terrible fall nearly broke every bone in the skier's body.

   _____

   _____

5. By the end of the war, twenty countries were almost involved in the fighting.

   _____

   _____

DANGLING MODIFIERS

You have learned that a misplaced modifier is incorrectly separated from the word or words it describes. In contrast, a **dangling modifier** has no word in the sentence to describe. Dangling modifiers usually begin a sentence. When a modifier begins a sentence, it must be followed right away by the word or words it is meant to describe. Look at this example:

Dangling modifier	Sitting in the dentist's chair, the sound of the drill awakened Ryan's old fears.

The modifier *sitting in the dentist's chair* is followed by *the sound of the drill*. This word order suggests that the sound of the drill was sitting in the dentist's chair. Clearly, that is not what the author intended. The modifier was meant to describe the word *Ryan*. Since the word *Ryan* is not in the sentence (*Ryan's* is a different form of the word), it is not possible to correct the dangling modifier simply by changing its position in the sentence.

Here are two common ways to correct modifiers.

● **METHOD I: Follow the dangling modifier with the word or words it is meant to modify.**

After the dangling modifier, write the word it is meant to describe, and then revise as necessary. Using this method, we could correct the sentence about Ryan's experience at the dentist's office like this:

> *Correct version*   Sitting in the dentist's chair, **Ryan found that** the sound of the drill awakened **his** old fears.

Now the modifier is no longer dangling. It is followed by the word it is meant to describe, *Ryan*.

Following is another dangling modifier. How could you correct it using the method described above? Write your correction on the lines below.

> *Dangling modifier*   Depressed and disappointed, running away seemed the only thing for me to do.

_____

_____

The dangling modifier in the above sentence is *depressed* and *disappointed*. It is meant to describe the word *I*, but there is no *I* in the sentence. So you should have corrected the sentence by writing *I* after the opening modifier and then rewriting as necessary: "Depressed and disappointed, **I felt that** running away **was** the only thing for me to do."

PRACTICE 3

Underline the dangling modifier in each sentence. Then, on the lines provided, revise the sentence, using the Method 1 style of correction.

1. Out of money, my only choice was to borrow from a friend.

_____

_____

2. While jogging, a good topic for Anton's English paper occurred to him.

_____

_____

3. Bored by the lecture, Jiao's thoughts turned to dinner.

_____

_____

4. Moving around the sun, Earth's speed is more than 106,000 kilometres per hour.

_____

_____

5. Loudly booing and cursing, the fans' disapproval of the call was clear.

_____

_____

- **METHOD 2: Add a subject and a verb to the opening word group.**

The second method of correcting a dangling modifier is to add a subject and a verb to the opening word group, and revise as necessary. We could use this method to correct the sentence about Ryan's experience at the dentist's office.

Dangling modifier	Sitting in the dentist's chair, the sound of the drill awakened Ryan's old fears.
Correct version	**As Ryan was** sitting in the dentist's chair, the sound of the drill awakened **his** old fears.

In this revision, the subject *Ryan* and the verb *was* have been added to the opening word group.

Following is the dangling modifier that you revised using the first method of correction. How could you correct it using the second method? Write your revision on the lines below.

Dangling modifier	Depressed and disappointed, running away seemed the only thing for me to do.

_____

_____

You should have revised the sentence so that I and the appropriate verb are in the opening word group: "**Because I was** depressed and disappointed, running away seemed the only thing for me to do."

Often, sentences with dangling modifiers will need to be significantly rewritten. Here are two examples from student essays:

Original	Being different and mysterious, people could not see the good heart of Boo Radley.
Problem	**Who** is different and mysterious—**people** or **Boo Radley?**
Revised	People could not see the good heart of Boo Radley because he was different and mysterious.
Original	Being a symbolic novel, Golding uses different symbols to stand for things.
Problem	**Golding** is not **a symbolic novel.**
Revised	William Golding's *Lord of the Flies* is a symbolic novel, which means that the author uses different symbols to stand for things.

PRACTICE 4

Underline the dangling modifier in each sentence. Then, on the lines provided, revise the sentence, using the Method 2 style of correction.

1. While waiting for an important call, Sameera's phone began making weird noises.

   _____

   _____

2. After being shampooed, Natalia was surprised by the carpet's new look.

   _____

   _____

3. Touched by the movie, tears came to my eyes.

   _____

   _____

4. After eating one too many hot dogs, Stella's stomach rebelled.

   _____

   _____

5. Born on Halloween, Rob's birthday party was always a costume party.

   _____

   _____

Misplaced and Dangling Modifiers

In each sentence, underline the **one** misplaced or dangling modifier. Then rewrite each sentence so that its intended meaning is clear.

1. The customer demanded that the waiter take her order rudely.

   _____

   _____

2. I peeled the potatoes before I cooked them with a paring knife.

   _____

   _____

3. In one week, the cat nearly had caught every mouse in the house.

   _____

   _____

4. The child playing on the jungle gym with curly red hair is my nephew.

   _____

   _____

5. We discovered an Italian bakery a few miles from our house that had just opened.

   _____

   _____

6. After visiting the bakery, the aroma of freshly baked bread filled our car.

   _____

   _____

7. Lying on the sunny beach, thoughts of skin cancer began to enter my mind.

   _____

   _____

8. Not meaning to be cruel, George's careless remark hurt Jackie's feelings.

   _____

   _____

9. Though not usually a fan of romantic movies, *Titanic* is one of Kyle's favourite movies.

   _____

   _____

10. Exhausted by his first day at school, Sam's eyes closed in the middle of his favorite TV show.

    _____

    _____

TEST 2   Name: _____   Section: _____   Date: _____

Score: (Number right) _____ x 20 = _____ %

Misplaced and Dangling Modifiers

Each group of sentences contains **one** misplaced modifier and **one** dangling modifier. On the lines provided, rewrite the sentences so that the intended meanings are clear.

1. I mailed a letter to my cousin who lives in Manitoba without a stamp. Embarrassed, the post office sent it back to me a week later.

   _____

   _____

   _____

2. Lin's mother answered the door, and Jim asked if he could speak to Lin politely. Impressed with Jim's manner, the answer was "Certainly. Please come in."

   _____

   _____

   _____

3. The thunderstorm ended, and Shannon saw the sun burst through the clouds. Searching the sky, a glorious rainbow appeared. It nearly lasted a minute and then faded from view.

   _____

   _____

   _____

4. Not meaning to embarrass you, but please answer a question about your birthday present. Will you wear the sweater that I bought for you ever? If you won't, I could exchange it for something else.

   _____

   _____

   _____

5. Most of Ms. Nichol's students were gazing blankly into space one warm spring day. In fact, Ms. Nichol noticed that two students only were paying attention. Clapping her hands together sharply, the students woke up from their daydreams.

   _____

   _____

   _____

Misplaced and Dangling Modifiers

The following sentences are taken from the essays of real first-year students. Identify the problem and rewrite the sentence in the space provided.

1. It is the story of King Arthur and his life that nobody has ever heard about.

   _____

   _____

2. Only people with cars that live in the dorms should be able to park in those lots.

   _____

   _____

3. At the beginning of the novel, Tom Joad comes across a turtle on his way home from spending four years in prison.

   _____

   _____

4. Where one parent would be quiet, polite, and conservative, the other parent would drive up in a black Trans Am full of arrogance and conceit.

   _____

   _____

5. Gertrude and Claudius have broken a couple of values which anger Hamlet.

   _____

   _____

TEST 4   Name: _____   Section: _____   Date: _____

Score: (Number right) _____ × 10 = _____ %

Misplaced and Dangling Modifiers

Rewrite the following paragraph about seasonal affective disorder correcting the **ten** modifier errors.

[1]People with short winter days living in northern countries know that moods are affected by the weather often. [2]Although noticeable, our daily lives aren't usually interrupted by these changes in mood. [3]However, there is a type of depression that is experienced by some people, following a seasonal pattern. [4]Called Seasonal Affective Disorder (SAD), the sufferers experience symptoms including weight gain, irritability, difficulty concentrating, and fatigue. [5]In extreme cases, sufferers experience suicidal thoughts. [6]Having many symptoms similar to those of other depressive disorders, it can be difficult to diagnose SAD. [7]Usually, doctors without any other reason for mood or behavioural changes diagnose SAD when a patient's symptoms have returned for at least two consecutive winters. [8]Individuals should consult their doctors who regularly experience more than one of the symptoms during the winter. [9]There are many effective treatments for SAD, depending on the severity of the symptoms. [10]People should spend more time outdoors during daylight hours with mild symptoms. [11]Monitoring diet, sleep patterns, and exercise levels might also relieve some of the symptoms. [12]In more serious cases, doctors using special fluorescent light boxes may recommend "light therapy." [13]If you are suffering from more severe symptoms, your doctor may prescribe antidepressant medication. [14]Finally, try to enjoy what little sunlight there is in the winter, and just remember... spring isn't far away!

_____

_____

_____

_____

_____

_____

_____

_____

_____

_____

_____

_____

_____

_____

PARALLELISM

Basics about Parallelism

Two or more equal ideas should be expressed in **parallel,** or matching, form. The absence of parallelism is jarring and awkward to read. Parallelism will help your words flow smoothly and clearly. Here's an example:

> **Not parallel:**   The new restaurant has fresh food, reasonable prices, and service that is fast.

The first two features of the restaurant—*fresh food* and *reasonable prices*—are described in parallel form. In each case, we see an adjective followed by the noun it modifies.

> fresh **food,** reasonable **prices**

But with the last feature, we see the noun first followed by the phrase modifying it.

> service that is **fast**

To achieve parallelism, the nonparallel item must have the same form as the first two:

> **Parallel:**   The new restaurant has fresh food, reasonable prices, and **fast service.**

EXAMPLES OF PARALLELISM

Some of the best, most memorable writing uses parallel structure. Read the following passages out loud to hear the effect.

In a moment the pirates were all around us, rolling their eyes, gnashing their teeth, and filing their nails.

> *Stephen Leacock, Canadian writer*

There was a valid distinction between an offensive and a defensive weapon; if you were in front of it, it was offensive; if you were behind it, it was defensive.

> *Lester B. Pearson, former Canadian prime minister*

The ultimate measure of a man is not where he stands in moments of comfort and convenience, but where he stands at times of challenge and controversy.

> *Martin Luther King, Jr., American civil rights leader*

One cannot think well, love well, sleep well, if one has not dined well.

> *Virginia Woolf, British writer*

Here are some additional examples of non-parallel structure that have been revised to make them parallel:

Not parallel   The children were arguing in the lobby, talked during the movie, and complained on the ride home.
Talked and **complained** are similar in form. But **were arguing** is not. It must be changed so that it has the same form as the other two.

Parallel   The children **argued** in the lobby, **talked** during the movie, and **complained** on the ride home.

Not parallel   Our neighbours spend a lot of time shopping, visiting friends, and they go to the movies.
The sentence lists a series of activities. **Shopping** and **visiting** both end in *-ing*. To be parallel, **they go to the movies** must be revised to include an *-ing* word.

Parallel   Our neighbours spend a lot of time **shopping**, **visiting** friends, and **going** to the movies.

Use the same verb form throughout the sentence.

Not parallel   My aunt is selfish, impatient, and she is not a kind person.
To be parallel, the modifying phrase **she is not a kind person** should be expressed in a single adjective to match **selfish** and **impatient**.

Parallel   My aunt is selfish, impatient, and **unkind.**

Not parallel   When Erlinda got up to deliver her presentation, her hands were sweaty, her voice was shaking, and she had an upset stomach.
To be parallel, the phrase **she had an upset stomach** should be expressed in a pattern that matches **her hands were sweaty** and **her voice was shaking.**

Parallel   When Erlinda got up to deliver her presentation, her hands were sweaty, her voice was shaking, and **her stomach was upset.**

Use the same type of modifier throughout the sentence (adjectives only or adjective-noun).

Understanding Parallelism

See if you can underline the **three** errors in parallelism in the following passage. Then look at the corrections below.

¹This is Jasmin Santana. ²In this picture, Jasmin is laughing, answering the telephone, and she works at the computer. ³It is typical for Jasmin to be doing several things at once. ⁴She is a full-time employee and a full-time student as well. ⁵Jasmin has to be very organized, efficient, and with discipline to get everything done. ⁶Sometimes she is discouraged by how busy she is. ⁷But she knows she will feel pride, happiness, and relieved when she earns her college degree.

1. _____working at the computer_____

2. _____disciplined_____

3. _____relief_____

Check Your Understanding

Underline the **three** mistakes in parallelism in the following passage. Then write the correct forms in the spaces provided.

¹Jasmin works for an organization that matches high school students with mentors and teaches them study skills. ²As the receptionist, Jasmin spends a lot of time answering the phone, she types letters, and greeting visitors. ³But she also works directly with the students in the program. ⁴She provides them with information, encouragement, and she is their friend. ⁵In this picture, Jasmin is shown with Virgen on the left, Julio in the middle, and on the right is Kimberly.

1. _____

2. _____

3. _____

PRACTICE I

Each of the short passages below contains errors in parallelism. Underline the errors. Then correct them in the spaces provided.

[1]When she lived at home, Jasmin loved her grandmother's cooking, but now she lives on her own, and she doesn't have much time to prepare meals. [2]After work, she usually makes a sandwich, heats up some soup, or she might scramble some eggs. [3]Every evening, she takes the bus to campus, where she spends the evening listening to a lecture, she takes notes, and asking questions. [5]But sometimes she has to take a break. [6]"I call Grandma and say, 'I am so stressed out!'" Jasmin says. [7]"And she says, 'Come over, and I'll cook for you.' [8]I go over and she feeds me, babies me, and is talking Spanish to me. [9]That always makes me feel better."

1. _____

2. _____

3. _____

[1]Jasmin moved into her own apartment when she was just 17. [2]She could have lived at home and saved money, time, and making a lot of effort. [3]But back in her neighbourhood, she was too distracted by friends who didn't understand why college was so important to her. [4]They were more concerned with hanging out, to go to clubs, and having fun. [5]Jasmin likes to have fun, too, but she made the decision to make school her first priority. [6]Sometimes living alone is boring, depressing, and it makes her feel lonely. [7]Other times she loves feeling independent, grown-up, and having a sense of responsibility. [8]Even when she feels lonely, she is sure her decision will pay off in the end.

4. _____

5. _____

6. _____

7. _____

¹When she gets home after a long night of classes, Jasmin reviews her notes, reads her next day's assignments, and is studying for any upcoming tests. ²She often falls asleep over her textbooks. ³It's hard to find time to clean her apartment, shop for groceries, and the doing of laundry. ⁴She sometimes envies other students who work only part-time or don't have to work at all. ⁵She sees them attending class during the day and go out with their friends when they want to. ⁶"I'd like to have more time for a social life," she admits, "but that's not my top priority right now."

8. _____

9. _____

10. _____

PRACTICE 2

Correct each sentence to make the parts parallel.

1. Arun would play video games night and day if it weren't for eating and to have to sleep.

_____

2. Smoking and to spit are both prohibited on the subway.

_____

3. That slice of pizza looks shrivelled, has a rancid smell, and tastes awful.

_____

4. Maryam usually either braids her hair or is putting it back in a ponytail.

_____

5. When arriving in a new country, a person can be overwhelmed with strange sounds, smells that surprise, and unusual sights.

_____

6. It is easier to wash dishes every day than letting them pile up for a week.

_____

7. The loud voices, air that has smoke in it, and stale smells in the room all made Jiang Li want to leave the party early.

   _____

8. After hiking Nova Scotia's Cape George Trail, many of us complained of blistered feet, backs that ached, or skinned knees.

   _____

9. Many young people move to Canada's big cities because of the diversity of the residents, activity going on constantly, and employment opportunities.

   _____

10. All this house needs is a fresh coat of paint, planting a few shrubs in the front yard, and a brand-new roof.

   _____

PRACTICE 3

The passage below contains **five** errors in parallelism. Underline the errors. Then correct them in the spaces provided.

[1]In spite of her difficult schedule, Jasmin works hard, stays positive, and is focusing on her goals, which include to do well in college and getting admitted to law school. [2]She wants to earn her law degree, become a judge, and working to help her community. [5]"I see so many people around me get in trouble, go to jail, and giving up on themselves," she says. [6]"As a judge, I'll be in a position to see that people get the help they need." [7]Jasmin is grateful for the support of her family as she works to achieve her dreams. [8]"My family would probably like to see me settling down, get married, and having kids, but if going to school is what makes me happy, they respect that, too."

1. _____

2. _____

3. _____

4. _____

5. _____

Parallelism

Rewrite each sentence to make the parts parallel.

1. Nina has a high fever and a throat that is sore.

   _____

2. On a busy highway, travelling too slow is almost as bad as to drive too fast.

   _____

3. Humming laptops, beeping pagers, and the ringing of cell phones are part of almost every college classroom.

   _____

4. The Okanagan Valley is an ideal place for growing grapes to make wine because of its earth that is rugged, long days, and cool nights.

   _____

5. The driving rain turned the park into a swamp and the highway was a river.

   _____

6. Tonight's menu includes chicken that is roasted, baked potatoes, and steamed broccoli.

   _____

7. Before I left home, I never thought I'd miss my sister's shrill laughter and jokes that are stupid, but I do.

   _____

8. All Kostas asks of a girlfriend is that she adore him, lending him money, and centre her entire life around him.

   _____

9. My New Year's resolutions were to stop talking so much, losing weight, and to do more reading.

   _____

10. The diner at the table next to me made choking noises, was turning red, and pointed to his throat.

   _____

TEST 2   Name: _____   Section: _____ Date: _____

Score: (Number right) _____ x 10 = _____%

Parallelism

Rewrite each sentence to make the parts parallel.

1. The movie featured terrible acting, excessive violence, and plot twists that were ridiculous.

   _____

2. Long hours, pay that was low, and unpleasant coworkers are the reasons I left my job.

   _____

3. Majestic trees, abundant wildlife, and the fact that it is close to the city core make Stanley Park a popular escape for Vancouver residents.

   _____

4. Writing a research paper and to study for a chemistry test are my tasks for the weekend.

   _____

5. Sukhi's neighbours include a dress designer, a person who teaches second grade, and a car salesperson.

   _____

6. My parents always taught me that it is better to give than to do the receiving.

   _____

7. On hot days I close the windows, turn on the fans, and am complaining a lot.

   _____

8. For exercise, Giancarlo either plays basketball at the park or lifting weights at the gym.

   _____

9. The house we wanted to buy had a big backyard, sunny rooms, and a kitchen that was modern.

   _____

10. The house we could afford had a backyard that was tiny and overgrown, cramped, dark rooms, and an outdated, grimy kitchen.

    _____

Name: _____   Section: _____   Date: _____

Score: (Number right) _____ x 20 = _____ %

Parallelism

Rewrite the following paragraph correcting the **five** problems with parallelism.

[1]The novel *Les Miserables* was written in the 1800s by French author Victor Hugo. [2]The story has become well-known through its many adaptations for radio, film, and it was also performed on the stage. [3]*Les Miserables* tells the story of Jean Valjean. [4]Poor and being full of hunger, Valjean stole a loaf of bread one day. [5]He was arrested and receiving a sentence of five years as a slave in a galley ship. [6]His attempts to escape added years to his sentence. [7]In the end, Valjean served nineteen years for stealing the bread. [8]He left prison bitter, vengeful, and full of anger, but a surprising event changed Valjean's mind and was softening his heart.

_____

_____

_____

_____

_____

_____

_____

_____

_____

_____

_____

_____

_____

_____

Name: _____ Section: _____ Date: _____

Score: (Number right) _____ x 20 = _____%

Parallelism

Rewrite the following paragraph correcting the **five** problems with parallelism.

[1]Valjean could find nothing to eat and no place for sleeping because everyone was afraid of him. [2]Finally, he stormed angrily into the house of a bishop. [3]He demanded a scrap of food and permission to sleep in the stable. [4]To Valjean's surprise, the bishop welcomed him kindly and in a warm fashion. [5]He ate dinner with Valjean and then led him to a comfortable bedroom. [6]During the night, Valjean snuck out of bed and was stealing the knives and forks from the dining room. [7]In the morning, soldiers brought him and the silverware to the bishop's door. [8]The bishop greeted him as a friend and was responding, "I am glad you took the silverware I gave you." [9]Convinced that Valjean was innocent, the soldiers went away. [10]Valjean spent the rest of his life helping people, sharing with them, and he showed them the kindness the bishop had shown him.

PART 4 PUNCTUATION

OBJECTIVES

By the end of Part 4, you should be able to use the following punctuation marks correctly:

- comma;
- apostrophe;
- quotation marks;
- period;
- question mark;
- exclamation point;
- colon;
- semicolon;
- hyphen;
- dash.

In the space provided, rewrite each sentence with the correct punctuation. *Answers are available on the Online Learning Centre.*

1. When I cleaned out the basement I found my sons collection of dead beetles.

   _____

   _____

2. The sign in the window of the hairdressers shop read, Help Wanted.

   _____

   _____

3. The tall thin, red haired man is my cousin.

   _____

   _____

4. "Whats a nice guy like you doing in a place like this." Amy asked Ron.

   _____

   _____

5. Jamie's favourite quotation is this one by Shakespeare. To thine own self be true.

   _____

   _____

THE COMMA (,)

Basics about the Comma

Here are four main uses of the comma:

1. The comma is used to separate three or more items in a series.

   - The school cafeteria has learned not to serve broccoli, spinach, or Brussels sprouts.

Note that the second comma (before the "or" or "and") is optional, but it helps with clarity.

   - The letters k, j, x, z, and q are the least frequently used letters of the alphabet.

   - Our tasks for the party are blowing up balloons, setting the table, and planning the music.

2. The comma is used to separate introductory material from the rest of the sentence.

   - After taking a hot shower, Arun fell asleep on the sofa.

   - If anyone calls while I am out, please take a message.

   - As the movie credits rolled, we stretched and headed toward the exits.

3. The comma is used between two complete thoughts connected by a coordinating conjunction (*for, and, nor, but, or, yet,* or *so*).

   - Lee broke her leg in the accident, and her car was badly damaged.

   - The forecast called for rain, but it's a beautiful sunny day.

   - My glasses broke, so I mended them with duct tape.

Note that a comma is not needed just because a sentence contains *and, but,* or *so.* Use a comma only when the *and, but,* or *so* comes between two complete thoughts. Each of the two thoughts must have its own subject and verb.

   - Lee broke her leg in the accident, and her car was badly damaged.
     A comma is needed because each complete thought has a subject and a verb: *Lee broke* and *car was damaged.*

   - Lee broke her leg in the accident and badly damaged her car.
     A comma is not needed because this sentence expresses only one complete thought. The subject *Lee* has two verbs: *broke* and *damaged.*

4. Two commas are used around non-essential groups of words that "interrupt" the main flow of a sentence.

   - Darryl's car, which had run out of gas, was still sitting by the side of the road.

To determine if commas are needed, try reading the sentence without the interrupting material. If the meaning doesn't change, then the word or group of words is non-essential and should be put between commas.

- Fahira, who sits next to me in English class, is going out of town for the weekend.

- Math, as you know, is my worst subject.

Understanding the Comma

Read the following passage about Farzana Jamal, and insert commas where needed. There are **three** missing commas.

[1]When asked to describe herself Farzana Jamal uses words such as passionate, dedicated, driven, creative, and ambitious. [2]She is currently in her fourth year at Ryerson University and she will soon be graduating with a Bachelor of Commerce (BComm). [3]She does not consider herself lucky, choosing instead to attribute her success to her strong support system her dedication, and her hard work.

1. When asked to describe herself, Farzana Jamal uses words such as passionate, dedicated, driven, creative, and ambitious.
   A comma is needed after introductory words or phrases.

2. She is currently in her fourth year at Ryerson University, and she will soon be graduating with a Bachelor of Commerce (BComm).
   A comma is needed between complete thoughts joined by *and*, *but*, or *so*.

3. She does not consider herself lucky, choosing instead to attribute her success to her strong support system, her dedication, and her hard work.
   Commas are needed to separate items in a series.

Check Your Understanding

Insert commas where needed in the following passage. **Five** commas are missing.

[1]Before pursuing her studies at Ryerson Farzana enrolled in Seneca College. [2]Like many other students Farzana found it difficult to manage school, work family, and her social life. [3]She was feeling very frustrated but her family gave her constant support. [4]Her family taught her that if she stays resilient and committed, she can survive any tests that life gives her. [5]Farzana decided to speak to her program co-coordinator, Sheilagh Stephenson. [6]After listening to Farzana's story Sheilagh helped her design a customized solution just for her.

PRACTICE I

Insert commas where needed in each of the short passages below. **Five** commas are needed.

¹From that point on the sky was the limit for Farzana. ²After graduating from Seneca with her Advanced Accounting and Finance Diploma Farzana didn't feel that a full-time job would be personally fulfilling at this stage in her life. ³She wanted a new challenge so she along with a friend began their own door-to-door drycleaning service. ⁴Business began at a very slow pace but it soon became successful. ⁵With this achievement and her newly found entrepreneurial interest Farzana decided to apply to Ryerson University for the Direct Entry Entrepreneurship program.

PRACTICE 2

Add commas where needed in each sentence.

NOTE To help you master the comma, explanations are given for the first three sentences.

1. My neighbour's dog dislikes children and it hates the mail carrier.
   A comma is needed before the word that joins two complete thoughts.

2. Before the video started there were ten minutes of commercials.
   Use a comma after introductory material.

3. This recipe calls for a can of tuna a bag of frozen peas a box of noodles and a can of mushroom soup.
   A comma is needed after each item in a series.

4. Our apartment was too small after the triplets were born so we started looking for a house.

5. Because of the bad weather school was delayed by two hours today.

6. The travel brochure showed lots of sunny skies blue water gorgeous beaches and tropical sunsets.

7. *The Wizard of Oz* which is my favourite movie is on TV tonight.

8. Ahmed came to the door stretching yawning and rubbing his eyes.

9. Looking embarrassed the man asked if he could borrow bus fare.

10. The movie was in French so I had to read the subtitles.

PRACTICE 3

Insert commas where needed in the short passages below. **Five** commas are needed.

[1]Within eight months of graduating with her diploma Farzana found herself back in school aiming to achieve more. [2]She went on to apply to the Ryerson Internship Program and she was granted acceptance based on her academic average. [3]Farzana is currently in her final year of the program and she will be graduating with her four-year BComm majoring in Entrepreneurship. [4]She continues to set and achieve high goals for herself. [5]When asked about the cause of her success she states confidently that her strong support system dedication, and hard work are what have brought her this far and will take her even farther.

PRACTICE 4

On the lines provided, rewrite each sentence, including all missing commas.

1. Although she is 75 my grandmother can do thirty pushups.

   _____

2. The bookcase was filled with magazines paperback novels and CDs.

   _____

3. Our apartment walls are very thin so we hear most of our neighbours' conversations.

   _____

4. After eating raw oysters from "Bob's Oyster Joint" Jessica and Enzo spent the rest of the evening being sick.

   _____

5. In horror movies as everyone knows characters often do incredibly stupid things.

   _____

6. The zookeeper fed raw meat to the lions gave fresh hay to the zebras and conducted a guided tour.

   _____

7. The sign said, "No Smoking" but many people were ignoring it.

   _____

8. I like everything about housework except vacuuming dusting making beds and washing dishes.

   _____

9. The iron which had been left on all morning had left a burn mark on the countertop.

   _____

10. My mother sank down into her chair looked at me and sighed.

    _____

TEST 1   Name: _____   Section: _____ Date: _____

Score: (Number right) _____ x 10 = _____%

The Comma ,

Add commas where needed in each sentence.

1. These shoes are my usual size but they are still too small for me.

2. The instructor handing out the exam papers wished the students good luck.

3. The car is badly rusted and the rear window is cracked.

4. Without a sound the thief quickly emptied the cash register.

5. While I enjoy reading books I hate having to write a book report.

6. The dog bared its teeth flattened its ears and snarled when it saw me.

7. Unused to the silence of the forest the campers found it hard to sleep.

8. Every day starts with bringing in the newspaper turning on a morning news show and feeding the cat.

9. Because it increases unrest among inmates prison overcrowding is dangerous.

10. I had forgotten my glasses so I could not read the fine print on the test.

TEST 2   Name: _____   Section: _____   Date: _____

Score: (Number right) _____ x 10 = _____ %

The Comma ,

In each sentence, add any missing commas.

1. On most television shows people live in impossibly beautiful homes.

2. Politics money and religion are topics that people often argue about.

3. A customer was waiting but the clerk kept chatting with her friend.

4. Greg has to work the night of his birthday so we will celebrate the night before.

5. By the end of the day we had painted the entire apartment.

6. The smoke detector was buzzing and we could smell something burning.

7. The driving instructor asked me to turn on my headlights windshield wipers and emergency flashers.

8. I woke up feeling cheerful but my mood soon changed.

9. Many people including me have an overwhelming fear of spiders.

10. The province of Quebec is divided into three main geological regions: the Canadian Shield the St. Lawrence Lowlands, and the Appalachian Region.

TEST 3   Name: _____   Section: _____   Date: _____

Score: (Number right) _____ x 10 = _____%

The Comma ,

In the following paragraph about Olympic athlete Bobbie Rosenfeld, add commas where needed. There are **five** commas missing. In the space below, provide a brief explanation of why a comma is needed.

[1]On December 28, 1904 Fanny "Bobbie" Rosenfeld was born in Katrinaslov, a town in the Ukraine. [2]When she was less than a year old her family emigrated to Canada. [3]Growing up, Bobbie excelled at sports, especially track and field, softball ice hockey, and basketball. [4]She won races against other girls but people found it hard to believe that she could win against boys. [5]In grade nine she beat the three fastest boys at her high school.

1. _____

2. _____

3. _____

4. _____

5. _____

TEST 4   Name: _____   Section: _____   Date: _____

Score: (Number right) _____ x 10 = _____ %

The Comma ,

In the following paragraph about Olympic athlete Bobbie Rosenfeld, add commas where needed. There are **five** commas missing. In the space below, provide a brief explanation of why a comma is needed.

[1]After Bobbie finished high school she took a shorthand course and went to work as a secretary for Patterson's Chocolate Company. [2]In the evenings she was the star player on the company women's hockey team. [3]In 1928 Bobbie won a spot on the Canadian Olympic women's track and field team. [4]Six Canadian women participated in the track and field events at the Amsterdam Olympics and they became known as the "Matchless Six." [5]At a time when there were very few women in sports Bobbie Rosenfeld followed her dream to become one of the first female Olympians.

1. _____

2. _____

3. _____

4. _____

5. _____

THE APOSTROPHE (')

Basics about the Apostrophe

There are two main uses of the apostrophe:

1. The apostrophe takes the place of one or more missing letters in a contraction. (A **contraction** is a word formed by combining two or more words, leaving some of the letters out.)

   - I am sleepy. —> **I'm** sleepy.
     The letter *a* in *am* has been left out.

   - Hank did not know the answer. —> Hank **didn't** know the answer.
     The letter *o* in *not* has been left out.

   - They would keep the secret. —> **They'd** keep the secret.
     The letters *woul* in *would* have been left out.

Here are a few more common contractions:

   it + is = **it's** (the *i* in *is* has been left out)

   does + not = **doesn't** (the *o* in *not* has been left out)

   do + not = **don't** (the *o* in *not* has been left out)

   she + will = **she'll** (the *wi* in *will* has been left out)

   he + is = **he's** (the *i* in *is* has been left out)

   we + have = **we've** (the *ha* in *have* has been left out)

   could + not = **couldn't** (the *o* in *not* has been left out)

   will + not = **won't** (the *o* replaces *ill*; the *o* in *not* has been left out)

2. The apostrophe shows that something belongs to someone or something. (This is called **possession**.)

   - the fin of the shark —> the **shark's** fin
     The apostrophe goes after the last letter of the name of the owner, *shark*. The *'s* added to *shark* tells us that the fin belongs to the shark.

   - the grades of Nina —> **Nina's** grades
     The apostrophe goes after the last letter of the name of the owner, *Nina*. The *'s* added to *Nina* tells us that the grades belong to Nina.

 NOTE Never use an apostrophe with a possessive pronoun (his, hers, its, ours, yours, theirs). These words already indicate possession and do not need an apostrophe added.

- Nikola's car has a dent in **its** bumper.

- Priya insists that the sweater is **hers.**

Understanding the Apostrophe

Notice how the apostrophe is used in the following passage about students in a school-to-work transition program at Ajax High School in south central Ontario.

[1]When your family is in need, it's important to have the support of your friends and community. [2]The students in Ronda Franco's class clearly know this well, as they showed when their classmate, Bryan Nedham, needed their help. [3]In August, 2007, Bryan's father, Phil, was injured in a fire while working under a motorhome at his job. [4]He was brought to an Ajax hospital with third-degree burns on 20 percent of his body. [5]Because all nearby hospitals with specialized burn units were full, he was later driven to Rochester, New York for skin grafts. [6]He was in a coma for a month, and when he woke up, he didn't remember what had happened. [7]He asked Bryan's sister to turn on CNN and bring him a cup of coffee, as if it were any normal morning.

1. **It's** means "it is." The apostrophe takes the place of the *i* in *is*.

2. The second apostrophe, in **Ronda Franco's class,** means "the class of Ronda Franco."

3. The third apostrophe, in **Bryan's father,** means "the father of Bryan."

4. The fourth apostrophe, in **didn't,** means "did not."

5. The fifth apostrophe, in **Bryan's sister,** means "the sister of Bryan."

Check Your Understanding

Read the passage below. Then write out the meaning of the contraction in each sentence in the space provided.

[1]When a bed became available in Sunnybrook Hospital's burn unit, Phil Nedham was transferred back to Toronto. [2]After a month, his recovery was going well, but his family's situation was less stable. [3]Phil didn't have insurance and, without a second income coming in, Bryan's mother had to work two jobs to keep the house running. [4]Although Bryan was one of six students attending the school-to-work program at Ajax High School, his classmates hadn't realized how difficult things were for Bryan at home.

1. **Sunnybrook Hospital's burn unit** means _____ .

2. **His family's situation** means _____ .

3. The apostrophe in **didn't** takes the place of the missing letter in the word _____ .

4. **Bryan's mother** means _____ .

5. The apostrophe in **hadn't** takes the place of the missing letter in the word _____ .

PRACTICE 1

Some of the sentences in each of the following short passages contain a word or words that need an apostrophe. Underline the **five** words. Then write the correct version of each in the space provided.

[1]When a story about the Nedham family was published in a local paper, Bryans class decided to do something to help. [2]Wendy Shimkofsky, one of the groups educational assistants, came up with the idea for a penny drive. [3]"It's a good way to clear off your dresser and get rid of money you won't really use anyway," she said. [4]However, they werent expecting the incredible response from the students, teachers, and community. [5]In the first day alone, the class raised $50 for the Nedham family. [6]Bryan couldn't believe how many people from the community were eager to help his family. [7]People gathered the pennies from their dressers, desk drawers, and pockets, and gave them to Bryan's class. [8]One womans contribution was a handful of pennies with a $100 bill attached. [9]The mayor also brought in pennies.

1. _____

2. _____

3. _____

4. _____

5. _____

¹It wasnt only adults who wanted to help—two small children from a local school wrote a letter explaining that they usually donate their pennies to The Hospital for Sick Children in Toronto, but this year they wanted to help Nedhams. ²Its inspiring to see how many people were willing to help. ³The class spent full days rolling pennies and taking them to the bank. ⁴On one trip alone, they brought eighty rolls to the bank. ⁵On the last day of school before the Christmas holidays, the class will present Bryans mother with a cheque for $1,500. ⁶Bryan and his family are very grateful; theyre planning to use most of the money to pay bills. ⁷Also, because of their community's generosity, theyll be able to have a Merry Christmas.

6. _____

7. _____

8. _____

9. _____

10. _____

Plural Possessives

Some plural nouns end in *s*.

- ladies

- athletes

- buses

To make a plural noun that ends in *s* possessive, place an apostrophe after the *s*.

- the ladies' coats

- the athletes' uniforms

- the buses' engines

> **NOTE** No apostrophe is used with simple plurals.

- The **fans** cheered when the team ran onto the field.

  Fans simply means **more than one fan.**

Some plural nouns do not end in *s*.

- women

- men

- children

To make a plural noun that does not end in *s* possessive, add an *'s* to the end of the word.

- the women's careers

- the men's clothing

- the children's grades

PRACTICE 2

Read each of the following sentences, adding an apostrophe (') where needed.

1. Franklin has an interest in mens fashion.

2. After the teacher held one-on-one tutoring sessions, most of the students grades improved.

3. The Northwest Territories largest city is Yellowknife.

4. My parents marriage has lasted for 25 years.

5. Domenico is spending the night at a friends house.

6. The childrens baseball is stuck on the roof.

7. All of the computers hard drives have been destroyed.

8. The Pediatric Academic Societies meetings are being held in Toronto this year.

9. Students are not allowed in the teachers lounge.

10. The Calgary Girls Choir is performing on Saturday.

PRACTICE 3

Read each of the following sentences, adding an apostrophe (') where needed.

1. Dr. Siddiqui keeps a shelf in her office for all of her patients thank you cards.

2. The coachs daughter is one of the best runners on the track team.

3. Smudges on the CDs surface made it skip while it was playing.

4. The house's windows are shattered, and the lawn hasnt been mowed for years.

5. Yolanda and Marco werent speaking six months ago, but now they are getting married.

6. Alert Bay, British Columbia, claims to be home to the worlds largest totem pole, measuring 56.4 metres.

7. The kitchens warmth and the coffee's aroma were very welcoming.

8. Banff, Alberta is one of the Canadian Rocky Mountains' most popular ski destinations.

9. The homeless mans feet were wrapped in pages of yesterday's newspaper.

10. You'll either love or hate the movies surprise ending.

PRACTICE 4

The following passage contains **five** words that need apostrophes. Underline the five words. Then, on the lines following the passage, write the corrected form of each word.

¹Bryans father still doesnt have any memory of the fire. ²He only remembers waking up in the hospital. ³Bryan says that his family cant talk about fire, as they are afraid of bringing back his fathers memories of the incident. ⁴His father is working again, but he has taken a different job. ⁵After what happened, he says he wont work on motorhomes anymore.

1. _____

2. _____

3. _____

4. _____

5. _____

TEST 1   Name: _____   Section: _____   Date: _____

Score: (Number right) _____ x 10 = _____%

The Apostrophe

Each of the sentences below contains **one** word that needs an apostrophe. Underline the word. Then write the word, with its apostrophe, in the space provided.

1. My fathers thunderous snores can be heard all over the house.

   _____

2. The celebrity wore a hat and dark glasses, but she couldnt fool her waiting fans.

   _____

3. The tigers pacing never stopped as it watched the crowd of zoo visitors.

   _____

4. Some students are unhappy about the schools decision to remove soft-drink machines.

   _____

5. Even though they didnt finish elementary school, my grandparents want me to get a college degree.

   _____

6. The grasshoppers powerful hind legs allow the insect to jump many times its own height.

   _____

7. Sheer white curtains and fresh lilacs added to the rooms simple charm.

   _____

8. The hypnotists only tools are a soothing voice and a watch that ticks very loudly.

   _____

9. If you keep eating the cheese dip, there wont be enough to serve our guests.

   _____

10. Since lemons are so cheap right now, Im going to buy enough to make lemonade, lemon cake, and lemon chicken.

    _____

Name: _____ Section: _____ Date: _____

Score: (Number right) _____ x 10 = _____%

The Apostrophe

Each of the sentences below contains **two** apostrophe errors. Rewrite each sentence, with corrections, in the space provided.

1. A lobsters claws are used to crush it's prey and then tear it apart.

   _____

2. We havent seen our server since she gave us our menu's twenty minutes ago.

   _____

3. My cousins' know the stores owner, a man named Mr. Sherwin.

   _____

4. Theres a display of three local artists paintings at the public library.

   _____

5. School wont be opening until noon because of the accident with the power line's.

   _____

6. A dogs collar should not be too tight around it's neck.

   _____

7. Wouldnt it be nice to live in a world where all different cultures' got along with one another?

   _____

8. Ms. Mamdanis classes' will all miss her when she retires.

   _____

9. There was a rumour that some employees' would be laid off, but it wasnt true.

   _____

10. That one models teeth were so white that they didnt look real.

   _____

TEST 3   Name: _____   Section: _____   Date: _____

Score: (Number right) _____ x 10 = _____ %

The Apostrophe

Find the **ten** apostrophe errors in the following paragraph. Rewrite the paragraph, adding necessary apostrophes and removing unnecessary ones, in the space provided.

[1]Some students' are morning people, and some just arent. [2]The morning people are awake as soon as the suns rays' hit the window, so theyre ready to hop out of bed and get ready for school. [3]But given a choice, many people would prefer a beds warmth for a few more hour's. [4]Their brain's dont start functioning until about 10 a.m. [5]Couldnt there be one school for the morning people and another for the rest of us?

_____

_____

_____

_____

_____

_____

_____

_____

_____

_____

_____

_____

TEST 4   Name: _____   Section: _____ Date: _____

Score: (Number right) _____ x 10 = _____%

The Apostrophe

Find the **ten** apostrophe errors in the following paragraph. Rewrite the paragraph, with corrections, in the space provided.

[1]If you could choose, would you rather be your familys only child, or would you want to have siblings? [2]Only children never have to share their toy's or compete for their parents attention. [3]There were times growing up when my three brothers' were so annoying that I wanted to advertise in the local newspaper's: "Boys' for Sale—10¢ each!" [4]But later I decided I didnt really want to be an "only." [5]While its true that life as a single child would be easier in some ways, without my brother's I wouldnt have had anybody to blame when I did something wrong!

_____

_____

_____

_____

_____

_____

_____

_____

_____

_____

_____

CHAPTER 18

QUOTATION MARKS (" ")

Basics about Quotation Marks

Use quotation marks to set off all exact words of a speaker or writer.

- Margaret Laurence's novel *The Diviners* begins with the line, "The river flowed both ways."

  The novel's exact words are enclosed within quotation marks.

- "I'm afraid," the mechanic muttered to Adam, "that your car needs a lot of work."

  The mechanic's exact words are enclosed within quotation marks.

- "Our math teacher is unfair," complained Rohan. "He assigns two hours of homework for each class. Does he think we have nothing else to do?"

  Rohan's exact words are enclosed within quotation marks. Note that even though Rohan's second set of exact words is more than one sentence, only one pair of quotation marks is used. Do not use quotation marks for each new sentence as long as the quotation is not interrupted.

- "We cannot solve a problem by hoping that someone else will solve it for us," wrote psychiatrist M. Scott Peck.

  The exact words that Dr. Peck wrote are enclosed in quotation marks.

NOTE

- Quoted material is usually set off from the rest of the sentence by a comma. When the comma comes at the end of quoted material, it is included inside the quotation marks. The same is true for a period, exclamation point, or question mark that ends quoted material:

Incorrect	"Aren't you ready yet"? Dad yelled. "Hurry up, or we're leaving without you"!
Correct	"Aren't you ready yet?" Dad yelled. "Hurry up, or we're leaving without you!"

- Notice, too, that a quoted sentence begins with a capital letter, even when it is preceded by other words:

Incorrect	The diner asked suspiciously, "is this fish fresh?"
Correct	The diner asked suspiciously, "Is this fish fresh?"

Understanding Quotation Marks

The following profile of the literacy organization Literature for Life contains **five** sets of quotation marks. Underline each quoted phrase.

[1]The website for Literature for Life describes the organization as "a charitable literacy organization committed to improving the lives of young, at-risk families in the GTA by conducting reading circles in high-need neighbourhoods." [2]There are currently ten reading circles operating in what Executive Director Jo Altilia refers to as "priority neighbourhoods." [3]Each group is made up of between eight and twelve young mothers who attend the circles at local parenting centres and agencies. [4]As Altilia says, the program is about more than simply teaching literacy: "It's about self-actualization, self-confidence, and being strong enough to make better judgements." [5]She speaks enthusiastically about the sense of hope that she sees in the young people who attend the reading circles. [6]According to Altilia, "they are developing social skills and breaking the cycle with their own kids." [7]She adds, "learning how to read and think critically helps them to make better choices."

Check Your Understanding

Use **three** sets of quotation marks (" ") to enclose the words that Jo Altilia says out loud.

[1]In the reading circles, the young women read and discuss a series of books, including Alice Walker's *The Color Purple*, Alice Sebold's *The Lovely Bones*, Margaret Atwood's *The Handmaid's Tale*, and *The Diary of Anne Frank*. [2]Altilia says that, For many of the girls, this is the first novel they've ever read. [3]She continues: We help them to understand how to read a novel, including how to understand cues such as italics and quotation marks. [4]Although most of these readers left school in grade eight or earlier, once they are able to connect their own experiences to those they are reading about, they quickly become interested. [5]As Altilia says, Once they get invested in a novel, they just go!

PRACTICE 1

Each of the short passages below contains words that need quotation marks. Add the **two** sets of missing quotation marks in the passage below.

¹The young women who attend the reading circles have not been well-served by the traditional school system. ²Many of these girls are frightened of authority, says Altilia. ³She adds that many of them have been told by their families: You are never going to be any better than what you are, so don't bother trying. ⁴They believe this message, and they accept the idea that their choices are limited. ⁵This is the cycle that Literature for Life is trying to break by encouraging young mothers to read, so that they in turn will bring a love, understanding, and appreciation for literature to their children.

Add the **two** sets of missing quotation marks.

¹In the reading circles, the participants examine what it means to be an individual, a member of a family, and a member of a community. ²In addition to reading novels, they also write journals, poetry, and prose. ³We don't grade their writing, says Altilia. ⁴She explains: Many of them have had a bad experience in the school system. ⁵It's important to listen to their voices without judging.

Add the **three** set of missing quotation marks.

¹When author and activist Maya Angelou was speaking at Roy Thomson Hall in 2007, Altilia contacted her and was sent six tickets. ²To determine who would go, Literature for Life held an essay-writing contest, but surprisingly, no one entered. ³Altilia asked the girls why no one wrote, and she was told: We don't want someone judging our writing. ⁴She then wrote to Maya Angelou herself, who responded by saying: They can all come! ⁵Forty girls went, and met with Dr. Angelou afterwards in the Green Room. ⁶Toronto's mayor, David Miller, was also there. ⁷There wasn't a dry eye in the room, says Altilia.

PRACTICE 2

Insert quotation marks where needed in the following sentences. Look at the example below.

Example   The game announcer called out, "Looks like we have a winner!"

1. I won't take any more criticism, Ana-Maria said to her boyfriend. Our relationship is over.

2. The operator stated, Please deposit another quarter in order to continue this call.

3. Let's all turn on our computers, the instructor said.

4. The label on the chlorine bleach says, Do not mix this product with other cleansers.

5. This is a movie that will scare everyone in the family, the reviewer said.

6. On this afternoon's cruise along the coast of Vancouver Island, said the guide, we will be seeing Steller sea lions, Orca whales, and Grizzly bears.

7. In his book *Think Big*, Dr. Benjamin Carson writes, I had been in the fifth grade not even two weeks before everyone considered me the dumbest kid in the class and frequently made jokes about me.

8. Cut the onions into thin slices, the cooking instructor explained. Then place them in the hot skillet.

9. Could you turn the radio down just a little? the passenger shouted to the taxi driver.

10. Anne Frank wrote the following in her diary: It's a wonder I haven't abandoned all my ideals, which seem so absurd and impractical. Yet I cling to them because I still believe, in spite of everything, that people are truly good at heart.

PRACTICE 3

Five sets of quotation marks are missing from the following passages—two from the first passage and three from the second passage. Insert the quotation marks where needed.

Passage I
   [1]One of the main barriers to success for young mothers is the belief that they are powerless and ignored. [2]Altilia explains: They feel they don't have a voice; they think no one listens to them. [3]Through participating in the reading circles and writing poetry and prose, these young women are learning to use their voices. [4]Literature for Life also runs a quarterly health and lifestyle magazine called *Yo' Mama,* written and produced by young mothers. [5]In addition to providing a forum for young mothers to write and read about issues that matter to them, the young women who work on *Yo' Mama* magazine become role models for other teen mothers. [6]They become what Altilia calls spokespeople for less risky behaviours.

Passage 2

[1]At the top of the Literature for Life website is this quotation: Books are mirrors, windows and doors, they show us who we are, where we've been and where we can go. [2]At the heart of Literature for Life is the belief that there is a link between literacy and empowerment. [3]The following statement from the organization's website emphasizes this link: Literacy is a powerful tool and a first step in breaking the cycle of poverty. [4]One young mother who graduated from Literature for Life was named a 2003 YWCA Young Woman of Distinction. [5]In her acceptance speech, she stated: I am living proof that teen mums, when supported, can do anything.

SOLACE

Relationships 101

TEST 1   Name: _____   Section: _____ Date: _____

Score: (Number right) _____ x 10 = _____%

Quotation Marks

On the lines provided, rewrite the following sentences, adding quotation marks as needed.

1. My mother said, Take some vitamin C for your cold.

   _____

2. Do not discuss the trial during your break, the judge reminded the jury.

   _____

3. That movie, my friend complained, is full of nonstop violence.

   _____

4. According to Wayne Gretzky, It's just amazing how many companies suddenly want you to hold up their products after you've held up the Stanley Cup.

   _____

5. My computer screen is frozen, I said to the instructor.

   _____

6. Let's eat, Rochelle said, before we go to the movie.

   _____

7. Can I talk to you about my midterm grade? Ameel asked his instructor.

   _____

8. Who would like another slice of turkey? Mr. Brandon asked the dinner guests.

   _____

9. Keep your voice down! the little boy shouted loudly to the woman using a cell phone.

   _____

10. Take a lot of notes, my friend warned, if you want to do well on tests.

   _____

TEST 2	Name: _____	Section: _____	Date: _____

Score: (Number right) _____ x 10 = _____ %

Quotation Marks

On the lines provided, rewrite the following sentences, adding quotation marks as needed.

1. It can't be time to get up yet, Isaac groaned as his alarm clock rang.

   _____

2. The server said, What'll it be, folks?

   _____

3. Get away from that hot stove! Maria ordered her daughter.

   _____

4. The tag on the hair dryer said, Do not use this product while taking a bath.

   _____

5. Where did you buy those shoes? a woman on the bus asked me.

   _____

6. The crowd chanted loudly, Defence! Defence! Defence!

   _____

7. On the front page of the *Globe and Mail* are these words: Canada's National Newspaper.

   _____

8. To pass this class, the instructor said, you must be here every day

   _____

9. John Lennon said, Life is what happens to you when you're busy making other plans.

   _____

10. Jan's voice-mail message says, I'm not home, or else I'm pretending not to be home.

    _____

Quotation Marks

Add quotation marks to each of the following sentences.

1. Mother Teresa said, Kind words can be easy to speak, but their echoes are truly endless.

2. John G. Diefenbaker, the former prime minister of Canada, once said, Freedom is the right to be wrong, not the right to do wrong.

3. The first line in the novel *1984* reads, It was a bright cold day in April, and the clocks were striking thirteen.

4. Alice Walker once said, Writing saved me from the sin and inconvenience of violence.

5. Reading is to the mind what exercise is to the body, wrote Richard Steele.

6. In *The Diary of a Young Girl*, Anne Frank writes I want to write, but more than that, I want to bring out all kinds of things that lie buried deep in my heart.

7. Margaret Atwood's *The Handmaid's Tale* ends with the line Are there any questions?

8. In Alice Walker's *The Color Purple*, the character Nettie says, The world is changing. It is no longer a world just for boys and men.

9. The main character of Alice Sebold's *The Lovely Bones* tells the reader, I was fourteen when I was murdered on December 6, 1973.

10. According to Maya Angelou, Any book that helps a child to form a habit of reading, to make reading one of his deep and continuing needs, is good for him.

TEST 4   Name: _____   Section: _____   Date: _____

Score: (Number right) _____ x 10 = _____ %

Quotation Marks

Place quotation marks where needed in the short passages that follow. Each passage needs **two** sets of quotation marks.

1. Robertson Davies believed that a job could be an opportunity. If you bring curiosity to your work, he said, it will cease to be merely a job and become a door through which you enter the best that life has to give you.

2. The interviewer poked her head out of the office door and called out, Please come in, Mr. Taylor. She asked him a few questions about his experience. Then she said, We've had twenty-five applicants for this position. Tell me why you deserve to be hired rather than any of those others.

3. The 5'5" actor Michael J. Fox explained the difference between being an actor and being a star as follows: When you're a short actor, he said, you walk on a ramp. When you're a short star, everybody else walks in a ditch.

4. We can achieve a great deal, if we work together in true partnership with governments and our other Aboriginal sisters, said Rosemarie McPherson, National Spokesperson for Women of the Métis Nation. Respecting our diversity and understanding the differences for each of us will assist us in addressing many issues and priorities for the women we represent.

5. During the Toronto International Film Festival, Sharon spotted a handsome man outside the hotel. Can I have your autograph? she asked, excitedly. When she read the signature, she sputtered, James Dixon? I thought you were George Clooney!

OTHER PUNCTUATION MARKS

End-of-Sentence Punctuation

The punctuation used at the end of a sentence clarifies the tone of the sentence and helps the reader understand what you are trying to say.

THE PERIOD (.)

Use a **period** at the end of a statement, a mild command, or an indirect question.

- Stephen Harper is the prime minister of Canada.
  (A statement.)

- Please hand me the red pen.
  (A mild command.)

- I wonder if there will be a surprise quiz today.
  (An indirect question.)

THE QUESTION MARK (?)

Use a **question mark** after a sentence that asks a question.

- Are you ready for the test?

- How did the car get scratched?

> **NOTE** Indirect questions tell the reader about questions, rather than asking them directly. They end with periods, not question marks.

- The teacher asked if we were ready for the test.

- I wonder how the car got scratched.

THE EXCLAMATION POINT (!)

Use an **exclamation point** after a word or statement that expresses extreme emotion or that gives a strong command.

- Help!

- That's amazing!

- I just got a huge raise!

- Stop that!

> **NOTE** Exclamation points lose their power if they are used too frequently. Use them only when you wish to emphasize strong emotion.

> PRACTICE I

Place a period, question mark, or exclamation point at the end of each of the following sentences.

Example   Will we see each other again?

1. Our car has trouble starting on cold mornings

2. What classes are you taking this semester

3. Watch out for that car

4. Please fill out an application, and then take a seat

5. May I borrow the car

6. The first official hockey rules were published in 1877 in the *Montreal Gazette* newspaper

7. The tarantula has escaped from its cage

8. My brother asked if he could use my computer

9. Do you think it's going to rain

10. Bicycles, which don't pollute, may be the world's best method of transportation

The Colon and the Semicolon

Colons and semicolons are used to separate independent clauses. Here are the common uses of each.

THE COLON (:)

The **colon** directs attention to what follows. It has four main uses:

1. Use a colon to introduce a list.

   - St. John's, Newfoundland is known for three things: its rich history, its spectacular coastlines, and its vibrant music scene.

2. Use a colon to introduce a long or formal quotation.

   - After he was inducted into the WWE Hall of Fame, Canadian wrestler Bret "The Hitman" Hart had this to say about how to be a success: "I've wrestled for 23 years and it's not easy to go out there every night and describe yourself as the best there is, the best there was, and the best there ever will be. The best chance you have if you want to rise to the top is to give yourself up to loneliness. Fear nothing and work hard."

3. Use a colon to introduce an explanation.

   - Nanaimo bars are quite simple to make: first, melt butter, sugar, and cocoa in a double boiler. Next, stir in a beaten egg, graham cracker crumbs, and nuts, and press the mixture into an ungreased pan. Then, combine butter, cream, custard powder, and icing sugar and spread over the first layer. Finally, melt chocolate chips in the microwave, and pour over the first two layers. Chill until firm and cut into bars.

4. Use a colon between a title and subtitle.

   ● My favourite TV show is *Degrassi: The Next Generation*.

PRACTICE 2

Add **one** colon to each sentence.

1. The following TV shows were filmed in Vancouver *Battlestar Galactica*, *The X-Files*, *Dark Angel*, *Intelligence*, and *The Outer Limits*.

2. The novel *Anna Karenina* begins with this famous observation "Happy families are all alike; every unhappy family is unhappy in its own way."

3. In the 2010 Winter Olympics, several events will be held in Whistler, 100 kilometres north of Vancouver Skiing, Ski Jumping, Biathlon, Bobsled, Luge, and Skeleton.

4. Annu had a full day planned shopping on rue Ste-Catherine, lunch at her favourite restaurant, and a movie with her friends.

5. Instead of the anger he expected, Darryl felt only one emotion when his son was brought home by the police great relief.

THE SEMICOLON (;)

A semicolon provides more separation than a comma, but less separation than a period. It has three main uses:

1. Use a **semicolon** to join two complete thoughts that are closely related, but are not connected by a coordinate conjunction.

   ● Our cat knocked over a glass of grape juice; the stain spread over the white carpet.

2. Use a semicolon to join two closely related complete thoughts with a transitional word or word group (such as **afterwards**, **however**, **instead**, **therefore**, and **on the other hand**). Follow the transitional word or word group with a comma.

   ● Gagandeep began school without knowing any English; nevertheless, she will graduate this spring at the top of her class.

3. Use semicolons to separate items in a series when the items themselves contain commas.

   ● This summer, we plan to visit Tofino, B.C.; Kelowna, B.C.; and Banff, Alberta.

PRACTICE 3

Add one or more semicolons to each sentence.

1. Many Canadian actors move to Hollywood most leave disappointed.

2. We went to the airport to pick up my cousin however, her flight had been cancelled.

3. The members of the Barenaked Ladies are Jim Creeggan, who plays bass Kevin Hearn, who plays keyboards Tyler Stewart, who plays drums and lead singers Steven Page and Ed Robertson, who both also play guitar.

4. The emergency room was crowded it was going to be at least a three-hour wait.

5. There was snow on the ground in April we were beginning to wonder if spring weather would ever arrive.

Hyphens and Dashes

THE HYPHEN (-)

Hyphens are used within a word or between two words. Following are three main uses of hyphens:

1. Use a hyphen to divide a word at the end of a line of writing.

    - The lawyer stood up, put on her jacket, shoved a bundle of papers into her brief-case, and hurried to court.

2. Use a hyphen to join two or more words that act together to describe a noun.

    - That blue-eyed, brown-haired girl is strong-willed and free-spirited. (*blue-eyed, brown-haired, strong-willed,* and *free-spirited* all describe the noun *girl.*)

3. Put a hyphen in any number from twenty-one to ninety-nine and in a fraction that is written out, such as one-fourth or two-thirds.

> **NOTE** Words made up of two or more words are sometimes hyphenated (for example, fine-tune). There is no clear rule to cover such cases, so when you're unsure about whether or not to hyphenate such words, check your dictionary.

PRACTICE 4

Add a hyphen to each sentence.

1. Polls show that two thirds of the voters would support higher taxes.

2. You've handed in a very well written story.

3. That angry looking boss actually has a sweet personality.

4. Although Trudy turned thirty last month, she tells everyone she's twenty two.

5. Josée was telling me about a handsome green eyed boy she saw on the subway.

THE DASH (—)

While the hyphen is used within or between individual words, the **dash** is used between parts of a sentence. Following are three common uses of the dash:

1. Dashes may be used to set off and emphasize interrupting material. Use them when you wish to give special attention to words that interrupt the flow of the sentence.

   - Everyone in that family—including the children—has a weight problem.

2. Use a dash to signal the end of a list of items.

   - Family support, prayer, and hope—these are what got Grady through all those months in recovery.

3. A dash may be used to introduce a final element—a list of items, an explanation, or a dramatic point.

   - Anne's refrigerator was packed with food for the party—trays of cold cuts, bottles of pickles, loaves of bread, and several pitchers of lemonade.

   - Ravi hurriedly left work in the middle of the day—his wife was having labour pains.

   - My wallet was found in a trash can—minus its cash.

> **NOTE**   As previously mentioned, the colon can also be used to introduce a list or an explanation. A colon tends to add more formality and less drama to a sentence than a dash.

When typing, form a dash with two hyphens, leaving no space between them; most word processing programs will automatically convert this to a dash.

PRACTICE 5

Add **one** or **two** dashes, as needed, to each sentence.

1. Several papers important papers are missing from my desk.

2. A year after their divorce, Oscar and Ruby did something surprising they got married again.

3. Delicious food, wonderful service, and low prices that's all I ask in a restaurant.

4. The maple tree in our front yard it had been standing there for sixty years blew down last night.

5. Debra arrived at the party wearing an odd outfit a floor-length silk ballgown, a pair of flip-flops, and a cowboy hat.

TEST 1	Name: _____	Section: _____	Date: _____
		Score: (Number right) _____ x 10 = _____%	

Other Punctuation Marks

Place a period (.), question mark (?), or exclamation point (!) at the end of each of the following sentences.

1. The moon is almost 385,000 kilometres from Earth

2. Are you ready for the test

3. That's a great white shark heading this way

4. I wonder if this water is safe to drink

5. I'm so angry I could scream

6. I can't figure out how to turn on this computer

7. Would you like some help with that suitcase

8. Your choices for breakfast are scrambled eggs, pancakes, or cereal

9. That man has a gun

10. Did you take any notes in the class

Other Punctuation Marks

Each of these sentences needs **one** of the following kinds of punctuation marks: colon, semicolon, hyphen, dash or dashes. Add that mark to the sentence.

1. Horrible acting, laughable dialogue, and a ridiculous plot if you like these things, you'll love this movie.

2. The soup simmered all morning its delicious aroma filled the house.

3. Marie-Louise Gay's *Stella* books feature a little red haired girl and her younger brother.

4. The beach was clean and inviting the water was cool and blue.

5. There will be auditions tomorrow for three parts in the play the father, the mother, and the twelve-year-old daughter.

6. Since the movie *Juno*, Ellen Page has become a well known actress.

7. My usually soft spoken brother began to shout angrily.

8. Before I waded into the pond, I noticed someone else was already there a baby alligator.

9. My grandfather actually, he's my great-grandfather will be visiting us over the holidays.

10. Four people were at the meeting: the president of the company, who had arranged the meeting; the vice-president, who attended by teleconference and two accountants, who flew in from Calgary.

TEST 3   Name: _____   Section: _____ Date: _____

Score: (Number right) _____ x 10 = _____%

Other Punctuation Marks

Add **one** colon and **one** semicolon to each of the following sentences.

1. We're reading four books in our Canadian Literature class Rawi Hage's *De Niro's Game,* which won the 2008 IMPAC Dublin Literary Award; Vincent Lam's *Bloodletting and Miraculous Cures,* which is a series of short stories Yann Martel's *Life of Pi,* which won the 2002 Man Booker Prize; and Miriam Toews' *A Complicated Kindness,* which won the 2004 Governor General's Literary Award.

2. In the five seasons of Canadian Idol, the winners have been Ryan Malcolm from Kingston, Ontario Kalan Porter from Medicine Hat, Alberta; Melissa O'Neill from Calgary, Alberta; Eva Avila from Gatineau, Quebec; and Brian Melo from Hamilton, Ontario.

3. Yesterday was a terrible day my alarm clock didn't go off therefore, I slept in and missed my biology exam.

4. A curling team is made up of four players the lead, who throws the first two rocks; the second, who throws the second two rocks; the vice skip, who throws the third pair of rocks and the skip, who is the team captain and throws the last two rocks.

5. There are three rules that I live by first, treat others as you wish to be treated; next, don't worry about things that can't be changed and finally, never tell a lie.

Other Punctuation Marks

Each of the following sentences contains **two** punctuation errors. Read the sentence, and then add the correct punctuation (colon, semicolon, dash or dashes, hyphen, period, question mark, or exclamation point).

1. The vice principal came to the classroom and asked the boys to follow her to the office?

2. Only 2 percent of the population is naturally red haired, however, many people dye their hair red.

3. Does full time Internet access in the classroom really help students learn better.

4. The first international Earth Hour was a huge success, On March 29, 2008, between 8 and 9 p.m.; people around the world turned out their lights.

5. Most newspapers contain at least four sections news, sports, entertainment, and business!

6. My ex husband was wealthy, successful, and had never been married before or so I thought.

7. Canadian golfer Mike Weir won The Masters, he became the second left handed golfer to win a major tournament. After winning, Weir spoke about his goals, "If I can raise more money for charities, or get more Canadian kids to play golf, the green jacket will mean even more."

8. The company agreed to all the union's demands even the request for free parking spaces which means that the workers will not be going on strike.

9. At the 2008 Academy Awards, all four acting awards went to non American actors: Daniel Day-Lewis, from Ireland, for best actor; Marion Cotillard, from France, for best actress; Javier Bardem, from Spain, for best actor in a supporting role, and Tilda Swinton, from England, for best actress in a supporting role.

10. Kyle decided to change to part time studies, since he made this decision, school has been much more manageable for him.

MECHANICS AND SPELLING

OBJECTIVES

By the end of Part 5, you should be able to:

- Correctly spell commonly used words;

- Use commonly confused words and idiomatic expressions correctly;

- Eliminate wordiness, slang, informal expressions, and clichés from your writing;

- Correctly use capital letters;

- Correctly use numbers and abbreviations.

Here are five sentences, each of which contains **two** of the types of errors covered in this section. Correct the errors in the spaces provided. *Answers are available on the Online Learning Centre.*

1. Jenna clings to the beleif that world piece is possible within her generation's lifetime.

   _____   _____

2. Some people find it difficult to seperate the things they want from the things they need; these people often end up going over there budget.

   _____   _____

3. Brenda wants to get in shape, so for her birthday in march, her husband bought her a book called *The Joy of Joging.*

   _____   _____

4. I ordered a dvd called *How to Save Your Money.* It cost ninety nine dollars and ninety-five cents.

   _____   _____

5. Sandy enrolled in the media studies program in two thousand and five.

   _____   _____

How many errors did you catch? _____/10

CHAPTER 20

SPELLING IMPROVEMENT

Use the Dictionary and Other Spelling Aids

The single most important way to improve your spelling is to get into the habit of checking words in a dictionary. But you may at times have trouble locating a given word. "If I can't spell a word," you might ask, "how can I find it in the dictionary?" The answer is that you have to guess what the letters might be. Although you may be tempted to rely on your word processor's spell-check program, without a basic knowledge of spelling rules, you will not be able to choose correctly from among the choices your spell-check gives you.

Here are some hints to help you make informed guesses:

HINT 1

If you're not sure about the vowels in a word, you will have to experiment. Vowels often sound the same. So try an *i* in place of an *a*, an *e* in place of an *i*, and so on.

HINT 2

Consonants are sometimes doubled in a word. If you can't find your word with single consonants, try doubling them.

HINT 3

The English language contains many letters and letter combinations that sound alike. If your word isn't spelled with one of the letters in a pair or group shown below, it might be spelled with another in the same pair or group. For example, if it isn't spelled with a *k*, it may be spelled with a *c*.

Sound-alikes	Incorrect	Correct
ai/ay	payr	pair
au/aw	auful	awful
c/k/ck	aktual	actual
f/ph	telefone	telephone
able/ible	terrable	terrible
ent/ant	elephent	elephant
tion/sion	extention	extension
er/or	terrer	terror

English pronunciation and spelling can be very confusing for non-native speakers. There are many irregularities, so you will probably need to memorize the correct spelling of words in order to improve your spelling.

Here is a commonly used example to show how irregular English spelling really is.

- First, how would you pronounce this word?   GHOTI

- Now, say the following words aloud:

  laugh

  women

  lotion

What sound does the **gh** make in "laugh"?
What sound does the **o** make in "women"?
What sound does the **ti** make in "lotion"?

- Now put them together:

  gh   +   o   +   ti

Based on these irregularities in spelling, GHOTI would be pronounced _____!

In reality, there is no such word in English, but this just shows how confusing English spelling and pronunciation rules are.

PRACTICE 1

Use your dictionary and the above hints to find the correct spelling of the following words.

1. divelop	_____	11. aukward	_____
2. diferent	_____	12. photografy	_____
3. sertain	_____	13. asemble	_____
4. chearful	_____	14. seazon	_____
5. sergery	_____	15. dependant	_____
6. skedule	_____	16. terrable	_____
7. fony	_____	17. dezign	_____
8. comfortible	_____	18. rilease	_____
9. mayer	_____	19. funcsion	_____
10. paiment	_____	20. awthor	_____

In addition to a dictionary, take advantage of a spell-checker on your computer. Also, pocket-size electronic spell-checkers are widely available.

Keep a Personal Spelling List

In a special place, write down every word you misspell. Include its correct spelling, underline the difficult part of the word, and add any hints you can use to remember how to spell it.

 If spelling is a particular problem for you, you might even want to start a spelling notebook that has a separate page for each letter of the alphabet.

Here's one format you might use:

How I spelled it	Correct spelling	Hints
recieve	receive	I before E except after C
seperate	separate	There's A RAT in sepARATe
alot	a lot	Two words (like "a little")
alright	all right	Two words (like "all wrong")

Study your list regularly, and refer to it whenever you write and proofread a paper.

Learn Commonly Confused Words

Many spelling errors result from words that sound alike or almost alike but that are spelled differently, such as *break* and *brake*, *wear* and *where*, or *right* and *write*. To avoid such errors, study carefully the list of words on pages 235–237 and 238–240.

Memorize Correct Spelling of Commonly Used Words

Memorization is often the only way to learn the correct spelling of words. Try choosing two words every day. Practice writing these words over and over again. Then, write the words in a sentence.

Learn Some Helpful Spelling Rules

Even poor spellers can improve by following a few spelling rules. Following are **six** rules that apply to many words.

RULE #1: *I* BEFORE *E* RULE

I before E except after C

Or when sounded like *A*, as in *neighbour* and *weigh*.

	I before E	*Except after C*	*Or when sounded like A*
Examples	bel**ie**f, ch**ie**f f**ie**ld	rec**ei**ve, c**ei**ling	v**ei**n, **ei**ght

Exceptions to the above rule include: **ei**ther, l**ei**sure, for**ei**gn, sc**ie**nce, soc**ie**ty

A. Complete each word with either *ie* or *ei*.

1. dec_____ve   **6.** pr_____st

2. bel_____ve   **7.** cash_____r

3. br_____f   **8.** w_____gh

4. fr_____ght   **9.** p_____ce

5. c_____ling   **10.** r_____ndeer

B. In each sentence, fill in the blank with either *ie* or *ei*.

11. I rec_____ved an interesting email today.

12. Many of the people in my n_____ghbourhood are retired.

13. Norah never gave up her bel_____f in her husband's innocence.

14. What do you like to do in your l_____sure time?

15. There's a lot of traffic now, so don't ignore this y_____ld sign.

16. The r_____gn of Queen Victoria of Great Britain lasted over sixty years.

17. My parents are working hard to ach_____ve their retirement goals.

18. I have never travelled to any for_____gn countries.

19. My _____ghty-year-old grandfather still does a daily twenty pushups.

20. A th_____f broke into Parker's Bakery last night and stole all the dough.

RULE #2: SILENT *E* RULE

If a word ends in a silent (unpronounced) *e*, drop the *e* before adding an ending that starts with a vowel. Keep the *e* when adding an ending that begins with a consonant.

	Drop the e with endings that start with a vowel	*Keep the e with endings that start with a consonant*
Examples	like + ed = liked	love + ly = lovely
	confuse + ing = confusing	shame + ful = shameful
	fame + ous = famous	hope + less = hopeless
	guide + ance = guidance	manage + ment = management
Exceptions	noticeable, argument, truly	

PRACTICE 3

A. Write out each word shown.

1. abuse + ing = _____
2. hope + ed = _____
3. have + ing = _____
4. desire + able = _____
5. ridicule + ous = _____
6. sincere + ity = _____

B. Write out each word shown.

7. sincere + ly = _____
8. peace + ful = _____
9. advance + ment = _____
10. noise + less = _____
11. large + ness = _____
12. grace + ful = _____
13. bare + ly = _____

C. Write out each word shown.

14. write + ing = _____
15. care + ful = _____
16. safe + ly = _____
17. hire + ed = _____
18. serve + ing = _____
19. notice + able = _____
20. excite + ment = _____

RULE #3: Y RULE

Change the final *y* of a word to *i* when both of the following are present:
a. the last two letters of the word are a consonant plus *y*. (Keep a *y* that follows a vowel.)
b. the ending being added begins with a vowel or is *-ful*, *-ly*, or *-ness*.

Exception	Keep the *y* if the ending being added is *-ing*.

	*Change the **y** to **i***	*Keep the **y***
Examples	happy + ness = happiness	destroy + s = destroys
	lucky + ly = luckily	display + ed = displayed
	beauty + ful = beautiful	grey + ed = greyed
	try + ed = tried	try + ing = trying
	carry + er = carrier	carry + ing = carrying

PRACTICE 4

A. Write out each word shown.

1. rely + ed   = _____

2. holy + ness   = _____

3. play + ful   = _____

4. cry + ing   = _____

5. cry + ed   = _____

6. plenty + ful = _____

7. lazy + ness   = _____

8. fly + ing   = _____

9. angry + ly   = _____

10. betray + ed = _____

B. Write out each word shown.

1. stay + ing   = _____   stay + ed   = _____

2. busy + est   = _____   busy + ly   = _____

3. silly + er   = _____   silly + ness = _____

4. employ + ed = _____   employ + er   = _____

5. bury + ing   = _____   bury + ed   = _____

6. dry + ing   = _____   dry + ed   = _____

7. happy + ly   = _____   happy + er   = _____

8. funny + er   = _____   funny + est   = _____

9. satisfy + ing = _____   satisfy + ed = _____

10. annoy + ed = _____   annoy + ance = _____

RULE #4: DOUBLING RULE

Double the final consonant of a word before adding an ending when all three of the following are present:

a. the last three letters of the word are a consonant, a vowel, and a consonant (CVC).

b. the word is only one syllable (for example, *stop*) or is accented on the last syllable (for example, *begin*).

c. The ending being added begins with a vowel.

	One-syllable words that end in CVC	*Words accented on the last syllable that end in CVC*
Examples	stop + ed = sto**pp**ed	begin + ing = begi**nn**ing
	flat + er = fla**tt**er	control + er = contro**ll**er
	red + est = re**dd**est	occur + ence = occu**rr**ence

PRACTICE 5

A. First note whether each one-syllable word ends in the CVC pattern or with another pattern (VVC, VCC, etc.), and write the pattern in the first column. Then add to each word the endings shown.

	Word	Pattern of Last Three Letters	-ed	-ing
Examples	trip	CVC	tripped	tripping
	growl	VCC	growled	growling
1.	jog			
2.	learn			
3.	slam			
4.	wrap			
5.	rain			
6.	dot			
7.	flood			
8.	beg			
9.	clip			
10.	burn			

B. First note whether each two-syllable word ends in the CVC pattern or with another pattern (VVC, VCC, etc.), and write the pattern in the first column. Then add to each word the endings shown. *If a word ends in CVC, remember to check to see if the final syllable is stressed or not.*

	Word	Pattern of Last Three Letters	-ed	-ing
Examples	admit	CVC	admitted	admitting
	recall	VCC	recalled	recalling
11.	expel			
12.	perform			
13.	enter			
14.	omit			
15.	murder			
16.	prefer			
17.	occur			
18.	explain			
19.	submit			
20.	reason			

RULE #5: RULES FOR ADDING -*ES* TO NOUNS AND VERBS THAT END IN *S, SH, CH,* OR *X*

Most plurals are formed by adding -*s* to the singular noun, but in some cases -*es* is added. For nouns that end in *s, sh, ch,* or *x,* form the plural by adding -*es.*

Examples	kiss + es = kiss**es**	coach + es = coach**es**
	wish + es = wish**es**	tax + es = tax**es**

Most third-person singular verbs end in -*s* (he runs, she sings, it grows). But for verbs that end in *s, sh, ch,* or *x,* form the third-person singular with -*es.*

Examples	miss + es = miss**es**	catch + es = catch**es**
	wash + es = wash**es**	mix + es = mix**es**

PRACTICE 6

Add *-s* or *-es* as needed to each of the following words.

1. bush   _____
2. mix   _____
3. pitch   _____
4. glass   _____
5. carpet   _____
6. crash   _____
7. box   _____
8. watch   _____
9. shine   _____
10. business   _____

RULE #6: RULES FOR ADDING *-ES* TO NOUNS AND VERBS THAT END IN A CONSONANT PLUS *Y*

For nouns that end in a consonant plus *y*, form the plural by changing the *y* to *i* and adding *-es*.

Examples   fly + es = fl**ies**   lady + es = lad**ies**

                   canary + es = canar**ies**

For verbs that end in a consonant plus *y*, form the third-person singular by changing the *y* to *i* and adding *-es*.

Examples   pity + es =pit**ies**   marry + es = marr**ies**

                   bully + es = bull**ies**

PRACTICE 7

Add *-s* or *-es* as needed to each of the following words. Where appropriate, change a final *y* to *i* before adding *-es*.

1. army   _____
2. try   _____
3. tray   _____
4. hurry   _____
5. attorney   _____
6. variety   _____
7. chimney   _____
8. baby   _____
9. journey   _____
10. sympathy   _____

> **NOTE**   When buying a dictionary, make sure that you buy a Canadian dictionary, as there are many differences between American and Canadian (and British and Canadian) spellings of words.

For example, many words that end in *-or* in American English, end in *-our* in Canadian English:

AMERICAN	CANADIAN
color	colour
honor	honour
labor	labour

Here are some other common variations between American and Canadian English:

AMERICAN	CANADIAN
canceled	cancelled
catalog	catalogue
center	centre
check	cheque (as in "I'll write you a cheque")
meter	metre
neighbor	neighbour
theater	theatre

However, you should not assume that Canadian English is the same as British English! Here are some of the most common variations between British and Canadian English:

BRITISH	CANADIAN
ageing	aging
analyse	analyze
civilisation	civilization
criticise	criticize

TEST 1   Name: _____   Section: _____   Date: _____

Score: (Number right) _____ x 4 = _____ %

Spelling Improvement

Use the spelling rules in the chapter to write out the words indicated.

A. Complete each word with either *ie* or *ei*.

1. gr_____f

2. dec _____ve

3. n_____ghbour

4. fr_____nd

5. rel_____ ve

B. Use the *silent e* rule to write out each word shown.

6. time + ed = _____

7. time + ly = _____

8. hope + ful = _____

9. fame + ous = _____

10. change + ing = _____

C. Use the *y* rule to write out each word shown.

11. fry + ed = _____

12. easy + ly = _____

13. stay + ed = _____

14. duty + ful = _____

15. lonely + ness = _____

D. Use the *doubling* rule to write out each word shown.

16. drop + ing = _____

17. pad + ing = _____

18. prefer + ed = _____

19. jump + er = _____

20. sad + est = _____

E. Add *-s* or *-es* as needed to each of the following words. Where appropriate, change a final *y* to *i* before adding *-es*.

21. box _____

22. enemy _____

23. country _____

24. valley _____

25. porch _____

Spelling Improvement

Circle the correct word in each pair. Remember to use Canadian spelling.

1. conceive   concieve
2. field   feild
3. sobriety   sobreity
4. studyed   studied
5. chief   cheif
6. comeing   coming
7. desireable   desirable
8. deceive   decieve
9. accurately   accuratly
10. chooseing   choosing

TEST 3   Name: _____   Section: _____   Date: _____

Score: (Number right) _____ x 10 = _____ %

Spelling Improvement

Circle the correct word in each pair. Remember to use Canadian spelling.

1. replyed   replied

2. theatre   theater

3. carried   carryed

4. glorious   gloryous

5. peice   piece

6. beautyful   beautiful

7. vien   vein

8. beginning   begining

9. extention   extension

10. believe   beleive

Spelling Improvement

Circle the spelling error in each of the following sentences. Rewrite the word using the correct Canadian spelling in the space provided.

1. Prairie dogs in Saskatchewan have many enemys, including coyotes, bobcats, foxes, weasels, hawks, and snakes. _____

2. Since 2003, Phil Fontaine has been the National Cheif of the Assembly of First Nations. _____

3. Gizman dreams of being a fameous singer someday. _____

4. She knows her dream isn't likely to come true, but she still remains hopful. _____

5. The groom's brother made a toast wishing the couple a lifetime of happyness. _____

6. The next toast was given by the maid of honor. _____

7. When you move to a new city, it's a good idea to visit a local community center to see what services and programs are available. _____

8. Huda was very excited when she heard that her brother and his family were comeing to visit for Eid. _____

9. All the clocks stoped when the power went out. _____

10. I couldn't study for my exams, because a theif broke into my car and stole all my textbooks. _____

COMMONLY CONFUSED WORDS

Basics about Commonly Confused Words

Homonyms are two or more words that have the same sound but different spellings and meanings.

The following four groups of homonyms cause writers the most trouble:

1.

its	belonging to it
it's	contraction of *it is*

• **It's** a shame that the shiny car lost **its** muffler and now roars like an old truck.
It is a shame that the shiny car lost *the muffler belonging to it* and now roars like an old truck.

 Whenever you write *it's*, you should be able to substitute *it is*. For example: The dog was wagging *it's* tail = The dog was wagging *it is* tail. Remove the apostrophe.

2.

their	belonging to them
there	(1) in or to that place; (2) used with *is, are, was, were,* and other forms of the verb *to be*
they're	contraction of *they are*

• Our neighbours are health-food addicts. When we attend parties at **their** home, they serve pizza with broccoli florets on top. **They're** also fond of serving carrot juice. I hope they won't be offended if we don't go **there** very often.
Our neighbours are health-food addicts. When we attend parties at the home *belonging to them*, they serve pizza with broccoli florets on top. *They are* also fond of serving carrot juice. I hope they won't be offended when we don't go *to that place* very often.

 Whenever you write *they're*, you should be able to substite *they are*. For example: I'll meet you over *they're* = I'll meet you over *they are*. Change the spelling to *there*.

Also, *there* has the word *here* in it; both words refer to places.

3.

to	(1) used before a verb, as in "to serve"; (2) expressing direction, aim, or purpose
too	(1) overly or extremely; (2) also
two	the number 2

- I'll take these **two** letters **to** the post office for you, but you'll need **to** put more postage on one of them. It is **too** heavy for only one stamp.

  I'll take these *2* letters *so as to reach* the post office for you, but you'll need *to put* more postage on one of them. It is *overly* heavy for only one stamp.

 Remember the spelling of too this way: Too has one *o*, and it **also** has another one. Too has **too** many o's.

4.

your	belonging to you
you're	contraction of *you are*

- **You're** going to need a first-aid kit and high boots for **your** camping trip. *You are* going to need a first-aid kit and high boots for the camping trip *belonging to you*.

 Whenever you write *you're*, you should be able to substitute **you are.** For example: Give me *you're* phone number = give me *you are* phone number. Change the spelling to *your*.

Understanding Commonly Confused Words

In the following passage about a college student, five homonym mistakes are underlined. The correct spelling of each word is then shown in the spaces below.

¹This is Rosarina Saw. ²Rosarina is a student at Kwantlen University College in Vancouver. ³She is taking courses <u>two</u> improve her English before applying <u>too</u> a nursing program. ⁴Her favourite course is Reading and Writing, because she loves <u>to</u> write about her experiences. ⁵Before moving to Vancouver, Rosarina spent to years in Victoria, after arriving <u>their</u> from a refugee camp in Thailand. ⁶Her family stayed behind in Thailand, but <u>there</u> now living in Australia.

1. The spelling before a verb (such as "to improve") is always **to.**

2. The word expresses purpose or intention, and should be spelled **to.**

3. The meaning is "the number 2," which is spelled **two.**

4. The meaning is "at that place," which is spelled **there.**

5. The meaning is "they are," which is spelled **they're.** The apostrophe takes the place of the missing *a* in they are.

Check Your Understanding

Underline the **five** mistakes in homonyms. Then write the correct spellings of the words in the five spaces provided.

[1]Rosarina was born in Burma and was given up for adoption at the age of three. [2]Her biological parents were very poor and wanted her too get a better education. [3]She and her family are members of the Karen ethnic minority in Burma, which was renamed Myanmar by the ruling military regime. [4]Rosarina's adopted father was one of the leaders of the resistance against the Burmese government, who were terrorizing the Karen. [5]Rosarina and her adopted family left Burma in 1995, afraid for there lives. [6]They hoped to cross the border into Thailand to become refugees. [7]After living in the jungle near the border of Thailand, they planned to cross into Thailand at night with a few other families. [8]The Burmese government found out about they're plan. [9]Rosarina's family was very lucky, but there are still many people living in the jungle without weapons, food, or any possessions. [10]They are not able to get into Thailand, but they can't go back to Burma because its too dangerous for them. [11]Rosarina knows that you should never take you're freedom for granted.

1. _____

2. _____

3. _____

4. _____

5. _____

OTHER COMMON HOMONYMS

brake — low or stop

break — to cause to come apart

hear — take in by ear

here — in this place

hole — an empty spot

whole — complete

know — to understand

no — the opposite of *yes*

right — correct

write — to form letters and words

whose — belonging to whom

who's — contraction of *who is* or *who has*

PRACTICE 1

In the passage below, underline the correct word in the **ten** sets of parentheses.

[1]While attempting to enter Thailand, Rosarina saw her friend's father killed by the Burmese troops. [2]She ran and was separated from everyone. [3]It was dark and quiet and she was alone and very scared. [4]She was afraid *(to, too, two)* go forward because she didn't *(know, no)* what was ahead, and she was afraid to go back because the Burmese troops would kill her. [5]After a while, she heard some branches *(brake, break)*, and then some people whispering. [6]At first she thought it was the troops, but it was her parents. [7]They had been looking for her but hadn't been able to call her name because the troops would *(hear, here)*. [8]When Rosarina and her family arrived in Thailand, they were helped by the Office of the United Nations High Commissioner for Refugees (UNHCR), and a few months later they moved to a refugee camp in Northern Thailand. [9]At first the government of Thailand didn't want the people in the camps to build anything permanent because it would mean that they were staying. [10]Soon, however, the people in Rosarina's camp built an elementary school so that the children could learn to read and *(right, write)*. [11]Later, they built a high school *(to, too, two)*, but there were no options for students who wanted to continue *(their, there, they're)* education. [12]Then, the World University Service of Canada (WUSC) came to Thailand and visited the refugee camps, encouraging high school students to continue *(their, there, they're)* education in Canada. [13]Rosarina filled out an application, but since only one student from each camp would be chosen, she never dreamed that she would be the one *(who's, whose)* application was accepted. [14]She came *(hear, here)* to study in 2003, eager to learn English and improve her life.

NINE MORE HOMONYMS

buy	—	to purchase
by	—	close to; no later than; through the action of
knew	—	past tense of *know*
new	—	opposite of old
passed	—	past tense of pass; handed to; went by; completed successfully
past	—	the time before the present
peace	—	absence of war; quiet
piece	—	a part of something
plain	—	not fancy; obvious
plane	—	airplane

principal — main; the person in charge of a school
principle — guideline or rule

threw — past tense of *throw*
through — into and out of; finished

wear — to have on (clothing)
where — in what place

weather — outside conditions
whether — if

 Can you think of any other homonyms? List them in the space provided, so that you have a reference for yourself.

Homonyms   Meaning

_____

_____

_____

_____

_____

PRACTICE 2

For each sentence, underline the correct word in parentheses.

1. There is only one *(write, right)* answer to a math problem.

2. I live by the *(principal, principle)* of treating others as I want to be treated.

3. We drove *(through, threw)* the entire province in only three hours.

4. Everyone wants *(piece, peace)* on Earth.

5. I forgot *(where, wear)* I stored the Christmas presents.

6. Are you going to order a half or a *(hole, whole)* barbecued chicken?

7. The *(weather, whether)* in England is rainy much of the time.

8. Ray and Coral, who just got married, want all *(new, knew)* furniture in their house.

9. Unfortunately, one of the cars that Marylou *(passed, past)* on the highway was a police car.

10. The sign in the bus said, "*(There, They're, Their)* is no excuse for domestic violence."

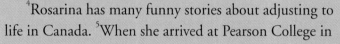

PRACTICE 3

In the passages below, underline the correct word in each set of parentheses. **Ten** corrections are needed.

¹After leaving the camp, Rosarina found herself in many unfamiliar situations. ²She had never been in a large city, in an airport, or on a *(plain, plane)* before. ³In the airport in Bangkok, she didn't know how to find information about her flight, and when she arrived in Hong Kong, she was amazed at how large and crowded it was.

⁴Rosarina has many funny stories about adjusting to life in Canada. ⁵When she arrived at Pearson College in Victoria in 2003, *(wear, where)* she would be living for the next two years, she didn't understand how anything worked—she didn't even know how to use the hot and cold taps in the shower! ⁶After settling in, she tried to phone her family in Thailand but did not *(know, no)* how to use a telephone. ⁷She dialed 911, and when the operator answered, she didn't know *(weather, whether)* or not to say anything, so she hung up. ⁸She was surprised when, a little while later, the police showed up at her residence!

⁹After struggling *(threw, through)* all of these new experiences, Rosarina has gotten used to life in Canada and feels like a real Canadian. ¹⁰However, when she sees a police officer, she still feels a rush of fear before she remembers that Canada is very different from Myanmar *(wear, where)* the police can arrest and torture innocent people with no reason. ¹¹ In addition to her studies, she volunteers with the Immigration Services Society in Vancouver, helping former refugees from Myanmar adjust to life in Canada. ¹²She interprets for them and helps them learn how to do things such as go to the bank, *(buy, by)* groceries, and take the bus. ¹³Many of them do not speak any English, and some have never been to school and never learned to *(right, write)* in any language.

¹⁴She has *(know, no)* thoughts of going back to Myanmar to live. ¹⁵That is part of her *(passed, past)*, and she feels strongly that her future is *(hear, here)* in Canada. ¹⁶She hopes to soon become a Canadian citizen, and she is very excited about moving on to the next stage in her education, becoming a nurse, and continuing to take care of other people and help them through difficult times in their lives.

OTHER CONFUSING WORDS

Here are some words that are not homonyms but are still confusing words. In most cases they have similar sounds and are often misused and misspelled.

1.

    a   used before words that begin with a consonant sound

    an   used before words that begin with a vowel or a silent *h* (as in *an hour*).

   • Would you like **an** ice-cream cone or **a** shake?

2.

accept (1) to receive; (2) to agree to take; (3) to believe in

except (1) excluding or leaving out; (2) but

- All the employees **except** the part-timers were willing to **accept** the new contract.

3.

advice opinion meant to be helpful

advise to give an opinion meant to be helpful

- Never take the **advice** of someone who **advises** you to act against your conscience.

4.

affect to influence

effect a result

- Divorce **affects** an entire family, and its **effects**—both good and bad—last for years.

 Remember that *effect* is a noun and *affect* is usually a verb—the exception is in the field of psychology, in which *affect* can also be a noun meaning "feeling" or "emotion."

5.

desert (1) a verb meaning "to leave or abandon"; (2) a noun meaning "a dry region with little or no plant growth"

dessert a sweet course eaten at the end of a meal

- The children were willing to **desert** the TV set only when **dessert** was served.

6.

fewer used for items that can be counted

less used for general amounts

- As our congregation ages, our church is left with **fewer** members and **less** financial support.

7.

loose (1) not tight; (2) free; not confined

lose (1) to misplace; (2) to not win; (3) to be deprived of something one has had

- If you don't fix that **loose** steering wheel, you could **lose** control of your car.

8.

quiet (1) silent; (2) relaxing and peaceful

quite (1) truly; (2) very; (3) completely

quit (1) to stop doing something; (2) to resign from one's job

- Giselle was **quiet** after saying she might want to **quit** her job but that she wasn't **quite** sure.

9.

    than   a word used in comparisons

    then   (1) at that time; (2) next

    ● First Dad proved he was a better wrestler **than** I am; **then** he helped me improve.

10.

    use   to make use of

    used (to) accustomed to or in the habit of

    ● I am **used to** very spicy food, but when I cook for others, I **use** much less hot pepper.

 Do not forget to include the *d* **with** *used to.*

11.

    were   the past tense of *are*

    we're   contraction of *we are*

    ● **We're** going to visit the village in Spain where my grandparents **were** born.

PRACTICE 4

For each sentence, underline the correct word in parentheses.

1. My daughter likes all types of food (*accept, except*) meat, fish, dairy products, and vegetables.

2. I (*loose, loose*) my keys at least once a week.

3. For me, a real (*desert, dessert*) must contain chocolate.

4. Your actions (*affect, effect*) those around you, whether you're aware of it or not.

5. James was looking forward to a (*quiet, quite*) evening at home, but he didn't know that Carol had planned a surprise party for him.

6. Since she is the youngest of four girls, Ellie is (*use, used*) to wearing hand-me-downs.

7. I find Sudoku puzzles more difficult (*than, then*) crossword puzzles.

8. Our relatives (*were, we're*) not surprised to hear of my brother's divorce.

9. Fruit contains (*fewer, less*) calories than ice cream.

10. Don't seek (*advice, advise*) from anybody you don't respect.

TEST 1   Name: _____   Section: _____   Date: _____

Score: (Number right) _____ x 10 = _____ %

Commonly Confused Words

Each sentence contains **one** homonym error. Circle the error and write the correct word in the space provided.

_____ 1. It's easy to see from your face that your very tired.

_____ 2. It isn't write to break your promise.

_____ 3. Does anyone know why this empty box is sitting hear?

_____ 4. Surely you're not going to eat that hole cake all by yourself.

_____ 5. Some people like winter more then summer.

_____ 6. Since beginning his karate class, Brian claims he can brake a stack of two bricks with his bare hand.

_____ 7. Its impossible to cancel the party—the guests are already on their way.

_____ 8. You're cat is going to break its leg if it jumps down from that tall tree.

_____ 9. Jamal used to always loose his textbooks, so he just stopped bringing them to school.

_____ 10. If their is life on other planets, it's probably very different from life on Earth.

Name: _____   Section: _____   Date: _____

Score: (Number right) _____ x 10 = _____ %

Commonly Confused Words

Each sentence contains **one** homonym error. Circle the error and write the correct word in the space provided.

_____ 1. Now that Mrs. Ringwald is in the hospital, no one knows whose going to teach her class.

_____ 2. Here in Oshawa, many people earn they're living in the automobile industry.

_____ 3. Excuse me, but your music is playing to loudly for the other passengers.

_____ 4. Two many people write unsigned letters to the newspaper.

_____ 5. It takes a hole lot of willpower to quit smoking.

_____ 6. Your wasting too much time worrying about things you can't control.

_____ 7. After too weeks, the lost cat returned, thin and dirty and without it's collar.

_____ 8. Unfortunately, it's easy to take you're family and friends for granted.

_____ 9. Their are too many empty storefronts in my neighbourhood.

_____ 10. Sometimes I wonder weather I should look for a different job.

TEST 3   Name: _____   Section: _____   Date: _____

Score: (Number right) _____ x 5 = _____ %

Commonly Confused Words

In the space provided, write the word that correctly fits each sentence.

by, buy; use, used

1. At first the motion of the airplane bothered Randall, but _____ the time the flight was over, he was _____ to it.

advice, advise; except, accept

2. Even people who won't usually take _____ somehow _____ it from Rosalie.

principal, principle; quit, quite, quiet

3. The _____ of my old school _____ his job to stay home and take care of his grandchildren.

effects, affects; loose, lose

4. Despite the terrible _____ of the earthquake, people didn't _____ their sense of humour.

less, fewer; less, fewer

5. One benefit of watching _____ TV is that you are exposed to _____ commercials.

past, passed; quiet, quite, quit

6. When Eleanor learned that she had _____ her GED exam, she disturbed her usually _____ house with a shout of joy.

a, an; Passed, Past

7. Tonight we're going to see _____ old movie called *Out of the* _____.

principal, principle; a, an

8. A basic _____ that _____ student doctor learns in training is "First, do no harm."

lose, loose; then, than

9. In order to _____ weight, it's better to exercise and eat sensibly _____ to starve yourself.

use, used; than, then

10. I am more _____ to spending an evening watching TV _____ reading or exercising.

Commonly Confused Words

Each sentence contains two homonym errors. Circle the errors and write the correct words in the spaces provided.

1. Tomorrow were going to by a present for Mom.

   _____   _____

2. Because it is so hot in the dessert, people there usually wear lose clothing.

   _____   _____

3. Rachel is a much better chess player then Ryan. In tomorrow's tournament, I think Ryan will loose.

   _____   _____

4. First we'll have salad, than a main course, and finally desert.

   _____   _____

5. If my daughter gets good marks on her report card, were going to by her a snake.

   _____   _____

6. Some medications, unfortunately, have quiet a few unpleasant side affects.

   _____   _____

7. Some of the best advise I ever got was this: "When you loose your temper, count to ten before you speak."

   _____   _____

8. People who are addicted to gambling find it impossible to quite, even when they know they are going to loose a lot of money.

   _____   _____

9. Even though the job doesn't pay much now, I strongly advice you to except it. It's a wonderful opportunity.

   _____   _____

10. My aunt is the principle owner of an hair salon in Montreal.

   _____   _____

 WORD CHOICE

Basics about Word Choice

Not all writing problems involve grammar. A sentence may be grammatically correct, yet fail to communicate well because of the words that the writer has chosen. This chapter explains three common types of ineffective word choice:

1. **Slang**

Slang	My sister is **awesome.**
Revised	My sister is **a very special person.**

2. **Informal Expressions**

Informal	I did **pretty badly** on that test.
Revised	I did **badly** on that test.
Or	I did **not do well** on that test.

3. **Clichés**

Cliché	This semester, I have **bitten off more than I can chew.**
Revised	This semester, I have **taken on more work than I can manage.**

4. **Wordiness**

Wordy	It is **absolutely essential and necessary** that you borrow some folding chairs for the party.
Revised	It is **essential** that you borrow some folding chairs for the party.

SLANG

Slang expressions can add liveliness and humour to conversational speech, but they should be avoided in formal writing. One problem with slang is that it is understood by a limited audience. Slang used by members of a particular group (such as teenagers or science-fiction fans) may be unfamiliar to people outside of the group. Also, slang tends to change rapidly. What was *cool* for one generation is *awesome* or *sick* for another. Finally, slang is by nature informal. So while it adds colour to our everyday speech, it is generally out of place in writing for school or work. Use slang only when you have a specific purpose in mind, such as being humorous or communicating the flavour of an informal conversation.

Slang	After working two shifts yesterday, I'm beat.
Revised	After working two shifts yesterday, I'm **exhausted.**

PRACTICE I

Underline the slang expression in each sentence, and revise the sentence in the space provided.

1. After exams, I'm going to chill for a couple of weeks before starting my job.

    _____

2. When Hannah met her new next-door neighbour, she was happy to discover that he was a hottie.

    _____

3. Everyone was grossed out when the cat brought home a dead rat.

    _____

4. After working a double shift, Karl just wanted to go home and pass out.

    _____

5. When my parents see, I will be dead.

    _____

 With a partner, list as many slang words and expressions as you can, along with the definition of the word. Are these expressions that you would use in conversation with your friends? In conversation with your parents? In an e-mail to your boss? In a school assignment? Discuss why some expressions are acceptable in oral conversation, but not in writing.

INFORMAL EXPRESSIONS

Other words and expressions, while not classified as slang, are nevertheless out of place in formal, academic writing. In your writing, you should be trying to achieve a knowledgeable, reliable, authoritative tone. By using words that are overly casual or informal, you may give the impression that you neither know nor care very much about your subject matter.

Here are some common examples of informal words or phrases that should be avoided.

Informal	More Acceptable
get	understand or obtain
goes, went	says, said
got	have
guy	man, boy, person
kid	child
kind of, sort of	somewhat, rather
pretty, somewhat,	rather
real, really	very
yeah	yes

Can you think of more examples of casual or informal expressions that, while appropriate in speech, should probably be avoided in academic writing?

PRACTICE 2

Underline the informal expression in each sentence, and revise the sentence in the space provided.

1. Flavio has been studying all night, but he still doesn't get Chapter 12.

_____

2. I would like to come to your party tonight, but I'm pretty tired.

_____

3. Shanique is like my best friend.

_____

4. We've known each other since we were kids.

_____

5. I asked Mr. Ramcharand for an extension, but he went, "I don't think so."

_____

CLICHÉS

A cliché is an expression that was once lively and colourful. However, because it has been used too often, it has become dull and boring. Try to use fresh wording in place of predictable expressions. If you don't know the precise meaning of a phrase, avoid it. Following are a few of the clichés to avoid in your writing.

Common Clichés

add insult to injury	in this day and age	rude awakening
avoid like the plague	in the nick of time	sad but true
better late than never	ladder of success	sick and tired
beyond the shadow of a doubt	last but not least	sigh of relief
bored to tears	light as a feather	sharp as a tack
cold, hard facts	like finding a needle	smart as a whip
easier said than done	in a haystack	straight and narrow
easy as pie	make ends meet	time and time again
face the music	playing with fire	tried and true
flat as a pancake	pretty as a picture	under the weather
green with envy	pride and joy	without a doubt
hit the nail on the head	ripe old age	

Cliché	After his one-week suspension from school, Ming resolved to **stay on the straight and narrow.**
Revised	After his one-week suspension from school, Ming resolved to **follow the rules.**

 Many clichés have become so overused that people have forgotten their meaning, but continue to use them anyway. Test yourself by writing the meanings of each of the phrases listed above.

- Are there any clichés that you know of that are not on the list? Add them.
- Why do you think you should avoid such expressions in your writing?

PRACTICE 3

Rewrite the cliché (printed in *italic type*) in each sentence.

1. My instructor taught us to avoid clichés *like the plague.*

   _____

2. *In this day and age*, teenagers face many temptations.

   _____

3. *Without a doubt*, my hiking trip in the Okanagan Valley was the highlight of my summer.

   _____

4. *Time and time again*, Fahira asked her parents for a car.

   _____

5. Dan bragged about his *tried and true* method for meeting girls.

   _____

WORDINESS

Some writers think that using more words than necessary makes their writing sound important. Actually, wordiness just annoys and confuses your reader. Try to edit your writing carefully.

First of all, remove words that mean the same as other words in the sentence, as in the following example.

Wordy	Though huge in size and blood-red in colour, the snake was harmless.
Revised	Though **huge** and **blood-red**, the snake was harmless.

Huge refers to size, so the words *in size* can be removed with no loss of meaning. *Red* is a colour, so the words *in colour* are also unnecessary. Following is another example of wordiness resulting from repetition. The author has said the same thing twice.

Wordy	Scott finally **made up his mind and decided** to look for a new job.
Revised	Scott finally **decided** to look for a new job.

Second, avoid puffed-up phrases that can be expressed in a word or two instead.

Wordy	**Due to the fact** that the printer was out of paper, Renee went to a store for the purpose of buying some.
Revised	**Because** the printer was out of paper, Renee went to a store to buy some.

In general, work to express your thoughts in the fewest words possible that are still complete and clear. For example, notice how easily the wordy expressions in the box below can be replaced by one or two words.

Wordy Expression	Concise Replacement
a large number of	many
at an earlier point in time	before
at this point in time	now
be in possession of	have
due to the fact that	because
during the time that	while
each and every day	daily
in order to	to
in the event that	if
in the near future	soon
made the decision to	decided

In the following wordy sentence, repetition has been eliminated by:

1. replacing one group of words and

2. eliminating two unnecessary words

- Owing to the fact that I was depressed, I postponed my guitar lesson until later.
  <u>Because I was depressed, I postponed my guitar lesson.</u>

The wordy expression *owing to the fact that* can be replaced by the single word *because* or *since*. The words *until later* can be eliminated with no loss of meaning.

PRACTICE 4

Underline the **one** example of wordiness in each sentence that follows. Then rewrite the sentence as clearly and concisely as possible.

Example   I suddenly realized that my date was not going to show up and had stood me up.

<u>I suddenly realized that my date was not going to show up.</u>

1. Due to the fact that Shani won the lottery, she won't be coming to work today.

_____

_____

2. My sister went ahead and made the decision to take a job in Montreal.

_____

_____

3. Jeff hid his extra house key and now has forgotten the location where it is.

_____

_____

4. I do not know at this point in time if I will be going to this school next year.

_____

_____

5. Daily exercise every day of the week gives me more energy.

_____

_____

 With the increasing popularity of text messaging, many people have become used to communicating in the shorthand known as "text language."

While abbreviations—such as txt for text and w for with—and acronyms (words formed from the first letters of the words of a phrase)—such as lol for laugh out loud—make text messaging easier, they are absolutely unacceptable in academic assignments.

Reducing language to as few letters as possible removes the subtlety and layers of meaning from language. It is impossible to communicate complex messages through text language, and it is very easy to misunderstand a text message.

In pairs, list as many examples of "text language," with their definitions, as you can.

TEST 1   Name: _____   Section: _____   Date: _____

Score: (Number right) _____ x 10 = _____ %

Word Choice

A. The following paragraph contains **five** examples of slang or clichés. Underline the slang phrase or cliché and then rewrite it, using more effective language.

[1]I usually avoid math like the plague, but I'm sick and tired of feeling totally clueless in class, so I promised myself that I would try harder. [2] As it turned out, that's easier said than done. [3]I tried to pay attention, but I was bored to tears. [4]When my parents see my grade they're going to freak out.

1. _____

2. _____

3. _____

4. _____

5. _____

B. Underline the **one** example of wordiness in each sentence that follows. Then rewrite the sentence as concisely as possible.

6. We were glad to hear the test had been postponed until a later date.

_____

7. Because of the fact that it was raining, we cancelled our trip.

_____

8. Please call me at the point in time when you are ready to go.

_____

9. I can't phone my grandmother yet because it is only 6 a.m. in the morning in Edmonton.

_____

10. Katya forgot her jacket and had to return back again to her house for it.

_____

TEST 2   Name: _____   Section: _____   Date: _____

Score: (Number right) _____ x 10 = _____%

Word Choice

Each item below contains **two** examples of ineffective word choice: slang, clichés, or wordiness. Underline the examples. Then rewrite the sentence as clearly and concisely as possible.

1. In the event that I get the part-time job, I will heave a sigh of relief.

   _____

   _____

2. Thirty-seven students signed up for the creative-writing class, but only twenty-four could be accepted. The other thirteen were really bummed out. They asked the teacher to consider opening a second section of the class, but he gave them the cold shoulder.

   _____

   _____

3. Gordon has decided to eat more carefully and to exercise each and every day, due to the fact that his doctor is concerned about his weight.

   _____

   _____

4. I was upset about not getting a raise, but then my boss added insult to injury when she told me that I wouldn't be getting my usual hours this week. I'd better face the cold, hard fact that I'll need to find another job.

   _____

   _____

5. The movie I saw last night was advertised as a comedy, but I didn't laugh once. Instead, it completely weirded me out. It showed married people who hated one another and parents who shouted at their children. Why do people in this day and age think it is funny for people to mistreat one another?

   _____

   _____

TEST 3   Name: _____   Section: _____   Date: _____

Score: (Number right) _____ x 20 = _____ %

Word Choice

The following paragraph about singer Nelly Furtado contains **five** examples of wordiness, cliches, or slang. Underline the examples and rewrite the passage in the space provided.

[1]In this day and age, when pop stars seem to be a dime a dozen and to disappear overnight, Nelly Furtado is one singer who has made climbing the ladder of success look easy. [2]Born in Victoria, B.C. to Portuguese immigrants, Furtado began singing and performing in Portuguese when she was a four-year-old kid. [3]In 1996, she moved to Toronto, which she calls "the most multicultural city in the world." [4]Due to the fact of living in Toronto, she was exposed to genres of music from all over the world, which influenced her own music and performing.

_____

_____

_____

_____

_____

_____

_____

_____

Name: _____   Section: _____   Date: _____

Score: (Number right) _____ x 20 = _____ %

Word Choice

The following paragraph about singer Nelly Furtado contains **five** examples of wordiness, clichés, or slang. Underline the examples and rewrite the passage in the space provided. Some sentences do not need revision.

[1]She recorded her first album, entitled *Whoa, Nelly!,* in 2000. [2]The album was wickedly successful, earning Furtado a Grammy Award for Best Female Pop Vocal Performance. [3]Since then, she has made two more albums and has collaborated with performers such as Timbaland and Justin Timberlake. [4]She has many fans, including many young people, who are down with her pride in her working-class, Portuguese background and her insistence on writing and performing many of her songs in Portuguese. [5]She is in possession of a strong voice and an even stronger work ethic. [6]She has given props to her mom, who was a housekeeper in Victoria, as the source of her willingness to work hard. [7]She continues to inspire young people in Canada and across the world to be proud of their heritage, their identity, and their language.

_____

_____

_____

_____

_____

_____

_____

_____

CHAPTER 23

CAPITAL LETTERS

Basics about Capital Letters

Here are seven main uses of capital letters:

1. Capitalize the first word in a sentence or direct quotation.

   - The ice-cream man said, "Try a frozen banana bar. They're delicious."

2. Capitalize the word "I" and people's names.

   - Because I was the first caller in the radio contest, I won two backstage passes to the Justin Timberlake concert. My friend Chantal Tremblay went with me.

3. Capitalize names of specific places, institutions, programs, and languages.

   - Janice, who lives in Toronto, Ontario and works as a lab technician at Mount Sinai Hospital, went to school at the University of Calgary in Calgary, Alberta.

   - James applied to the General Arts and Sciences program at Humber College, and his girlfriend is at Ryerson University, in the School of Journalism.

   - Emily is taking French Immersion at Humbercrest Public School. She speaks both French and English.

4. Capitalize names of specific groups and organizations.
   Capitalize the names of races, religions, nationalities, companies, clubs, and other organizations.

   - Edward, who is Polish-Canadian, sometimes cooks Chinese dishes for his Etobicoke Chess Club meetings.

   - Arlene, the local president of Mothers Against Drunk Driving, is a part-time real estate agent for Century 21.

5. Capitalize calendar items.
   Capitalize the names of days of the week, months, and holidays.

   - In Canada, Thanksgiving is celebrated on the second Monday in October.

6. Capitalize titles.
   Capitalize the titles of books, TV or stage shows, songs, magazines, movies, articles, poems, stories, papers, and so on.

   - Sitting in the waiting room, Dennis nervously paged through issues of *Maclean's* and *Time* magazines.

   - Gwen wrote a paper titled "Portrayal of Women in Rap Music Videos" that was based on videos shown on *MuchMusic* and MTV.

The words *the, of, a, an, and*, and other short, unstressed words are not capitalized when they appear in the middle of a title. That is why *of* and *in* are not capitalized in "Portrayal of Women in Rap Music Videos."

7. Capitalize product names.
   Capitalize the brand name of a product, but not the kind of product it is.

   • Every morning Ben has **T**ropicana orange juice and **R**aisin **B**ran cereal with milk.

Understanding Capital Letters

Notice how capital letters are used in the following passage about Laura Pettersen, a student at Langara College in Vancouver.

¹This is Laura Pettersen. ²She is a student at Langara College in Vancouver, B.C. ³She is currently taking courses in science, math, and English. ⁴Laura is very busy, with school five days a week and night classes on Tuesdays and Thursdays. ⁵Out of all her subjects, Laura says, "I like biology and chemistry the best." ⁶Laura wants to transfer to Kwantlen University College for their Environmental Protection Technology program.

1. Capitals are used for the first word in the sentence (and the first words in all the sentences that follow) and for Laura Pettersen's first and last names.

2. In the next two sentences capitals are used for specific institutions (Langara College), places (Vancouver, B.C.), and languages (English).

3. Capitals are used for days of the week (Tuesdays and Thursdays).

4. Capitals are used for Laura's name and the word "I."

5. Capitals are used for specific institutions (Kwantlen University College) and programs (Environmental Protection Technology).

Check Your Understanding

The following passage contains **five** errors in capitalization. Underline those words, and then write them, properly capitalized, in the spaces that follow.

> [1]Laura is a recovering drug addict. [2]She grew up in the town of hope, in British Columbia, where she began taking drugs at age thirteen, beginning with acid and progressing through cocaine to crystal meth. [3]She overdosed at age sixteen. [4]her mother, donna, found her unconscious in her basement and took her to the hospital. [5]Now, Laura can't even imagine what that must have been like for her mother. [6]"that must have been the worst day of her life," she says.
>
> [7]Laura went to Hope Secondary school, and managed to graduate, although she says that she manipulated her way through, making up excuses and blaming others. [8]Although she passed her courses, she doesn't remember any of the material she was taught.

1. _____

2. _____

3. _____

4. _____

5. _____

PRACTICE 1

Each of the short passages that follow contains **five** errors in capitalization. Underline the words that need capitalizing. Then write these words correctly in the spaces provided.

> [1]Laura continued using drugs in the years after leaving high school, moving from place to place and job to job. [2]She lived in several towns in Alberta, including lethbridge, Coleman, Lundreck, and Coaldale. [3]She took advantage of her employers, treated her family badly, and had no real friends. [4]She refers to herself at that time in her life as being like a zombie, a shell of a person. [5]she knew that she wanted to stop using drugs, but she couldn't do it on her own. [6]A close family friend helped her find an alcohol and drug treatment counsellor, and she moved into a local vancouver recovery house for six and half months. [7]Before she asked for help, she says, "i had no idea that there were so many facilities for recovering addicts." [8]She was amazed at the love and acceptance she received from both counsellors and other recovering addicts. [9]She has been officially "clean" since march 11, 2005.

1. _____

2. _____

3. _____

4. _____

5. _____

[1]Laura is now in a twelve-step recovery Program and has worked hard at rebuilding the relationships that she destroyed during her years of drug use. [2]"Between the ages of thirteen and twenty-two, i didn't go through the normal growing-up period that most people go through," She says. [3]Laura has had to learn the social skills and coping mechanisms that she missed during her years of Addiction. [4]after years of using drugs to numb herself to the world, she is learning how to take responsibility for her actions.

6. _____

7. _____

8. _____

9. _____

10. _____

PRACTICE 2

Underline the **two** words that need capitalizing in each sentence. Then write these words correctly in the spaces provided.

1. Our brother's usual breakfast of pepsi and doritos makes me shake my head.

   _____   _____

2. For christmas, my friend bought her parents tickets to the musical wicked.

   _____   _____

3. my parents asked, "why did you get in so late last night?"

   _____   _____

4. On monday, which is my birthday, i am going out to dinner with my boyfriend.

   _____   _____

5. Yasmin is going to mexico in march.

   _____   _____

6. Adam wants to study english at york university

   _____   _____

7. Naomi's family celebrates both chanukah and kwanzaa.

   _____   _____

8. Every january, our grandparents travel to florida for a winter vacation.

   _____   _____

9. Over march break, Vivien's drama camp performed the show *Charlie and the Chocolate factory.*

   _____   _____

10. My friend jamila was born in Nigeria.

   _____   _____

MORE USES OF CAPITAL LETTERS

Here are five more uses of capital letters:

1. Capitalize a word that is used as a substitute for the name of a family member. Also, capitalize words like *aunt* and *uncle* when they are used as part of people's names.

   - My biggest fan at the dirt-bike competitions was **M**om.
   - Go help **G**randfather carry those heavy bags.
   - Phil is staying at **U**ncle Raymond's house for the holidays.

   BUT Do not capitalize words such as *mom* or *grandfather* when they come after possessive words such as *my, her,* or *our.*

   - My grandmother lives next door to my parents.
   - Phil and his uncle are both recovered alcoholics.

2. Capitalize the names of specific school courses.

   - This semester, Jody has **D**ance 101, **G**eneral **P**sychology, and **E**conomics 235.

   BUT The names of general subject areas are not capitalized.

   - This semester, Jody has a gym class, a psychology course, and a business course.

3. Capitalize the names of specific periods and famous events in history.

   - During the **M**iddle **A**ges, only the nobility and the clergy could read and write.
   - My grandparents met during the **G**reat **D**epression of the 1930s.
   - Peter's uncle fought in the **G**ulf **W**ar in 1990.

4. Capitalize the opening and closing of a letter.

   Capitalize words in the salutation of a letter.

   - **D**ear **M**s. **A**xelrod:
   - **D**ear **S**ir or **M**adam:

   Capitalize only the first word of the closing of a letter.

   - **S**incerely yours,
   - **Y**ours truly,

5. Capitalize common abbreviations made up of the first letters of the words they represent.

- TV
- VCR
- CD
- DVD
- AIDS
- USA
- UK
- NATO
- CBC
- NDP
- IBM
- RCMP
- CSIS
- CIA
- YMCA
- FBI

PRACTICE 3

Each of the short passages that follow contains **five** errors in capitalization. Underline the words that need capitalizing. Then write these words correctly in the spaces provided. Some sentences contain more than one error, and some sentences are correct.

[1]Laura attends her recovery group on saturday nights. [2]She is now the Treasurer of her group. [3]She is very proud of this, as it shows how far she has come. [4]She also works at a franchise of white spot, a chain of restaurants with over sixty locations in alberta and B.C. [5]She is now a responsible, trustworthy young woman who enjoys life in vancouver and looks forward to the future.

1. _____

2. _____

3. _____

4. _____

5. _____

[1]Today, Laura's only addictions are to relatively harmless things such as crossword puzzles and the tv show *CSI las vegas*. [2]She likes the scenes that involve lab work, as the program she plans to enter—Environmental Protection Technology—involves lab work, too. [3]Laura also enjoys watching dvds of movies such as *The Boondock Saints, Kiss Kiss Bang Bang*, and *10 Things I Hate About You*. [4]She feels that the movie *American History X* has some relevance to her story because it shows a character "recovering from a bad choice and way to live." [5]Laura is constantly reminded of the consequences of her addiction: she experiences frequent short-term memory loss, a short attention span, and anxiety in crowded environments. [6]However, she does not dwell on her mistakes, instead choosing to live for the present and the future. [7]"life," she says, "is awesome."

6. _____

7. _____

8. _____

9. _____

10. _____

TEST 1   Name: _____   Section: _____   Date: _____

Score: (Number right) _____ x 10 = _____ %

Capital Letters

For each sentence, underline the word that needs to be capitalized. Then write the word correctly in the space provided.

1. Dear sir, you may have already won $1,000,000.

   _____

2. I am returning the cd player I purchased from your store.

   _____

3. Yao invited us over to celebrate chinese New Year.

   _____

4. My cousins live in Langley, b.c.

   _____

5. Next weekend, uncle Harry is coming to visit for the holidays.

   _____

6. On the weekends, Jenna volunteers at the hospital, helping people living with aids.

   _____

7. This semester, my favourite course was theories of Art.

   _____

8. In history class, we learned about the events leading up to world War I.

   _____

9. Dear mom, I miss you.

   _____

10. My parents are both catholic, but I haven't been to church since I was a child.

   _____

Name: _____   Section: _____   Date: _____

Score: (Number right) _____ x 5 = _____ %

Capital Letters

Underline the **two** words that need to be capitalized in each sentence. Then write the words correctly in the spaces provided.

1. Last summer, my mother and i visited my aunt in New orleans.

   _____   _____

2. Guy, who is french-canadian, signed up for introductory french because he thinks it will be easy for him to get an A+.

   _____   _____

3. Every wednesday after school, Cara goes to chinese-language school.

   _____   _____

4. The november issue of *prevention* magazine had an article you could use for your report.

   _____   _____

5. My grandfather's real name is henrik, but when he left norway, he started calling himself Hank.

   _____   _____

6. When i was a little girl, I thought that cheerios grew on a cereal bush.

   _____   _____

7. My mother is Mexican and a baptist, while my dad is italian and a Catholic.

   _____   _____

8. Every other july, the members of the baker family get together for a big reunion.

   _____   _____

9. To celebrate my birthday next thursday, my family is taking me out to my favourite vietnamese restaurant.

   _____   _____

10. At least once a year, my cousin james and I make popcorn, sit down, and watch the movie *The wizard of Oz*.

    _____   _____

| TEST 3 | Name: _____ | Section: _____ | Date: _____ |

Score: (Number right) _____ x 5 = _____ %

Capital Letters

Underline the **two** words that need to be capitalized in each sentence. Then write the words correctly in the spaces provided.

1. Dear auntie Ida,
   Thank you so much for your generous birthday cheque. I can certainly put it to good use! with love, Rachel

   _____   _____

2. During the period known as the dark ages, the rate of literacy fell in europe.

   _____   _____

3. The disc jockey said, "be the ninth caller and win a trip to beautiful bermuda!"

   _____   _____

4. Next term in english class, we'll be reading Margaret Atwood's *The Handmaid's tale*.

   _____   _____

5. Ramel is taking Media studies at Humber college.

   _____   _____

6. This issue of *glamour* magazine has an article called "Look Like a million Dollars for Ten Bucks."

   _____   _____

7. This year, the month of february will contain a friday the thirteenth.

   _____   _____

8. Our neighbourhood has many asian-language newspapers and a buddhist temple.

   _____   _____

9. everybody in my mother's family speaks greek as well as English.

   _____   _____

10. The italian renaissance, which took place from 1420 to 1600, is known as a time of great artistic accomplishment.

    _____   _____

Capital Letters

Underline the **two** words that need to be capitalized in each sentence. Then write the words correctly in the spaces provided.

1. Dear sir:
   Your microwave has been repaired and can be picked up at your convenience.
   sincerely,
   Rick's Repairs

   _____   _____

2. Because yesterday was a jewish holiday, our chemistry 101 class did not meet.

   _____   _____

3. The great Depression began in 1929 on Black tuesday, the day the stock market crashed.

   _____   _____

4. Stephen harper was sworn in as Canada's 22nd prime minister on february 6, 2006.

   _____   _____

5. Since september, my brother has worked as a physical therapist at Vancouver General hospital.

   _____   _____

6. When is mom getting back from the usa?

   _____   _____

7. In 1869, Louis Riel led the metis of Manitoba in a movement of self-determination known as the Red River rebellion.

   _____   _____

8. Our teacher asked us to write a paper called "the Dangers of television."

   _____   _____

9. The man on the phone said, "would you like to purchase a membership to the ymca?"

   _____   _____

10. Last march, on our trip to Florida, we swam in the gulf of Mexico.

    _____   _____

CHAPTER 24

NUMBERS AND ABBREVIATIONS

Basics about Numbers and Abbreviations

This chapter explains the following:

1. When to write out numbers (*one, two*) and when to use numerals (*1, 2*)

2. When to use abbreviations and which ones to use

NUMBERS

Here are guidelines to follow when using numbers.

1. Spell out any number that can be written in one or two words. Otherwise, use numerals.

   - When my grandmother turned **sixty-nine**, she went on a **fifteen**-day trip across **nine** states.

   - The mail carrier delivered **512** pieces of mail today.

   > **NOTE** When written out, numbers twenty-one through ninety-nine are hyphenated.

2. Spell out any number that begins a sentence.

   - **Eight hundred and seventy-one** dollars was found in the briefcase.

   > **NOTE** To avoid writing out a long number, you can rewrite the sentence.

   - The briefcase contained **$871**.

3. If one or more numbers in a series need to be written as numerals, write all the numbers as numerals.

   - When the school held a fundraising drive, I sold 125 chocolate bars, Emily sold 87, and Jacob only sold 19.

4. Use numerals to write the following:

   a. **Dates**

   - My grandfather was born on July **4, 1949**.

   b. **Times of the day**

   - The last guest left at **1:45** a.m.

But when the word *o'clock* is used, the time is spelled out:

- I got home at **six o'clock**.

Also spell out the numbers when describing amounts of time:

- Jessica worked **fifty** hours last week.

c. Addresses

- The bookstore is located at **3608** West 4th Avenue.

d. Percentages

- Nearly **70** percent of the class volunteered for the experiment.

e. Pages and sections of a book

- Jeff read pages **40–97** of the novel, which includes chapters **2** and **3**.

f. Exact amounts of money that include change

- My restaurant bill was **$8.49**.

g. Scores

- The Calgary Flames beat the Colorado Avalanche **5-2**.
- A normal IQ ranges between **85** and **115**.

5. When writing numerals, use commas to indicate thousands.

- Angie has **1,243** pennies in a jar.
- The population of Charlottetown, P.E.I. is approximately 65,000.

> **NOTE**   Do not use commas in telephone numbers (1-800-555-1234), street numbers (1355 Hornby Street), social insurance numbers (620 423 785), or years (2008).

Do not use numerals to begin a sentence.

INCORRECT $10 was lying on the table.

Either write out the number or rephrase the sentence so that it begins with another word

CORRECT   Ten dollars was lying on the table.

CORRECT   A ten dollar bill was lying on the table.

PRACTICE 1

Cross out the **one** number mistake in each sentence. Then write the correction in the space provided.

_____   **1.** No wonder these cookies cost $5.25 each—they're fifty percent butter!

_____   **2.** The pro football player wore a gold earring and 2 diamond rings.

_____   **3.** By 7 o'clock, the temperature had dipped below freezing.

_____   **4.** Nelson began working at his present job in two thousand and one.

_____   **5.** For next week, please read pages 1–forty in Chapter 1.

ABBREVIATIONS

Abbreviations can save you time when taking notes. However, you should avoid abbreviations in papers you write for classes. The following are among the few that are acceptable in formal writing.

1. Abbreviate titles that are used before and after people's names.

- **Ms.** Glenda Oaks
- **Dr.** Huang
- Keith Rodham, **Sr.**

2. A person's name may be abbreviated by using the first initial(s).

- John **A.** MacDonald
- **T.S.** Eliot

3. Abbreviations of time and date references are also acceptable.

- The exam ended at 4:45 **p.m.**
- Cleopatra lived from about 69 to 30 **B.C.**

4. Organizations, agencies, technical words, countries, or corporations known by their initials. They are usually written in all capital letters and without periods.

- YMCA
- CSIS
- VCR
- AIDS
- USA
- CBC
- TVO
- NDP
- IBM
- RCMP
- CD

PRACTICE 2

Cross out the **one** abbreviation mistake in each sentence. Then write the correction in the space provided.

_____   **1.** Buddhism was founded in the sixth cent. B.C. by Buddha.

_____   **2.** Dr. Diamond works for the CBC in T.O.

_____   **3.** Mr. Ostrow emigrated from Russia to Can. in 1995.

_____   **4.** On Mon., I have an appointment at IBM with Ms. Janice Grant.

_____   **5.** In 1970, the FBI expanded the no. of criminals on its most-wanted list from ten to sixteen.

TEST 1 Name: _____ Section: _____ Date: _____

Score: (Number right) _____ x 10 = _____%

Numbers and Abbreviations

Cross out the **one** number or abbreviation mistake in each of the following sentences. Then write the correction on the line provided.

_____ 1. 102 patients visited Dr. Jamison's clinic today.

_____ 2. Jonathan won 3 CDs by entering a contest on CBC Radio.

_____ 3. That univ. has 143 professors and 894 students.

_____ 4. Radville, Saskatchewan, has a population of approx. 850.

_____ 5. The hosp. has treated eighteen patients with AIDS.

_____ 6. Mr. Pidora has been supt. of schools for the past nine years.

_____ 7. We finally reached the outskirts of New York City at 8 o'clock.

_____ 8. Only thirteen percent of the customers preferred the new brand of cereal.

_____ 9. 26 students helped out at the homeless shelter at 31 Lake Street.

_____ 10. Last night I woke up at midnight and didn't fall asleep again until two forty five.

TEST 2   Name: _____   Section: _____   Date: _____

Score: (Number right) _____ x 10 = _____ %

Numbers and Abbreviations

Cross out the **one** number or abbreviation mistake in each of the following sentences. Then write the correction on the line provided.

_____ 1. Ms. Bradley begins her day at 5 o'clock.

_____ 2. The NDP MP will give an interview on Tues.

_____ 3. Shelly watched a program on CTV for 30 minutes before going to work.

_____ 4. On September eleven, 2001, terrorists attacked the World Trade Center and the Pentagon.

_____ 5. The vendors sold eighty soft pretzels, 145 soft drinks, and 106 hot dogs.

_____ 6. For their wedding, the couple invited 210 of the bride's friends and relatives and fifty of the groom's.

_____ 7. The twenty-seven students in Mrs. Greene's class are learning about S. America.

_____ 8. In Feb., the representative from CUSO announced plans to study the response to climate change in Nigeria.

_____ 9. Since the meal cost ten dollars, the tip should be at least one dollar and fifty cents.

_____ 10. I listed Dr. Keenan as a ref. on my résumé.

PART 6   PROOFREADING

OBJECTIVES

By the end of Part 6, you should be able to successfully proofread a draft of your paper for the following errors:

- Sentence fragments;
- Run-on sentences and comma splices;
- Incorrect verb forms;
- Lack of subject–verb agreement;
- Shifts in verb tense;
- Incorrect capitalization;
- Incorrect use of commas and apostrophes;
- Missing endings;
- Missing words;
- Misspelled words.

Here are five sentences, each of which contains **two** of the types of errors covered in the previous sections. Correct the errors by rewriting the sentence to eliminate or add words or punctuation marks. **Corrections may vary. Answers are available on the Online Learning Centre.**

1. Helena is taking two english course in school this semester.

_____

_____

2. I feel sorry for Donnas dog, it lost a leg in a car accident.

_____

_____

3. Its easy too do well in college, as long as you're willing to take the time to study.

_____

_____

4. My mother take night classes at college, wear she is learning to use a computer.

_____

_____

5. When the power came back on. All the digital clocks in the house began to blink, the refrigerator motor started to hum.

_____

_____

How many errors did you catch? _____/10

CHAPTER
25

PROOFREADING YOUR WORK

An important step in becoming a good writer is learning to proofread. When you proofread, you check the next-to-final draft of a paper for grammar, punctuation, and other mistakes. Often you would not have found and fixed these errors in earlier drafts of a paper because you were working on content.

All too often, students skip the key step of proofreading in their rush to hand in a paper. As a result, their writing may contain careless errors that leave a bad impression and result in a lower grade. This chapter explains how to proofread effectively and suggests a sequence to follow when proofreading. The chapter also provides a series of practices to improve your proofreading skills.

How to Proofread

Proofreading is a special kind of reading that should not be rushed. Don't try to proofread a paper minutes before it is due. If you do, you are likely to see what you intended to write, rather than what is actually on the page. Instead,

1. Read your paper out loud. (If you're afraid of bothering others or looking "silly," or if you're proofreading an essay written in class, try reading "aloud" in your head, perhaps moving your lips as you read.)

In either case, listen for words and phrases that do not read smoothly and clearly. You will probably be able to hear where your sentences should begin and end. You will then be more likely to find any fragments and run-ons that are present. Other spots that do not read smoothly may reveal other grammar or punctuation errors. Take the time needed to check such spots closely.

2. Read through your paper several times, looking for different types of errors in each reading. Here is a good sequence to follow:

First Reading:	Look for sentence fragments, run-ons, and comma splices.
Second Reading:	Look for verb mistakes.
Third Reading:	Look for capital letter and punctuation mistakes.
Fourth Reading:	Look for missing words or missing -s endings.
Fifth Reading:	Look for spelling mistakes, including errors in homonyms.

This chapter will give you practice in proofreading for the above mistakes. In addition, as you proofread your work, you should watch for problems with pronoun and modifier use, word choice, and parallelism.

3. Using your dictionary or spell-check program, check for any misspelled words that you might have missed. Be aware that spell-check programs miss many errors, so it is important not to rely too much on these programs.

4. Keep a "red flag" list of your own personal recurring errors. If your instructor is repeatedly writing CS (for comma splice) in the margins of your paper, you will know that you have to look carefully for comma splices as you proofread.

5. If your instructor allows it, have a friend read your paper, looking for specific errors. This is often referred to as "peer reviewing" or "peer editing." After spending a lot of time and effort on writing a paper, you might be too close to the material to catch all the errors. A fresh pair of eyes might be very helpful in making sure that the version of the paper you hand in for grading is as close to perfect as it can be. Have them use the following list of questions (this list is also useful when proofreading your own paper).

Questions for Peer Review

- Does the tone sound intelligent, knowledgeable, and appropriate to the subject matter?
- Do the ideas progress in a logical manner?
- Does the essay stay on topic?
- Is there unnecessary "filler" or repetition that can be removed?
- Are the main points well supported?
- Does the essay read smoothly?
- Are there any errors in grammar, spelling, sentence structure, or punctuation?

Common Errors to Look for when Proofreading

1. SENTENCE FRAGMENTS, RUN-ONS, AND COMMA SPLICES

Sentence Fragments

A **sentence fragment** is a group of words that lacks a subject or a verb, or does not express a complete thought.

When proofreading for sentence fragments, remember to look for the following:

- Dependent-word fragments
- Fragments without subjects
- Fragments without a subject and a verb. These include:
  - *-ing* and *to* fragments
  - example fragments

In general, correct a fragment by doing one of the following:

1. Connect the fragment to the sentence that comes before or after it.

2. Create a completely new sentence by adding a subject and/or a verb.

To further refresh your memory about fragments, turn to pages 131–144.

2. RUN-ON SENTENCES AND COMMA SPLICES

When proofreading for run-on sentences and comma splices, keep the following definitions in mind:

- A **run-on sentence** results when one complete thought is immediately followed by another, with nothing between them.

 A sentence does not need to be long to be a run-on sentence. **"It's raining I forgot my umbrella."** That is a run-on sentence!

- A **comma splice** is made up of two complete thoughts that are incorrectly joined by only a comma. To correct run-on sentences and comma splices, do one of the following:

    1. Use a period and a capital letter to create separate sentences.

    2. Use a comma plus a joining word (such as *and, but,* or *so*) to connect the two complete thoughts into one compound sentence.

    3. Use a dependent word to make one of the complete thoughts dependent upon the other one.

    4. Use a semicolon to connect the two complete thoughts.

To further refresh your memory about run-on sentences and comma splices, turn to pages 145–156.

PRACTICE 1

Read each of the following short passages either aloud or to yourself. Each passage contains a sentence fragment, a run-on, or a comma splice. Find and underline the error. Then correct it in the space provided.

1. That bookcase is too heavy on top it could fall over. Take some of the big books off the highest shelf and put them on the bottom one.

_____

_____

2. The detective asked everyone to gather in the library. He announced that he had solved the mystery. And would soon reveal the name of the murderer. Suddenly the lights went out.

_____

_____

3. That rocking chair is very old. It belonged to my great-grandfather, he brought it to Canada from Poland. I like to think about all the people who have sat in it over the years.

_____

_____

4. Before you leave the house. Please close all the windows in case it rains. I don't want the carpet to get soaked.

_____

_____

5. Xiaojing is from Beijing, she uses the English name Sharon, which is easier for her Canadian friends to say. Everyone in her family has both a Chinese and an English name.

_____

_____

6. My aunt took a trip on a boat off the coast of British Columbia. She wanted to see whales. Whales are always sighted there. At a certain time of the year.

_____

_____

7. For vacation this year, we are going to rent a cottage in Muskoka. It is on a lake we can swim, fish, and canoe there. Everyone in the family is looking forward to that week.

_____

_____

8. Rosalie went to the hair salon on Friday. To get just a few centimetres trimmed from her long hair. However, she changed her mind and had it cut very short.

_____

_____

9. The Webbs put a white carpet in their living room. Now they feel that was a foolish choice. Every bit of dirt or spilled food shows on the white surface. And is nearly impossible to get rid of.

_____

_____

10. That waiter is quick and hard-working, he is not friendly with customers. For that reason he doesn't get very good tips. The manager tells him to smile and be more pleasant, but he doesn't seem to listen.

_____

_____

 ## COMMON VERB MISTAKES

When proofreading, look for the following common verb mistakes:

- The wrong past or past participle forms of irregular verbs (pages 50–60)
- Lack of subject–verb agreement (pages 41–49; 119–130)
- Needless shifts of verb tense (pages 50–60)

PRACTICE 2

Read each of the following sentences either aloud or to yourself. Each contains a verb mistake. Find and cross out the error. Then, write the correct version in the space provided.

_____   1. The girls swimmed all the way to the raft.

_____   2. The rock climbers wears safety ropes in case they fall.

_____   3. Because my brother studied hard, he does very well on the exam.

_____   4. The strange-looking puppy growed up to be a beautiful dog.

_____   5. Neither of our cars are working right now.

_____   6. The phone rang twenty times before someone answers it.

_____   7. The public swimming pools in the city is not open yet.

_____   8. Somehow, I sleeped through last night's loud thunderstorm.

_____   9. There are poison ivy growing all over that empty lot.

_____   10. Emmanuel tells everybody it's his birthday and then claimed he doesn't want presents.

CAPITAL LETTER AND PUNCTUATION MISTAKES

When proofreading, be sure the following begin with **capital letters**:

- The first word in a sentence or direct quotation
- The word _I_ and people's names
- Family names
- Names of specific places and languages
- Names of specific groups
- Names of days of the week, months, and holidays (but not the seasons)
- Brand names
- Titles
- Names of specific school courses
- Names of historical periods and well-known events
- Opening and closing of a letter

When proofreading, look for **commas** in the following places:

- Between items in a series
- After introductory material
- Around words that interrupt the flow of a sentence

- Between complete thoughts connected by a joining word

- Before and/or after words of direct address and short expressions

- In dates, addresses, and letters

When proofreading, be sure **apostrophes** are used in the following:

- Contractions

- Possessives (but not with pronouns)

When proofreading, look for quotation marks around direct quotations. Eliminate any quotation marks around indirect quotations.

Finally, remember to also watch for problems with colons, semicolons, hyphens, dashes, and parentheses.

To further refresh your memory, turn to "Capital Letters," pages 255–264; "The Comma," pages 180–188; "The Apostrophe," pages 189–198; "Quotation Marks," pages 199–207; and "Other Punctuation Marks," pages 208–216.

PRACTICE 3

Read each of the following sentences either aloud or to yourself. Each sentence contains an error in capitalization, an error in comma or apostrophe use, or two missing quotation marks. Find the mistake, and correct it in the space provided.

_____   1. I loaded up my low-fat frozen yogourt with fudge sauce peanuts, cherries, and whipped cream.

_____   2. Bobs uncle is a contestant on a reality show.

_____   3. Between you and me I don't like scary movies.

_____   4. Our flight to london was delayed two hours because of mechanical problems.

_____   5. Please call me Tom, our business instructor said.

_____   6. I dread the Summer because I get hay fever so badly.

_____   7. A person doesnt have to be great at a sport to be a great coach.

_____   8. Although he's only a cartoon character Mickey Mouse is loved by millions.

_____   9. Is that book his or her's?

_____   10. "I'd like to ask you a question, Marvin told June. I hope you don't think it's too personal."

 MISSING -*S* ENDINGS AND MISSING WORDS

Since you know what you meant when you wrote something, it is easy for you not to notice when a word ending or even a whole word is missing. The following two sections will give you practice in proofreading for such omissions.

Missing -s Endings

When you proofread, remember the following about noun and verb endings:

- The plural form of most nouns ends in *s* (for example, two *cups* of coffee).

- Present tense verbs for the singular third-person subjects end with an *s*.

PRACTICE 4

Read each of the following sentences either aloud or to yourself. In each case an *-s* ending is needed on one of the nouns or verbs in the sentence. Find and cross out the error. Then correct it in the space provided, being sure to add the *s* to the word.

_____ 1. I've been on hold for half an hour because all of the operator are currently busy.

_____ 2. You should check your front left tire because it look a little flat.

_____ 3. My uncle is always telling terrible joke.

_____ 4. Most barn are painted a dark red color.

_____ 5. Ella make new friends quite easily.

_____ 6. Martin got his job because he speak French and English equally well.

_____ 7. The drugstore close at nine o'clock, but the other mall stores stay open till ten.

_____ 8. The grass always grow faster whenever we have a heavy summer rain.

_____ 9. There are two carton of ice cream hidden in the back of the freezer.

_____ 10. My cousin Darcy has red hair and get sunburned easily in the summer.

Missing Words

When you proofread, look for places where you may have omitted such short words as *a, of, the,* or *to.*

PRACTICE 5

Read each of the following sentences either aloud or to yourself. In each sentence, one of the following little words has been omitted:

    a   and   by   of   the   to   with

Add a caret (∧) at the spot where the word is missing. Then write the missing word in the space provided.

Example _____*of*_____ My new pair ∧ jeans is too tight.

_____ 1. Several pieces this puzzle are missing.

_____ 2. When she went to the grocery store, Louise forgot buy bread.

_____	**3.** Some the programs on TV are too violent for children.
_____	**4.** That blue shirt looks great the brown pants.
_____	**5.** I didn't think I had a chance of winning prize in the contest.
_____	**6.** James plays both the piano the bass guitar.
_____	**7.** Sandra became tired climbing up steep hill.
_____	**8.** Everyone was surprised the school principal's announcement.
_____	**9.** Do you drink your coffee milk or just sugar?
_____	**10.** It's hard pay attention to a boring speaker.

CONFUSED WORDS

When proofreading, pay special attention to the spelling of words that are easily confused with other words.

To refresh your memory of the commonly confused words listed in this book, turn to pages 233–244.

PRACTICE 6

Read each of the following sentences either aloud or to yourself. Each sentence contains a mistake in a commonly confused word. Find and cross out the error. Then correct it in the space provided.

_____	**1.** We left the cottage early because there were to many black flies.
_____	**2.** It's you're own fault that you missed the deadline.
_____	**3.** No one knows who's sweatshirt this is.
_____	**4.** If your hungry, fix yourself something to eat.
_____	**5.** I can't get close enough to the stray dog to read the tag on it's collar.
_____	**6.** My cousins have promised that their coming here soon for a visit.
_____	**7.** I can think of too practical reasons for staying in school: to improve your skills and to prepare for a better job.
_____	**8.** These greeting cards have pictures on they're covers, but there's no message inside.
_____	**9.** Although its tempting to keep the money, you should return it to the man whose name appears in the wallet.
_____	**10.** As we waited in the emergency room to hear whether our sick friend would be all right, time past slowly.

TEN PROOFREADING TESTS

In this chapter, you will find ten tests on which you can practise your proofreading skills. Please note that there may be more than one error in a sentence, and that some sentences are error-free. Also note that corrections may vary.

TEST 1   Name: _____   Section: _____   Date: _____

Score: (Number right) _____ x 20 = _____ %

Proofreading Test

Read the following passage either aloud or to yourself, looking for the following **five** mistakes:

    1 fragment
    1 apostrophe mistake
    1 missing word
    1 missing comma
    1 verb mistake

Correct the mistakes, crossing out or adding words or punctuation marks as needed.

[1]Can you tell the difference between an alligator and a crocodile? [2]In order to do so, you'd probably need to see the two animals side by side. [3]An alligators snout is shorter and broader than that of a crocodile. [4]When an alligator's mouth is shut. [5]You can see only the top teeth protruding outside the mouth. [6]But with crocodile, you can see several of its bottom teeth as well as its top teeth. [7]The most important difference, however, is in behaviour rather than looks. [8]Although alligators are dangerous they does not often attack people, but crocodiles are definitely aggressive toward humans.

Name: _____ Section: _____ Date: _____

Score: (Number right) _____ × 20 = _____ %

Proofreading Test

Read the following passage either aloud or to yourself, looking for the following **five** mistakes:

> 1 **comma splice**
> 2 **verb mistakes**
> 1 **missing word**
> 1 **confused word**

Correct the mistakes, crossing out or adding words or punctuation marks as needed.

[1]My aunt is the thriftiest person I have ever known. [2]She will do just about anything to save money. [3]For example, she never throws away old socks, she uses them as dust rags. [4]Instead of using a sandwich bag once and disposing of it, she wash and re-uses it. [5]When she receives a gift, she carefully unwraps it without tearing the wrapping paper. [6]She'll use that paper to wrap next gift she gives. [7]Her old milk cartons become bird feeders. [8]Her tin cans become flowerpots. [9]Plastic bags from the grocery store becomes liners for her wastebaskets. [10]When her family's blue jeans are too worn out to where, she recycles them into cozy quilts for the beds. [11]She really is a model of thriftiness.

TEST 3   Name: _____   Section: _____   Date: _____

Score: (Number right) _____ x 20 = _____ %

Proofreading Test

Read the following passage either aloud or to yourself, looking for the following **five** mistakes:

> **2 fragments**
> **1 comma splice**
> **1 missing quotation mark**
> **1 confused word**

Correct the mistakes, crossing out or adding words or punctuation marks as needed.

[1]When I was twelve, my family moved to a new town. [2]Our new house was in a large development. [3]On my first day there, I went for a walk. [4]As I left, my mother told me, Don't get lost." [5]I rolled my eyes at her silly warning and walked for a long time. [6]Hoping to meet some of the kids who lived near us. [7]Finally, I got tired and hungry. [8]And turned to go back home. [9]That's when I realized how much alike all the houses looked. [10]I realized, too, that I didn't know my new address. [11]All I new was that the street was named after a tree. [12]I began looking at street signs and read, "Plum Lane," "Poplar Street," "Elm Court," and "Maple Avenue." [13]They were all named after trees. [14]I walked around the development for more than two hours, too embarrassed to ask for help, then I spotted my family's car parked outside our house.

TEST 4   Name: _____   Section: _____   Date: _____

Score: (Number right) _____ × 20 = _____ %

Proofreading Test

Read the following passage either aloud or to yourself, looking for the following **five** mistakes:

1 **fragment**
1 **comma splice**
1 **missing capital letter**
1 **missing apostrophe**
1 **verb mistake**

Correct the mistakes, crossing out or adding words or punctuation marks as needed.

When I was nineteen, I lived in Costa rica for a few months. This beautiful country is filled with fruits and flowers growing everywhere. [3]The country is also blessed with rain forests, mountains, and inactive volcanoes. [4]One of my favourite memories are of a time I stayed overnight on the beach with some friends. [5]At about midnight, we decided to stand waist deep in the warm ocean water. [6]A gentle rain began to fall, we could see lightning flashing in the clouds many miles away. [7]Suddenly, we all gasped in amazement. [8]Lines of flickering green light were dancing across the tops of the waves. [9]As they rolled toward us. [10]We learned later that the light was caused by tiny glowing animals which live on the oceans surface. [11]That night was a magical time for us.

TEST 5   Name: _____   Section: _____   Date: _____

Score: (Number right) _____ x 20 = _____ %

Proofreading Test

Read the following passage either aloud or to yourself, looking for the following **five** mistakes:

    1 **fragment**
    1 **run-on sentence**
    1 **missing comma**
    1 **missing apostrophe**
    1 **verb mistake**

Correct the mistakes, crossing out or adding words or punctuation marks as needed.

[1]In the fall of 2006, residents of a rooming house in Toronto's west end discovered an eight-foot-long cobra coiled behind their refrigerator. [2]A week later, the landlord peered into a gap in the basement ceiling and seen the snake hissing at him. [3]Described as white with brown and red markings. [4]The cobra belonged to a resident of the other half of the semi-detached house. [5]The man had a history of keeping dangerous animals in the previous year, Animal Services removed a crocodile, Komodo dragon, and a viper from the residence. [5]The rooming house was shut down for more than four months while the police, fire fighters, paramedics, and experts from the Toronto Zoo and Animal Services searched for the snake. [6]This is not the only recent case of exotic pets causing havoc in the Toronto area; in 1992, a Brampton man was strangled to death by his pet Burmese python, and in 1992, a sixteen-year-old Ontario boy was killed after entering a cage containing two Siberian tigers and a cougar. [7]More recently, in September, 2006 a Barrie man was treated after being bitten by a friends pet viper. [8]Animal experts caution people to avoid purchasing exotic animals unless they fully understand the responsibilities and risks involved in caring for such animals.

Name: _____   Section: _____   Date: _____

Score: (Number right) _____ x 20 = _____ %

Proofreading Test

Read the following passage either aloud or to yourself, looking for the following **five** mistakes:

    1 sentence fragment
    1 missing -*s* ending
    1 missing capital letter
    1 missing apostrophe
    1 verb mistake

Correct the mistakes, crossing out or adding words or punctuation marks as needed.

[1]In 2002, CBC Radio started Canada Reads. [2]A national project to encourage more Canadians to read Canadian literature. [3]Every spring, several Canadian celebrities participates in an on-air panel in which each celebrity chooses one work of Canadian fiction as the book that all Canadians should read. [4]Each panelist defends his or her choice and votes on the others' choices. [5]In april, 2002, the panel included former prime minister Kim Campbell, writers Leon Rooke and Nalo Hopkinson, actor Megan Follows, and musician Steven Page. [6]Each day, one book was voted off the list until only Steven Pages choice was left. [7]That book, *In the Skin of a Lion* by Michael Ondaatje, was the first winner of the contest. [8]The next few winners were Hubert Aquin's *Prochain Episode*, Guy Vanderhaeghe's *The Last Crossing*, Frank Parker Day's *Rockbound*, and Miriam Toews's *A Complicated Kindness*. [9]According to Canadian authors, publishers, librarian, and teachers, the Canada Reads program has greatly increased public interest in Canadian fiction.

| **TEST 7** | Name: _____ | Section: _____ | Date: _____ |

Score: (Number right) _____ x 10 = _____ %

Proofreading Test

Read the following passage either aloud or to yourself, looking for the following **ten** mistakes:

    2 fragments
    2 comma splices
    2 missing apostrophes
    1 missing comma
    1 missing word
    1 confused word
    1 verb mistake

Correct the mistakes, crossing out or adding words or punctuation marks as needed.

[1]On TV, people who sleepwalk generally act like zombies, they stagger along with their arms held stiffly in front of them. [2]In fact (as you know if youve ever seen one), most sleepwalkers walk around quite normally. [3]They may even perform routine tasks. [4]Such as getting dressed or brushing their teeth. [5]Sometimes they talk, although there conversation may not make a lot of sense. [6]Sleepwalking is a fairly common behavior. [7]Especially among children. [8]It occurs during periods of very deep sleep. [9]In most cases, a person sleepwalks just a few times, then the sleepwalking stops forever. [10]If sleepwalking becomes a frequent problem the sleepwalker may need a doctor help. [11]What should you do if you see someone sleepwalking? [12]Leading the sleepwalker back bed is usually all that is necessary. [13]But if the sleepwalker be in danger of injury, gently wake him or her up.

Name: _____   Section: _____   Date: _____

Score: (Number right) _____ x 10 = _____ %

Proofreading Test

Read the following passage either aloud or to yourself, looking for the following **ten** mistakes:

1 **missing capital letter**
2 **verb mistakes**
2 **missing apostrophes**
2 **confused words**
2 **comma splices**
1 **missing comma**

Correct the mistakes, crossing out or adding words or punctuation marks as needed.

[1]George Orwells famous novel *Animal Farm* is an example of an allegory. [2]In an allegory, characters and events act as symbols of other things. [3]In the book, the horses, sheep, pigs, cows, and other animals of Manor Farm rebels against their drunken owner, mr. Jones. [4]With the pigs taking the lead, the animals drive all humans away from the farm, they take control of it themselves. [5]They intend to turn the farm into a sort of paradise, where all the animals will work hard and live together in piece and equality. [6]But soon the pigs begin taking advantage of the situation. [7]They work less than the other animals and changed the societys rules for they're benefit. [8]By the time the book ends the pigs are almost identical to human beings. [9]You can enjoy *Animal Farm* simply as a story, you can also read it as a warning against how a well-intentioned revolution can go wrong.

TEST 9   Name: _____   Section: _____   Date: _____

Score: (Number right) _____ x 10 = _____ %

Proofreading Test

Read the following passage either aloud or to yourself, looking for the following **ten** mistakes:

- **1 missing word**
- **1 missing -s ending**
- **2 capital letter mistakes**
- **1 missing quotation mark**
- **3 verb mistake**
- **1 comma splice**
- **1 run-on sentence**

Correct the mistakes, crossing out or adding words or punctuation marks as needed.

[1]Elaine and Don was driving from Vancouver to Calgary. [2]They were hungry and thirsty, so they stop at a convenience store. While Elaine picked up bottles of water, fruit juice, and pepsi, Don browsed through the snacks. [4]He decided that it would be fun to try something new and unusual, so he bought pickled hard-boiled eggs, a bag of pork rinds, and a tasty-looking sausage. [5]Back in the car, Elaine nibbles on a pickled egg, Don tried a sausage. [6]"Hey, I like this," she said. [7]Do you want to try one?" [8]Don didn't answer her question he just made choking sound as he hurriedly opened a bottle and gulped down some water. [9]"Don't eat that sausage!" he finally gasped. [10]Elaine picked up the Sausage package and read the label. [11]"Fire-Eater's Favourite Chilli Sausage," she said. [12]"Maybe you should have read label first."

Name: _____ Section: _____ Date: _____

Score: (Number right) _____ x 10 = _____ %

Proofreading Test

Read the following passage either aloud or to yourself, looking for **ten** mistakes. Correct the mistakes, crossing out or adding words or punctuation marks as needed.

[1]One of the most amazing things about the Internet is the way it makes a hole world of facts available to you. [2]Have you ever wondered for instance what that little bump of flesh just in front of your ear canal is called? [3]Connect to the Internet and type in the address of your favourite search engine. [4]In the search field, type "What is the bump in front of the ear called?" [5]In less than a second, youve learned that little bump is called the "tragus." [6]And by the way, the pale half-moon at the base of your fingernail is the "lunula." [7]You dont even have to search for weird, interesting facts. [8]Just go to one of the hundreds of trivia sites online and read the items collected there. [9]Thanks to such sites, I now know that Murphy's Oil Soap is what most zookeepers use to wash their elephants. [10]Believe it or not, the people of Des Moines, Iowa, eats more Jell-O than the people of any other city. [11]Another interesting fact is that more films have been made about Dracula than about any other fictional character. [12]Getting weird facts off the Internet can be habit-forming you may find it very hard to stop with just one...or two...or ten. [13]Before you know it you have spent an hour at the computer. [14]And completely forgotten what you wanted to look up in the first place.

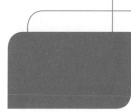

PHOTO CREDITS

Chapter 1: p. 3: Peanuts, reproduced by permission of United Feature Syndicate, Inc.; p. 8: Photo by Suzanne Simpson Millar.

Chapter 2: p. 24: © United Media.

Chapter 4: p. 42: CP Photo/Adrian Brown; p. 43: Stockbyte; p. 45: CP Photo/Frank Gunn; p. 49: Steve White/CP Images.

Chapter 6: p. 62: Brian Wilson Photography Inc.; p. 63: Brian Wilson Photography Inc.; p. 64: Brian Wilson Photography Inc.; p. 64: Brian Wilson Photography Inc.

Chapter 7: p. 81: CP Photo/Fred Chartrand; 7-2: CP Photo/Tobin Grimshaw.

Chapter 9: p. 102: Canadian Press/Jonathan Hayward; p.102: CP Photo/Paul Chiasson; p.102: Canadian Press/Edmonton Sun – Jason Franson.

Chapter 10: p. 115: CP Photo/Toronto Star-Bernard Well; p. 113: CP Photo/Aaron Harris.

Chapter 11: p. 120: © BananaStock/Punch Stock; p. 121: © Image100 Ltd.; p. 127: © Image100 Ltd.; p. 130: CP Photo/Frank Gunn; p. 130: © Sullivan Entertainment Inc.

Chapter 12: p.142: © Lynsey Addario/Corbis.

Chapter 13: p. 146: © Ashley Watson Images; p. 147: © Ashley Watson Images; p. 150: © Ashley Watson Images; p. 151: © Ashley Watson Images.

Chapter 16: p. 181: © Ashley Watson Images; p. 181: © Ashley Watson Images; p. 182: © Ashley Watson Images; p. 183: © Ashley Watson Images; p. 187: Canada's Sports Hall of Fame; p. 188: Canada's Sports Hall of Fame.

Chapter 17: p. 190: © Scott Simpson Millar; p. 190: CP Photo/Peterborough Examiner-Clifford Skarstedt; p. 191: Courtesy Ronda Franco, Ajax High School; p. 192: Courtesy Ronda Franco, Ajax High School.

Chapter 18: p. 200: Courtesy of Literature for Life; p. 200: Courtesy of Literature for Life; p. 201: Courtesy of Literature for Life; p. 201: Courtesy of Literature for Life; p. 201: Courtesy of Literature for Life; p. 203: Courtesy of Literature for Life.

Chapter 21: p. 234: Courtesy of Rosarina Saw; p. 235: Courtesy of Rosarina Saw; p. 236: Courtesy of Rosarina Saw; p. 238: Courtesy of Rosarina Saw.

Chapter 22: p. 253: CP Photo/Geoff Howe.

Chapter 23: p. 256: © Brent Richter; p. 257: © Brent Richter; p. 260: © Brent Richter.

INDEX